Cambridge Studies in French

Tradition and Desire

Cambridge Studies in French
General Editor: MALCOLM BOWIE

Also in the series:

Tradition and Desire

From David to Delacroix

NORMAN BRYSON

Fellow of King's College, Cambridge

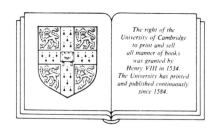

The right of the
University of Cambridge
to print and sell
all manner of books
was granted by
Henry VIII in 1534.
The University has printed
and published continuously
since 1584.

CAMBRIDGE UNIVERSITY PRESS

Cambridge
New York   New Rochelle
Melbourne   Sydney

Published by the Press Syndicate of the University of Cambridge
The Pitt Building, Trumpington Street, Cambridge CB2 1RP
32 East 57th Street, New York, NY 10022, USA
10 Stamford Road, Oakleigh, Melbourne 3166, Australia

First published 1984
First paperback edition 1987
Reprinted 1988

Printed in Great Britain at the University Press, Cambridge

Library of Congress catalogue card number: 83–20985

British Library cataloguing in publication data

Bryson, Norman
Tradition and desire: from David to Delacroix.
1. Painting, Modern – 17th-18th centuries
– France
2. Painting, Modern – 19th century – France
I. Title
759.4   ND546

ISBN 0 521 24193 6 hard covers
ISBN 0 521 33562 0 paperback

For Margaret Pinder

Je suis ce malheureux comparable aux miroirs
Qui peuvent réfléchir mais ne peuvent pas voir
Comme eux mon œil est vide et comme eux habité
De l'absence de toi qui fait sa cécité

Louis Aragon

Contents

Illustrations

xi

Jacket illustration: this study for *The Oath of the Horatii* by David is reproduced by kind permission of the Musée Bonnat, Bayonne

Preface

This book offers itself as a discussion of the problem of artistic tradition as it manifests in the work of three French painters: David, Ingres and Delacroix. It is not intended as a comprehensive account of these painters' achievements, or as a history of their work in any inclusive sense, but rather as an exploration of the different ways in which David, Ingres and Delacroix perceive, and cope with their perception of, their place in artistic tradition. Faced with the enormous output of these artists, I have selected those works which, in my judgement, best illustrate their individual response to tradition, and their highly personal solutions to the problems which tradition presents. Even within these limits I have, necessarily, been obliged to omit discussion of many works I would have liked to see included: notably the portraiture of David and of Ingres and the easel painting of Delacroix. Omission has, in all such cases, been attended by its full measure of pain and regret. I can only ask the reader to consider what is there, in the discussion, rather than point out – what I am well aware of – everything that is not; and hope that from those works which are discussed the reader may extend his or her set of inferences towards those which have been excluded.

In the first chapter I ask the question, in what sense *is* tradition a problem? The answer must be, I think, that for most viewers, and by extension for most historians of art, tradition supplies every reason for activity and celebration; but that for the artist who is obliged by a stylistic consensus (such as that of Neo-classicism) to imitate the art of the past, or who perceives his place in tradition as one of latecoming, or both, tradition can assume a less beneficent guise; one that threatens the foundation of his self-definition as painter, that is, as one who gives to the world what the world never saw before. Here my argument owes much to the work, within literary history, of W.J. Bate and of Harold Bloom; though I would maintain that for literature, a practice whose access to the flow of language across society provides it with a permanent possibility of escape from tradition's burdens, the case for the pressure of tradition is harder to make than it is for the image, which lacks access to any comparable flow (at least before the mass dissemination of imagery). In the second chapter I outline certain manipulations of tradition, which I call tropes, in the early work of David. Discussion of the tropes is by no means exhaustive – it is likely that many more strategies of 'turning' tradition are deployed xvii in the history painting promoted by the Académie, and in David, than I have identified; but the idea of the trope is useful not least in the way it alerts one to David's increasing preoccupation with on the one hand (in his narrative material) a principle of alterity or dispossession in human vision, and on the other (in his manipulation of artistic inheritance) a principle of alterity or dispossession in artistic vision, the latter increasingly identified with the art of the past. The interplay between those forces of dispossession is the matter of the third chapter, on the *Oath of the Horatii*.

While the years of Revolution may have temporarily pushed the vicissitudes of tradition to the margins, there can be little doubt that in the wave of eclecticism, antiquarianism, and stylistic multiplicity that followed, the question of the 'source' returns to the centre, above all in the theoretical anxieties of Quai and his circle, and practically in the early work of Ingres. To the difficulties enunciated by Quai, Ingres devises unprecedented solutions; and in my discussion, in chapter four, of the portraits of Napoleon and of the Rivière family, I try to locate a shift or reworking of the status of tradition, in which Ingres comes deliberately to intensify the invocation his paintings make to the past, but as a result is able to claim his images as uniquely his own. This strategy makes his painting strangely evacuative, or self-emptying, and in chapter five I trace some of the strategy's consequences for the odalisque, for the 'bourgeois' portraits, and for the major *tableaux d'histoire*: arguing that, for Ingres, tradition itself supplies the means for overcoming the problems it sets in motion, until the desire to produce new and unique images, which had been formerly threatened by tradition, eventually comes to join forces with its antagonist, tradition and desire mutually re-enforcing each other in a highly sophisticated, allusive, and self-deconstructing technique. In the case of Delacroix's cycle in the Bourbon Library, a rather different configuration is found: by modelling cultural inheritance less as an accumulative weight than as a transformation of pre-cultural or acultural energies, Delacroix turns from culture as product to culture as process, at the same time applying this 'dynamic' view to his own narrative of cultural tradition, with radical consequences for the terms of viewing proposed and assumed by the cycle as a whole.

This work is the third part of a larger project, the overall aim of which is to elaborate the implications, for the history of art, of the proposition that painting is an art 'of the sign'. I cannot say that I have pursued the implications to anywhere near their limit. In *Word and Image* I considered the possibility that, painting being a matter of signs, it would therefore be accessible to description not only in painterly or stylistic terms, but in terms of narrative analysis and narrative history. In *Vision and Painting* I took issue with the proposition that painting is derived from, and may be theorised around, perception. That second stage of investigation presented painting as unable to deliver the 'original' perceptions which, in its classical and realist dispensations, it nevertheless claims to reproduce. Denied an 'outside', or window looking away from the representation on to a world beyond it, painting seemed increasingly to raise before me the problem of the degree to which its representations were self-referring and their meanings to be found not within perception, but within representation. This consideration brought to the forefront the problem of tradition, and of the apprehension of tradition not just in theoretical terms, for aestheticians, but in practical terms, for the painters themselves. The present study is an analysis of what painting can become in the hands of those who both fear and desire that the meaning of a painting is, always, another painting.

Acknowledgements

This book is practically indebted to two institutions without whose support it simply could not have been written: to King's College, Cambridge, which awarded the Fellowship enabling me to carry out the research project of which this study is the third part; and to the British Academy, for the generosity that made possible a number of vital field trips outside the United Kingdom.

In the course of writing this book I have been helped by more individuals than it is possible to name. Among those colleagues and friends with whom on many occasions I have discussed topics directly or indirectly related to the book I especially want to thank John Barrell, Anita Brookner, Michael Camille, Rana Kabbani, Su Kappeler, Joseph Koerner, Margaret Pinder, Martin Powers, and Tony Tanner. I must also thank Malcolm Bowie, Annie Cave and Terence Moore for the detailed attention they gave to the manuscript. Maurice Sérullaz and Jean Baudry de Vaux generously supplied photographs of the Delacroix paintings in the Palais Bourbon.

Author and publisher gratefully acknowledge the permission of the following to reproduce their illustrations in this book: the Trustees, the National Gallery, London (1, 11, 69, 97, 99); the Mansell Collection, London (2, 6, 7, 12, 58, 66, 68); Musée du Louvre, Paris (3, 15, 18, 24, 25, 28, 29, 32, 33, 38, 40, 41, 42, 48, 49, 55, 56, 57, 59, 60, 61, 64, 65, 70, 74, 75, 76, 78, 85, 86, 87, 88, 91, 92, 93, 98); Vatican Museum, Rome (4, 5); Museo Poldi-Pezzoli, Milan (8); Isabella Stewart Gardner Museum, Boston (9); Freer Gallery of Art, Smithsonian Institution, Washington, DC (10); Burghley House (13); National Gallery of Scotland, Edinburgh (14); Ville de Paris, Musée du Petit Palais, Paris (16); Bibliothèque Nationale, Paris (17, 39, 45, 46); The Minneapolis Institute of Arts (19); École Nationale Supérieure des Beaux-Arts, Paris (20, 22); Witt Library, London (21); Musée des Beaux-Arts, Marseilles (23); Walker Art Gallery, Liverpool (26); Musée des Beaux-Arts, Lyons (27); Albertina Graphics Collection, Vienna (34); the Fotografia Soprintendenza per i beni artistici e storici delle Marche – Urbino (35); Musées Royaux des Beaux-Arts, Brussels (copyright A.C.L. Bruxelles) (36, 77); Musée Carnavalet, Paris (photo Giraudon) (37, 47); the Trustees, the British Museum, London (43); Kunsthalle, Hamburg (44); Musée d'Art Moderne, Liège (50); National Gallery of Art, Washington, DC, Samuel H. Kress Collection (51); Musée Condé, Chantilly (photo Giraudon) (52, 62); (photo copyright) Musée de l'Armée, Paris (53, 54); Musée des Beaux-Arts, Nantes (63, 94, 95); Musée Granet, Palais de Malte, Aix-en-Provence (67); Library of Congress, Washington, DC (71); Fogg Art Museum, Harvard University (72); Walters Art Gallery, Baltimore (73); © Arch. Phot. SPADEM, Paris (81, 82, 83); Museu de Arte de São Paulo (84); Musée Bonnat, Bayonne (90); Frick Collection, New York (96); Éditions du Temps, Paris (100–22).

Chapter 3 first appeared as an article in *French Studies*. It is slightly revised in this book.

Tradition and its discontents

I

THE CIVILISATION of the West possesses the oldest tradition of representational painting which exists on our planet. Though the civilisation of China stretches back further in time than our own, of its surviving paintings even the earliest are comparative latecomers: the *Admonitions of the Instructress*, chosen by Waley to mark the beginnings of Chinese brush-painting, dates from only the fourth century AD.[1] The art of the Far East is greatly preoccupied with its own tradition, to a degree that makes the attribution of its paintings a hazardous and in many ways an irrelevant exercise: for the classical painter of China the art of copying or paraphrasing work by previous artists is by no means confined to the stage of apprenticeship; the copy is not relegated to a side-category of authentic production; and indeed the moments of major innovation in the tradition occur when the master takes it on himself to refashion and reinterpret the classic images of his inheritance.[2] Yet no Chinese painter, of however late a date, has ever found the vista of continuously vital tradition that enabled Ingres, in 1856, to interpret *Mme Moitessier* (illustration 1) through an image that pre-dated his work by over two thousand years, the fresco at Herculaneum known as *Herakles and the Infant Telephos* (illustration 2). Nowhere in China will we find an equivalent, in terms of temporal chasm and temporal bridging, to the back of Phlegyas in Delacroix's *Dante and Vergil* of 1822 (illustration 3), a reverential distortion of the Belvedere Torso (illustration 4), interpreted across its own earlier re-imagining by Michelangelo, in the Sistine Chapel (illustration 5).

The art of Europe is old, and it is art history that must count her days. That is to sound a note of elegy. Yet the history of art, as it is currently perceived, remains curiously insensitive to what one might call the necessary elegaic tone. When art history reveals that Herculaneum stands behind *Mme Moitessier*, or that Antiquity and Michelangelo combine in Delacroix's figure of Phlegyas, that part of its work which concerns itself with sources is almost done. Its method is vigilantly retrospective – a good art historian develops a truly hawk-like instinct for the cues which point backwards from a given work to its predecessors: but the manner in which the sources, once found, are presented or written up is insistently forward-looking, or proleptic. Art history expends considerable effort on the discovery of sources, and when it has located a source it will probably go on to examine the ways in which the source is adapted to later use; but its temporal perspective is committed primarily to ideas of fulfilment or entelechy: it is for the predecessor to sow the seed, and for his successor to reap the harvest.

This perspective is understandable enough, and accords well with art history's preferred tone, which is one of informed celebration. As we survey the art of the past, we may well congratulate ourselves on having been born into a culture so crammed with visual riches. But let us be clear in identifying the viewpoint of that festive survey: it is that of the viewer, not the painter. Nowhere is the gulf – the opposition of interests – between viewing and painting more evident than in this area, of the preception of tradition. When we learn for the first time that *Mme Moitessier* owes its inspiration to a remote and little-known antique fresco, there need be no substantial change in our apprehension of the painting: this new fact is ancillary, of specialised and limited importance, and to deal in such facts is perhaps to deal in little more than the exchange of learned footnotes. For the viewer it is the activity of seeing the painting *now*, in the presence of the gaze, which counts. The present form of the image is, after all, that to which the source yielded, in the process of its transformation into the painting we now have; and this in itself may be a persuasive

1 Jean-Auguste-Dominique Ingres, *Mme Moitessier* (detail)

2 *Herakles and the Infant Telephos*
(detail); Roman copy of the
fresco from Herculaneum

3 Eugène Delacroix, *Dante and
Vergil crossing the Styx* (detail)

enough reason for consigning the source to the margins of knowledge. It may be true that Ingres was thinking of Herculaneum as he contemplated the figure of his sitter, but in making his painting Ingres refashioned that source almost to the point of obliteration. If the painting freed itself from its frail, comparatively uninteresting predecessor, its very success in doing so perhaps justifies that we relegate information about the fresco to the realm of polite pedantry.

But the perspective of the viewer is not the only one available, nor is it the only perspective within painting itself; for although to the viewer the art of the past may appear a treasure-house where all the riches are available for simultaneous inspection, to the painter it may well seem that the tradition has grown too wealthy to need anything further. Where the viewer's activity takes place in the essentially timeless zone of the gallery or study, and collapses the

4 *Belvedere Torso*

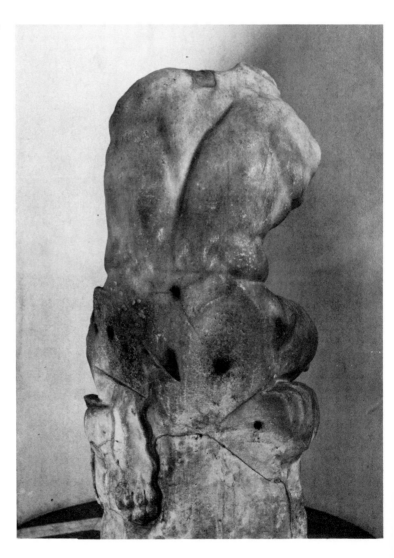

long process of tradition into a presence that seems to stand outside of history, the painter is condemned to work within time, within history, and within a tradition which may already have said everything he has to say. And though the viewer who loves painting will properly seek to be flooded by the images of the past, if the painter yields to the same desire he risks disaster, for in that flood his own images may drown: if he yields to that invasion he will cease to be who and what he is, a painter, and become the being he must always fight to overcome, that is, only a viewer.[3]

The development of the painter necessarily involves struggle against the viewer in himself, yet to that struggle the forward-looking and ruthlessly optimistic perspective of source-hunting need pay no attention. The error here originates in a persistent tendency of 'academic' reasoning: the analyst projects into the object of his investigation the principle of his *own* relation to the object.[4] Since to the viewer, and to the art history that aligns itself with his perspective, all the paintings can be seen together at once, in timeless plenitude, so surely it must be within painting itself: to the painter also, tradition must have appeared in just this way, outside the *duration* of its own making. The painter is not seen to labour within the tradition: he is simply its heir. The fecundity of

5 Michelangelo, figure from the Sistine Chapel

the past can only energise his talents, and without that stimulus his gifts may lie fallow, as they do in the young painters to whom Reynolds issues the recommendation to develop 'the habit of contemplating and brooding over the ideas of great geniuses, till you find yourself warmed by the contact'.[5] Besides, in those cases where we trace an image back to its lair, we nearly always find that the source exists only as a lesser element in the later production: the Belvedere Torso and the Sistine ceiling, those stupendous works, are found responsible for only a fraction of Delacroix's painting of *Dante and Vergil*, the back of Phlegyas; and this fragmentary result of influence may then be evinced as proof of the marginal role of the predecessor. The Herculanean fresco lies behind what is only a minor component of Ingres' portrait – Mme Moitessier's pose: perhaps Ingres could have dispensed altogether with this catalyst. To view influence as primarily forward-directed – the source nudges or coaxes its user into creative action – suppresses the equally available reading of the same evidence in the *opposite* direction: that the finally minor role of the Torso, or the fresco, or the Sistine ceiling, may be the outcome of a massive effort to *overcome* the weight and authority of Antiquity, of Michelangelo. Yet faced with evidence that points equally towards the felicitous borrowing and the struggle to overcome, the aesthetic of viewing (as opposed to painting) will project on to that evidence its own *pacific* relation to the past. The viewer is not troubled; *he* experiences no difficulty in what he does; for the painter also this is how tradition must have appeared.

We can begin to sensitise ourselves to the blind spot of the viewer-oriented aesthetic – its tendency to lose sight of the *problem* of tradition in its praise of tradition's wealth – by citing an extreme statement of the power of innovation, from Nietzsche:

> Great men, like great ages, are explosives in which a tremendous force is stored up; their precondition is always, historically and psychologically, that for a long time much has been gathered, saved up, and conserved by them – that there has been no explosion for a long time. Once the tension in the mass has become too great, then the most accidental stimulus suffices to summon into the world the 'Genius', the 'deed', the great destiny. What does the environment matter then, or the age, or the 'spirit of the age', or 'public opinion'?[6]

Genius, according to this description, produces itself by collecting together energies which in lesser men lie in disarray: the genius is strong because he resists the tendency of his fellows to dilute or squander their force. Yet the impact on the surrounding world of genius so conceived is precisely to crush it in its weakness and dispersal; to drive the age, the public, the creative community, into still greater weakness. The source here, though self-produced, is measured exactly against its power to diminish those around it and those who follow. Nietzsche's celebration of the powers of genius adumbrates a price the viewer never has to pay in his dealings with art, for unlike the painter he is never called on to work within an orbit of influence, a style, a school; just as it indicates that the qualities which the aesthetic of viewing most prizes may be those which for the painter are the most to be dreaded for their power to crush. The viewer, contemplating the productions of genius, is contemporary with them, in the eternal presence of the gaze; but the painter must always come *after*. Truer to the aesthetic of painting, as opposed to that of viewing, is Ruskin:

It being required to produce a poet on canvas, what is our way of setting to work? We begin, in all probability, by telling the youth of fifteen or sixteen, that Nature is full of faults, and that he is to improve her; but that Raphael is perfection, and that the more he copies Raphael the better; that after much copying of Raphael, he is to try what he can do himself in a Raphaelesque, but yet original manner. . . . And we wonder we have no painters.[7]

II

If the business of source-hunting – art history in its professional and obsessive mode – is so forward-looking and by the same token so insensitive to the burden of the past, this may stem in no small measure from the equally vigorous futurism of the customary account of painting's history and evolution. Many figures might be chosen from among the proponents of that account, but let us stay with those whose influence is still most strongly felt in the discipline of art history. At three crucial junctures the painting of the past has been portrayed to art history as the passage from winter to spring: in Antiquity, by Pliny; in the Renaissance, by Vasari; and by Gombrich, in our own time. For those who come in their wake, and work in the discipline still marked by their impress, it is these three accounts that must be challenged and questioned, if their collective burden is ever to lift: Pliny's *Natural History*; Vasari's *Lives*; and Gombrich's *Art and Illusion*.

For Pliny it is not the past which poses problems to the painter, but nature; a nature so perplexing and many-faceted that it requires for its successful representation many painters, a community of specialists, each concentrating on a particular natural aspect, and each contributing to the sum of collective knowledge. The underlying conceptual figure here is that of Pliny's own *Natural History*, a work which divides the universe into categories of knowledge (Concerning the World, Elements and Stars; Concerning the Inventions of Men; Concerning the Creatures of the Land; Concerning Gold and Silver, etc.) in order then to collect the information into a definitive *summa* or encyclopaedia. Thus we find Eumarus of Athens, the first to distinguish the male from the female in painting; Cimon, the first to depict 'image in three quarters' (*obliquae imagines*); Parrhasius, the first to give proportion to painting, and to give vivacity to the expressions of the face; Aristides of Thebes, the first to depict the mind and to express the inward feelings (*ethe*) of men.[8] Each has conquered his own minor province of knowledge, though it is left to the great ones to gather these separate skills into a synthesis whose aim is clear: the perfect registration of the objective world. At this Olympian level the field narrows to a few divinely gifted painters, and in the end to only two – Apollodorus, and Zeuxis. Of Apollodorus' actual paintings Pliny has little to say: what he insists on is Apollodorus' reputation, and that, although there were many good painters prior to his career, with Apollodorus the art enters a new phase. 'There is no painting now on view by any artist before Apollodorus', Pliny says, 'still capable of holding our attention' (*quae teneat oculos*): he is the first true luminary of the art.[9] And his greatest achievement was to 'throw open the gates' to Zeuxis of Heraclea, whose career completed the task Apollodorus had begun.[10] The degree of Zeuxis' success is, of course, indicated by that central anecdote in Western aesthetics, the story Pliny tells of the painting of the grapes, so lifelike that the birds flew down to eat from the Zeuxian vine. Equally important, though consistently overlooked, is what Pliny has to say about the relation that existed between Apollodorus, he who began art, and Zeuxis, he who fulfilled it. Given the intense rivalry between artists which Pliny likes to describe – Apelles drawing on Protogenes' work even finer lines than Protogenes could produce, Parrhasius tricking Zeuxis with his *trompe-l'œil* curtain, and so forth – between the two strongest of the painters we might expect some kind of titanic clash. What we find instead is resignation: 'Of Zeuxis, Apollodorus wrote an epigram to the effect that Zeuxis robbed his teachers of their art, and carried it off with him' (*artem ipsis ablatam Zeuxis ferre secum*).[11] The master is made obsolete by his pupil, and by an act of robbery. Yet if there is pathos in Apollodorus' epigram, Pliny does not dwell on it, since the important concern is not Apollodorus' exhaustion in Zeuxis, but simply Zeuxis' triumph (though Parrhasius, with his ingenious curtain, may well take over where Zeuxis' talent leaves off: this is a marathon race).

Vasari's *Lives of the Painters*, a humanist refashioning of Pliny's account of painting in the *Natural History*, repeats and reinforces the model of progress, with the difference that for Apollodorus, Vasari substitutes Cimabue, and for Zeuxis, Giotto.

But to return to Cimabue: although Giotto's fame obscured his, this was only in fact in the way that a great light dims the splendour of a lesser. Cimabue was, as it were, the first cause of the renewal of the art of painting. Giotto, although he was his pupil, inspired by a worthy ambition and helped by providence and his natural gifts, aspired even higher. And it was Giotto who opened up the door of truth to those who have subsequently brought the art of painting to the greatness and perfection it can claim in our own century. In our time there have been so many marvels and so many miraculous, indeed, well-nigh impossible artistic triumphs to see every day, that we have come to the point where no matter what is done, even if it seems superhuman, no one is astonished.[12]

Just as Apollodorus is the first luminary of antique painting, so Cimabue is the first cause of its renewal in Italy; as Zeuxis outstripped Apollodorus, so Giotto's light outshines that of Cimabue, in a continuous ascent that culminates in the miraculous realism of the High Renaissance; a perfection which articulates together all the knowledge of the past and which, for Vasari, reaches its technical zenith in Raphael, its emotional zenith in Michelangelo. Yet what the passage also states, as the shadow of its optimism, is that exactly because the present state of painting consummates the past, because the art is complete, perfect, fulfilled, there is no clear direction in which painting may now develop. The future of painting is hardly touched on by Vasari, and in a sense it cannot exist: the viewer in Vasari's age is no longer astonished, as were the first viewers of Cimabue and Giotto; not even the miraculous, the artistically impossible, can surprise, because the age of perfection in which Vasari lives is also the era of the *end*, when everything that was to be done, has been done already. In his own painting, Vasari is painfully unable to continue within the tradition which he so admires in his capacity as viewer; yet even as a viewer, he feels himself to exist in a period of anaesthesia and belatedness; he and his age are so flooded by tradition that the perception of beauty is no longer easily available and must be assigned backward in time, to the first generations to see the work of Cimabue and Giotto. The burden of the *Lives* is that of its tense, the aorist past, for Vasari the painter is drowned out by Vasari the viewer, while the viewer must reach into himself and project himself into restropective time if he is to be even a viewer. One rhetorical effect of the theme of 'triumph' now becomes clear, in that it is by means of the idea of artistic triumph that Vasari may diminish or repress its opposite, the fear of belatedness in tradition: it is by heightening the sense of sweeping onward movement that he can subsume and overcome his perception of the finality and paralysis of his own time; just as in Vasari's model, Pliny, the triumph of Zeuxis incorporated and neutralised Apollodorus' recognition of being made a latecomer in the new Zeuxian age.

If I stress the sense of belatedness in Vasari, and point to the suppression of an incipient sense of belatedness in Pliny, it must be understood that nevertheless both Pliny and Vasari are fully committed to the idea of painting's progressive history – the gradual accretion of artistic knowledge which enables the art to approximate ever closer to its goal, the Essential Copy of the real. Artistic knowledge, in this progressive history, does not differ in kind from the knowledge acquired by the inductive method in science. According to the theory of induction, the scientist carries out experiments which yield precise observations of the natural world; these observations he duly records, and, as the corpus of observation grows, recurrences within data begin to appear, regularities which the scientist abstracts from the data and formulates as propositions of a general nature, which is to say, as laws.[13] Science is the name given to the collective body of such propositions; the stock of propositions is derived by direct observation of the universe, and grows as more and more phenomena in the natural world are subjected to controlled examination, and their regularities recorded and classified. In the same way, Pliny's and Vasari's 'classical' account of painting describes artistic evolution as an accumulation of controlled observations: from unmediated observation the painter abstracts patterns of recurrence, and these patterns he records in his work as forms. The stock of artistic forms develops as more and more visual phenomena are subjected to detailed examination. According to both views, of science and of painting, the progress of knowledge moves smoothly and inevitably towards its goal, the perfect understanding and representation of the surrounding world.

Tradition is never a problem here, since the past supplies only support for the present: the body of lawlike propositions, in science, and of accurate forms, in painting, develops by simple addition. The findings of the present are cast into the existing repertoire of knowledge: they do not emerge from that repertoire; it is to nature they owe their origin, and since the laws of nature may be supposed to be unchanging, inductive knowledge therefore knows no historical dimension. In its view observations from the past and from the present are on equal footing: both past and present knowledge are *contemporary*, in that the universe which is the object of knowledge is static in its laws and forms; it makes no difference when those immutable laws and forms are discovered. Reference to a changeless universe from which observations are perpetually drawn thus annuls tradition as problem, by making art timeless in the fashioning of its truths. The only orientation of which an artistic tradition is susceptible is therefore towards the future, for it is in the future that finer observations will be made, more accurate propositions and forms developed, until a point is finally reached at which knowledge will be total, and the orientation towards futurity will be abolished in a synthesis where science and art meet, in convergent presence with their object.

To place Gombrich alongside Pliny and Vasari may at first sight seem anomalous, since the model of knowledge on which Gombrich structures his theory of art so conflicts with inductive method. If we read Gombrich through his own precursor, Sir Karl Popper, the description of knowledge which he advances seems to bear little resemblance to that of the 'classical' account.[14]

According to Popper, who in turn is refashioning Hume, we cannot know phenomena absolutely, since even if in every recorded instance event Y has always followed event X, observation has no bearing on prediction: science cannot construct 'laws', only hypotheses, hypotheses which may at a later date be proven false.[15] A necessary provisionality enters the scene: science must renounce its ambition to construct a perfect map of the way things are. *Art and Illusion* transposes Popper's position into its own domain. As with science, so with art: the painter does not depict the visual field in absolute terms; he, too, must deal in hypotheses, hypotheses constantly to be tested against the visual field, but hypotheses only: there can be no more hope of an Essential Copy in art, than there can be hope in science of an ultimate blueprint, or final chart of universal laws. Let us take a classic illustration of Gombrich's argument: Giotto is at work depicting the Crucifixion (illustration 6). Tradition suggests to him certain ways of proceeding: in particular, the model of Cimabue's handling of the

6 Giotto *The Crucified Christ* (detail of painted cross); S. Maria Novella, Florence

Crucifixion subject presents and recommends itself (illustration 7). The inherited formula, or *schema*, is tested against what Giotto discovers for himself in the visual field: here the schema coincides with reality – Cimabue has clearly understood the effects of torsion on the musculature of the ribs and the arms; there the schema is inadequate to reality – Cimabue has no sense of the individuation of the muscles, nor of the modelling of skin over muscle in actual lighting conditions. Where the schema is found inadequate, Giotto corrects it. In turn, the new image will become a schema for later

7 Cimabue, *The Crucified Christ* (detail of painted cross); S. Domenico, Arezzo

artists, in whose hands it will be subjected to further testing, further modification, and further transmission.

The concept of the schema, central to Gombrich's work, does not seem to imply a pessimistic understanding of the art of the past: the story told by *Art and Illusion* is one of advancing knowledge, and it is only when we stand back and survey what the account chooses to omit, that we can see hidden within it another, and darker, view of tradition. When Giotto comes to paint the Crucifixion, Cimabue's prior example provides an instrument through which to perceive the visual field more clearly than Cimabue himself was able to do: the earlier work supports and sustains the later; and indeed without Cimabue's contribution, Gombrich argues, Giotto would be lost – he would literally not know where to begin. The sense of tradition here is resolutely that of progress towards the ever-increasing accuracy of represen- tations. Moreover, once the painter actually confronts the visual field, tradition becomes *weightless*. The work of 'testing' the inherited schema against the world of actual appearances con- stantly points beyond inheritance: in discovering how skin really does curve and inflect over the bone-structure of the body, and how these curves and inflections actually look when bathed in light, at exactly these points Giotto ceases to be Cimabue's heir: he moves out of legacy into a fresh, uncharted zone of exploration where he, the latecomer, is the first to tread. Giotto may well have been unable to find that zone unaided, and to that extent his visual discoveries are circumscribed by his predecessor; but what the predecessor has supplied is a schema that indicates beyond itself, towards virgin land. The concept of 'testing' allots to tradition a role as positive as it is delimited: positive, in that it supplies the painter with an indispensable repertoire of instruments with which to confront the visual field; delimited, in that once the painter scans the world of appearances through the instruments the past supplies, he will see beyond the old gridwork to those phenomena which emerge precisely in the gaps or shortcomings of past formulae: tradition presents of itself the means of its own undoing.

It is in the emphasis which Gombrich places on art as the testing of hypotheses, that he rejoins the company of Pliny and Vasari: once again painting is affirmed in its forward movement and the past need never be a burden, since its historical dimension is at every point of 'testing' annulled at the touch of facts disclosed for the first time. In this respect Gombrich's work remains curiously close to the optimistic vein of Reynolds' *Discourses*: for Reynolds also, the study of previous masters was justifiable on instrumental grounds, as the straightest route to the appearance of nature. Given many lifetimes, the apprentice might eventually rediscover on his own the truths already stated by Raphael, Michelangelo, and the antique; but such solitary and redundant striving is made un- necessary by the very fact of latecoming, since exactly because he comes late in tradition the newcomer is able to take advantage of the previous generations' work, to incorporate their discoveries, to see more clearly and to work more closely with nature, than they. Reynolds, like Gombrich, practises optimism as official policy – each generation stands on the shoulders of the last. Yet from the very optimism of that policy there emerges, as a consequence which must be kept hidden if optimism is to prevail, the opposite view: arriving late on the stage of painting's history, the neophyte painter on his own can do nothing, in the short life before him, that will equal the knowledge of accumulated generations that is stored within tradition. It is the Masters who have already wrested from nature her secrets, her 'central forms', and the newcomer's efforts can only consist in the retracing of problems already solved: before he can continue within tradition, he must absorb into himself the vast corporate sum of the Old Masters' expertise. The more Reynolds and Gombrich praise the support that the past supplies the present, the closer they come to saying, by the same token, that compared with the corporate achievement embodied in tradition, the achievement of the newcoming or latecoming painter must be minute: if achievement can exist at all – for the greater the tradition, the harder it will be for the painter to discover terrain that the tradition has not yet fully exhausted. Yet this is an implication hardly consistent with the onward progress which Reynolds, like Gombrich, officially celebrates, and though the argument in praise of tradition is on the point of conversion into its opposite with every plaudit Reynolds accords the Old Masters, it is in fact Hazlitt who brings the *reversible* nature of the argument into sharpest focus:

Michel Angelo, the cartoons of Leonardo da Vinci, and the antique, your correspondent tells us, produced Raphael. Why have they produced no second Raphael? What produced Michel Angelo, Leonardo da Vinci, and the antique? Surely not Michel Angelo, Leonardo da Vinci, and the antique?[16]

Hazlitt's question, expressing here as everywhere in his writings on art the pain of the painter unable to subdue the viewer in himself, gives an exact and Janus-like balance to both sides. There is no need for the newcomer to study the art of the past since he has, and should be left to enjoy, access to unmediated perception of the only true source of art, the world of natural forms. And yet the newcoming artist *cannot* enjoy access to that world exactly because Michelangelo, Raphael, and the antique have preceded him there: it is precisely because there has been Raphael, that there can be no *second* Raphael.

One might describe the rhetorical figure Hazlitt employs as peripeteia, taking that word from the pivotal moment in classical theatre when, with all the forces present in the dramatic situation visibly at work, the wheel of fortune begins to turn. It is the figure which dominates the tradition we are presently examining. In

Pliny, the celebration of Zeuxis' achievement generates out of itself its concealed consequence, the demise of Apollodorus, for whom Zeuxis' achievement is felony. In Vasari, hagiography produces from its own excess the recognition that the tradition's brilliance inevitably leads to its own eclipse, and that to complete or perfect its history is also to proclaim its end. And for Gombrich, the analysis of the formative role of the schema in tradition produces, as its unacknowledged consequence, the first complete and negative vision of artistic tradition, as a perpetual dependency upon the past.

To be sure, this is not at all Gombrich's official story, which is one of tradition robust as never before, and of the wholly beneficial legacy of forms and schemata which each generation passes on to the next. Yet the corollary of such 'positive transmission' is that no generation of painters can stand in direct relation to the world or to the visual field: always the schema, tradition's instrument of deflection, comes to intervene; and if the neophyte painter is to see the world with his *own* eyes, he must therefore direct his effort towards surpassing the schemata of his inheritance. Let us return to Giotto's *Crucifixion*. If Giotto is to represent the play of light over flesh and bone, first he must dismantle the rigid scaffolding of Cimabue's figure, and the hard, bracketed curves which prevent the modelling of the body in three dimensions; he must interrupt the smooth and artificial continuum of the torso, by placing a pronounced depression at the sternum; to articulate the eyebrows with the nose he must remove the imaginary muscle between the eyebrows; he must replace geometric with volumetric expressions in the face. In order to carry out his own enterprise, Giotto must *break* Cimabue's format: a necessary iconoclasm begins to emerge.

Iconoclasm is not a phenomenon Gombrich chooses to analyse, yet once one is alerted to the breaking of tradition that is an intrinsic condition of the forward movement which Gombrich's account celebrates, it becomes possible to view the Western tradition as propelled by an iconoclastic impulse as deep as its commitment to 'realism'. For Pollaiuolo to make the Milan *Portrait of a Lady* his own (illustration 8), he cannot remain with the received formula for the profile portrait as it comes to him from his gothic predecessors (illustration 9).[17] A neck that had been little more than a stem connecting head to shoulders, must bend at its corners to meet the lines of the chin and the upper body, the back of the head and the in-curving spine; the line of the eyebrow must move in order to register the orbit beneath; the necklace must rise at the back and fall at the front, to describe the complex oblate curve of the neck. If we look at Gombrich's schema in practice, in the actual making of the image, what we discover is the opposite of the gradualism of tradition to which the account remains officially committed; the relation of neophyte to precursor is in fact one of intrinsic *antagonism*. We are not dealing here simply with the improvement of details, but rather with radical effacement of the *principles* of the precursor's work: the prototype becomes deficient point by point when viewed across its later remodelling, yet when taken on their own the features Pollaiuolo is at such pains to undo possess a strong original coherence. We might characterise the earlier portrait by saying that it is structured around the principle of the *edge*, and that by dramatising the hard, bright edges against their background of darkness the prototype unites as positives the features Pollaiuolo will later work hardest to erase: the (to him) unnaturally long lines running from the bridge of the nose into the hairline, and from the back of the head into the spine. For Pollaiuolo, no attempt at analysis or refinement of the elements may take place until the leading principle which holds the prototype together is destroyed. That earlier painting has had to

8   Antonio Pollaiuolo, *Portrait of a Lady*

cope with its own problems of wresting from tradition an image that will cohere on its own terms, and its solution has been an intensification of edges; yet what constitutes the success and the coherence of the earlier image, when viewed in the retrospective time of tradition, is a barrier to be torn down. Pollaiuolo must deliberately misregard the prototype, actively misinterpreting its leading principle of the edge as a deficiency in Pollaiuolo's own leading principle, of volume. Pollaiuolo is not only appropriating the earlier image for his own use; in order to achieve that, he is also denying the principle by which the predecessor had claimed possession of that image – the edge; which means that his first

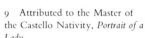

9 Attributed to the Master of the Castello Nativity, *Portrait of a Lady*

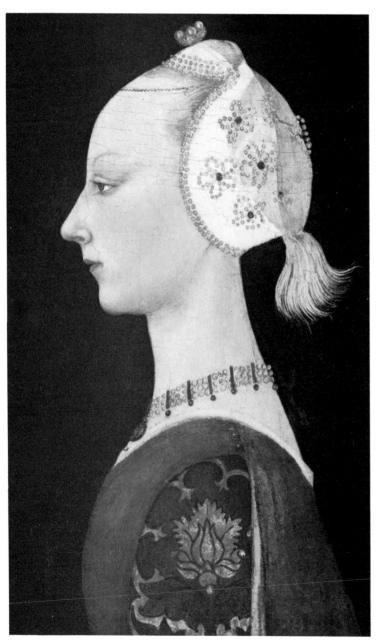

priority must consist in denying possession to the precursor.

With cases such as these, it is pointless to appeal to an idea of smooth and incremental advances towards the Essential Copy, or to tradition's primarily supportive role; Pollaiuolo and Giotto have creatively corrected their predecessors, but if this is so it is by the way of a vigorous miscognition of the principles at work in the earlier images, principles holding those images, so to speak, in place, and therefore working against the interests of later appropriation. The myth of the peaceful transmission of the schema through time may open up consoling vistas of tradition and its continuities, yet in practice a schema may be dislodged and made to function in a new way only by transgression of the earlier work: for the child to become a changeling it must first be successfully unhoused, and for this to happen the later work must deny the rationale of its prototype. Gombrich's official celebration of artistic heritage as a system of beneficent patronage takes us, paradoxically, to the brink of the first tragic account of tradition, as perpetual warring across the generations and as continuous iconoclasm: the denial of original possession which Apollodorus names, in Zeuxis, as theft.

III

Although in Gombrich the negative appraisal of tradition is largely concealed by the idea of benign legacy, in his hands the schema fulfils such wide-ranging functions that (whether or not this result was intended) his analysis of the schema entails an almost complete description of inheritance as dispossession. If we take the schema to be an inheritance of an *executive* nature, a craft-formula handed down (directly or otherwise) from master to apprentice, and existing as it were in the musculature of the painter – absorbed by him in the physical activity of the studio – its effect is to maintain a steady state of inertia. The apprentice sets out to record on canvas the visual field before him: the scene contains an infinity of aspects, any number of which he may wish to set down; yet the moment he takes up his brush, the dead hand of the schema lays itself across his own, binding his fingers to the repetition of the ways things have been done in the past. Tradition here behaves as a kind of manual paralysis, an ebbing of the hand's natural vitality, forcing it back into tracks or furrows which its own energies will cut still deeper. The failure of the present to overcome the past does not end with its immediate defeat in local time, but passes into the future as additional entropy; not the sins, but the obediences of the fathers are visited on their sons. And if we take the schema to be an inheritance of a *phenomenal* order, the consequences are still more drastic. When the neophyte painter opens his eyes on the visual field, what he will see there will depend on what, from tradition,

he already knows. To break the circuit of repetitions he must fight
to go beyond what he has been permitted or set up to see, which is
to say that in him the antagonism of tradition is introjected, and
what must be dislodged is his *own* vision. The schemata which
open up the visual field also close it down, so that memory
becomes a kind of darkening or blindness. Again, few have
described this occlusion better than Nietzsche:

> For the rapture of the Dionysian state with its annihilation of the ordinary
> bounds and limits of existence contains, while it lasts, a *lethargic* element in
> which all personal experiences of the past become immersed. This chasm
> of oblivion separates the worlds of everyday reality and Dionysian
> reality. But as soon as this everyday reality re-enters consciousness, it is
> experienced as such, with nausea: an ascetic, will-negating mood is the
> fruit of these states.[18]

Memory, the mother of the Muses, is the faculty the seer of the
new must activate if he is to fix the fleeting forms of the vision that
lie on the far or Dionysian side of perception; yet it is the influx of
remembrance of past forms that drowns the moment of disclosure
or revelation in its own Lethean waters. In order to escape that
influx the painter must continue to rise above everything he has
known before; he must pull himself above his own habitual
processes of cognition in a willed forgetfulness that seeks to empty
itself of all remembered contents. In order to see clearly, the past
must be shed as it persists in the painter's own being: yet to record
the perceptions revealed in that higher state of vision he must again
fall into the quotidian or the customary, and if he is to paint what
he saw in the higher state he must somehow contrive to return to
the customary without losing what it is he has seen – a task as
elusive as catching a dream when we are on the point of leaving it,
and one which depends on screening out from consciousness the
faculty of memory that threatens to reduce everything that was
seen to a repetition of the already-known.

Though the rhetoric of progress is at pains to deny it, what the
idea of the schema centres upon is the combat of the painter with
the past both *around* and *within* himself. It is a struggle far more
demanding in the case of painting than it is for the other arts, and
particularly for literature. Literature's medium, the Word, is in
constant circulation throughout society, and reflects with instant
sensitivity the slightest variations in social existence.[19] While a
society may dispense altogether with the production of images, as
certain historical societies have done, if any society were to
dispense with the Word it would at once grind to a halt: the Word
is present at every point of social and material activity; it is
indispensable to the functioning of the social organism. And this
means that literature, a specialised body of language withdrawn
from collective movement into a privileged and sheltered domain,
is always able to renovate itself by permitting the inflow of
discourse from the outside; we can even say that in the global life of

languages, the sequestration of literature is an artificial stillness in the general turbulence, and that its clearing of a zone of aesthetic contemplation of the Word is exceptional within the primarily *functional* economy of language. But apart from certain primitive systems, the medium of the image has no knowledge of this functional life. Even in reduced systems, such as advertising, public information, and propaganda, where our own societies find an instrumental role for images, these can easily be replaced by verbal devices, and indeed it is primarily as a shorthand, which rapidly translates back into language, that in such systems the image is deployed.[20] Since the ubiquity and social pervasiveness of the Word is exactly lacking to the image, the latter cannot directly renew itself, as literature can, by seeking or permitting an inflow into tradition from the outside. Moreover, for images the barriers which mutually divide the national languages do not exist; and while this ensures an immeasurably greater accessibility of images to the viewer and from his standpoint must represent a total gain, for the painter it entails also that the field of pressure from the precursors is that much greater. Mobile in its internationalism, painting is by the same token exposed to tradition's physical mass and gravity. It is, of course, the repertoire of available schemata which now comes to clear the stage, narrowing what might be an unintelligible bombardment of influence to humanly manageable scale, and, in this, functioning in a similar fashion to the canon in literature: out of the chaos or babel of conflicting representations, only a few are singled out and posited as models for repetition.[21] Yet once again, it is the power of the schema that is thereby reinforced, since only by its aid may the pressure of influence be reduced, in a movement that converts the schema's capacity to organise the oppressive disparateness into a further legitimation of its own authority. The means to organise the tradition cannot easily flow in from the outside, but must be forged from within: in order to introduce a principle of intelligibility, tradition must, in other words, suppress or neutralise large spans of its own extant being, and the instrument whereby this is achieved, the schema, is accordingly invested with the full force of what it has been able to overcome.

Yet however intense may be the pressure of tradition's schemata on the painter, it is not only there that we discover the seriousness of the problem of the past for the life of the image. Here we must shift our attention away from the painter and from the practical difficulty of *beginning* towards the circuit of recognition which underpins the activities equally of painter and of viewer. As we have seen, the spokesmen for tradition are always in a position to appeal against the weight of the past by invoking a continuous presence of nature; in the end, they argue, the painter need not fear his latecoming in time, since the world of changeless natural forms is as available to him as it had been to the ancients – the ancients had themselves no preceding tradition to fall back upon, and the greatness of their achievement, despite that hindrance, testifies to what can be done by an art that works from nature alone. It is this argument which enables a theorist of classicism such as Reynolds to retain his buoyancy: the address to Nature or to Truth allows the painter to go behind his predecessors and to contact that which ante-dates tradition; by this means the newcomer can drink directly from the source, and cast his predecessors into their own belatedness. In Gombrich also it is the alleged perceptual access to natural forms which still works to preserve the concept of a tradition permanently open to the outside, and therefore a house of welcome. But what the painter deals in is *representations, not perceptions*, and even as he is recording for the first time an aspect of nature that has eluded all his predecessors, for his image to be recognised it must participate in the economy of signs; and, once we take it on ourselves to consider painting as an art of the sign, then a deeper aspect of belatedness, and one which affects the whole circuit of viewing and of painting, must strike us: that the recognition of signs can never occur in presence.

The logic of recognition is difficult to hold steady, but let us take some simple cases first. When an individual makes a statement such as 'I know that face' or 'I wasn't sure before, but now I know where we are', what he is doing is comparing a present with a past occurrence. A face appears: it looks familiar; a rapid search is carried out in the memory-bank to see if the face is on file. It is: the present and the past instances match; the face is recognised. An individual is unsure of the way: perhaps the road is the same as the one he took before, but perhaps there has been a wrong turning. Now a landmark appears: it matches the recollection of its earlier appearance; he recognises that he is on the right road. With examples such as these, only the individual concerned is capable of performing these acts of recognition, since only he possesses the original data: these are purely private transactions. But now consider two people looking at an image; for example, the representation of a *Pietà*. They cannot 'recognise' the image in the same way that they might recognise a face or a landmark, since the original datum is missing. Recognition is constructed by social codes and acquired through instruction: we learn to identify a certain class of representations as a *Pietà*. Mistakes can be made. If asked what we see before us, in ignorance of the code of recognition we might very well answer that it is an old woman with a corpse; but that would be an error – such a response is at odds with the socially constructed codes, and is simply mis-recognition.

The two types of recognition – public and private – are readily confused. It is tempting to think that the recognition of painting is a purely private affair, since it seems to link together two self-enclosed and private worlds of sensation: the painter's, and the viewer's. The painter is at work in his studio, transcribing on to canvas the data of the visual field: the viewer is alone in the gallery, contemplating the result; and we might suppose that we are dealing here with a kind of *transmission* of perception, from the painter to the viewer, across the *relay* of the image. The rest of the world seems excluded, so silent is the communication; and just as recognising a face involves private linking between a present and a past sensation, so we might fall into supposing that perceptions are again being linked together, in the privacy of art. Recognition here seems to take place when the two mental fields, of painter and viewer, become *congruent*, and the viewer feels an 'inner experience' of recognising. The criterion of recognition might then seem to be just this inner experience, of 'Now I see what this is'; an experience occurring invisibly and inwardly, in private recesses of the mind.

But such a criterion for recognition will be clearly seen as false if we consider sign-systems other than painting. With mathematics, for example, I may indeed experience a vivid sensation of understanding a formula, but the criterion of my knowing it was a *formula* (in the first place) would be my awareness of its mathematical application. The test of whether or not I had understood the formula is not to be looked for in the inner recesses of my subjectivity, but rather in my ability to place the formula in the context of mathematical techniques, to carry out related calculations, and so forth: in my executive competence. Again, in the case of a child learning to read, it is hard to determine the sense of the question, 'Which was the first word the child *read*?' The question looks as though it appeals to some inward accompaniment to the physical progress of the eye through the sequence of letters, an accompaniment which eventually crystallises into a 'Now I can read' sensation. But the criterion for right reading cannot be this: the child might well have such a sensation, yet be quite unable to read correctly. Reading, like mathematics – and like the recognition of images – can be said to take place only when the individual is able to 'go on'; not when he experiences an inner sensation of recognising symbols, but rather when he is able to meet the executive demands placed upon him by the outside and social world.[22]

When the painter sets down on canvas his representation of the new aspect of nature that eluded all his predecessors, he is therefore not as alone as he might wish to think. While drinking at the source, and contemplating with Adamic gaze the phenomenon which so interested him, then perhaps he had gone beyond his precursors in discovering the thing each of them had missed; but the moment he begins to articulate his sensation or his vision into painting, he enters a domain of symbolic relations which is, from the first, communal. The criterion of right recognition involves *always more than one observer*: only *across* individuals and in an *arc* of recognition, does the medium of signs take shape.[23] For his private sensation to be recognised, it must be passed into a symbolic register of painting where it ceases to be his alone. Maybe to him the image he makes will always recall the lost Adamic sensation; but if it does, that inward recollection will be, with respect to the image, both contingent and redundant; it will exist to one side of the sign, not within the sign itself. Signs cannot exist outside of social formations, since only in as much as they have achieved consensual regularity do they exist as signs: the sign has its being in the interval *between those who recognise it*, and beyond that individual arc of recognition, ceases to exist.

If the concept of the *schema* allows us perhaps for the first time to see into the intrinsic pain of creative process, it is the concept of the *sign* which reveals the permanent belatedness of every representation. Let us imagine that the painter has succeeded in lifting himself above the Lethean tide of tradition, and is seeing an aspect of the world with innocent eyes: before he saw nature as through a glass, darkly, but now face to face. For as long as he stays with his perception, in the vernal freshness of discovery, he is sole possessor of the prospect. But as soon as he tries to communicate his perception, he must join a circuit of recognition which pre-dates his perception, and which ends at a stroke both his solitude and his original ownership of the scene. The perspective of recognition, to which the painter must now submit, is subject to constraints wholly different from those present in his original vision. In order to communicate what he has seen, he must take the scene of his vision and re-envision it from the viewpoint of others; putting himself in their place he is obliged to reinvent himself not as painter, but as viewer of the work he sets out to make. The conditions surrounding the installation of this other viewpoint are not at all like those that attended the original scene. There he had been alone in his perceptual horizon, and the new aspect of the world that disclosed itself to him emerged only when he discovered or attained that solitude.[24] Now he must undo his achievement. The viewpoint of the others must again take over, or there will never be recognition of what he has seen.

Once articulated and set down on canvas, the vision is subject to a complex fate. Let us take the example of a viewer gazing at a version of the Nativity: for him also, the viewpoint of others must be installed, since if he is to recognise the representation for what it is, a Nativity, he must have mastered the appropriate code of iconography. The present Nativity can be known in itself only by referral back to previous engagements of the viewer with the same scene, and to the series of instructions that taught him to classify and identify similar representations as belonging to *this* iconographic category. Perhaps we can more clearly picture the belatedness immanent in recognition by means of the following imaginary experiment. Let us place the viewer in the dark of a lecture room;

projector and screen are in place. An image is beamed on to the screen first as an indecipherable blur; the viewer has no way to decode it. As the lens of the projector moves into focus, certain edges of figures, in a hazy architectural setting, are performing some as yet obscure transaction. The lens moves more exactly into focus: there is a central female figure and a child – perhaps the image is a Madonna Enthroned; there are trees and rocks – perhaps it is a Flight into Egypt; now there are cattle, and that is enough: it is a Nativity. If we give to this stage of the image, which is not yet in full focus, the name of the *minimal schema of recognition*, we can see that at least at the level of generic categories, the minimal schema refers the present image back to the sum of representations known previously to the viewer as the Nativity subject. To recognise this new image, the viewer has not attended to the form it takes now, in the present of viewing, but to the past of remembrance – to the entire class of images which can be substituted for the present one; it is by mobilising the set of substitutions that recognition proceeds. We might perhaps pause at this point, and accord to the axis of substitutions the limited role of providing broad, generic outlines: once the primitive stage of the minimal schema of recognition has been reached, then (we might suppose) the perception of what is unique in the new image may commence. Yet the recognition of *all* the forms in the painting repeats the same pattern, of the invasion of the present by the past: similar schemata of recognition are mobilised at every point and *in every detail*. Recognition *is* this activity of referral to the sets of past cognition, and when it comes to the uniqueness of the present image, this is perceived not in the presence and plenitude of the image the viewer sees before him now, but in the distance of the image from those whose recollection it activates. The unfolding of recognition is not so much a discovery of identity as of *difference* between present and past configurations.[25] The image's identity is the *gap* between 'itself' and the repertoire of images in play; though we now must hesitate in assigning clear outlines to the image 'itself', since its 'self' is not something it possesses in any absolute way. What is perceived in and as the image is relative to the acts of substitution carried out in recognition, and for the viewer these will vary, both historically and individually.

Origin is, in other words, just as problematic for the viewer as for the painter. The viewer may feel, just as much as the painter during his original vision, that the image is uniquely his. He would be quite correct to do so: only he can have experienced precisely his history of exposure to previous visual experience; personal memory stamps that experience as his alone. But memory equally takes from him, through its substitutions, the presence and immediacy of what he sees now; and this has been true *from the beginning*. To ask which was the first painting, or the first form, that the viewer recognised, is to repeat the question, 'Which was the first word the child read?' There may have been any number of occasions when the viewer *thought* he recognised what he saw, but those inward sensations cannot count as criteria of what is meant by recognition. The 'first' image, or the 'first' form, is the first one to be referred *back* to a previous instance in the way consensually defined by recognition's codes. Perhaps it is the previous instance which we should name as 'the first'? But that can hardly be claimed: the previous only becomes *prior* when appropriated by the future as recollection; it can only become a source retroactively.

The world of perception, as it is lived out in organic experience, is radically asymmetrical with the world instituted by the painterly trace. When I look out into the world, it is I who bring into being this world that only I can see in this specific way: I am a consciousness, immediately present to the world, and nothing can claim to exist within this world without in some way being caught in the net of my experience. Within that presence of my perception, at the centre of my lived horizon, I am not this particular person or face, this finite being: I am a pure witness without position and without age, equal to the world's infinity. Yet when I engage in any kind of transaction that involves communication of what I perceive, whether I am a neophyte painter or a neophyte viewer, I must engage with others. My perception can easily retain its self-possession, its composure, when dealing only with things, but to deal with the existence of other people is harder, is *obdurate*; for if another person exists, then he too has a consciousness, occupying the centre of *his* lived horizon; and if he is a consciousness, then I must consent to be for him a finite object, obdurate also, *visible* at a certain place in the world. To communicate my existence, I must draw out of myself signs which may, for me, be saturated in the light that floods the centre of my lived horizon, but these strokes of paint, these marks on canvas, are for him only further objects and obduracies added to the material field. The world as it appeared to me was a constant emergence of order: as I looked, it disclosed itself intermittently and in partial views, and as I saw the aspect of the world that seemed uniquely my possession, for nowhere in the legacy of representation could I find its equivalent, it was exactly as the emergence of the new that I saw it. Yet as I try to translate my experience into signs, there is no way I can convey this fact of lived emergence: the signs I produce to transmit the perception precisely cannot show the latter's emergent character, because the system of signs, no matter how I deploy it, can only appropriate it in terms of its own fully existent nature. I might make a stroke that 'to me' conveys the experience I had, of the material world organising itself in process before my eyes: but for the stroke to become a sign it must engage in the articulation of these signs which come to me from the world of the others, a world that does not know what it is I have experienced: it must engage with the signs that come to me from the past and *as the past*.

Whereas the painter's struggle with the inheritance of the schema was his alone – a kind of solo combat against the ancestors – the bitter jolt from cognition to recognition is shared equally by the painter and by the viewer. In its root form the word 'anxiety' refers to the latin *angustiae*, the narrowing of a road between cliff-sides, the traveller's transit from a landscape of panorama to the enclosure of the mountain-pass; and it is in this sense also that we should understand the anxiety of influence in art, since each stage of painting and of viewing is marked by the same loss of a lived horizon and by the same passage from a vista of continuity-without-limit, through the narrow defiles of the signifier.[26]

The mark of this passage is the painterly trace, but the trace here is not characterised by its following in the track or train of something else, as a wake follows the cleaving of water: there is no retention of original presence in the painterly sign, despite its Zeuxian appearance. Not in the representation of things does the painterly sign have its being, but in a double kind of loss: loss, for the painter, of the plenary possession of his lived horizon; loss, for the viewer, of *this* image, as it passes into the interval between 'this' and the past where alone recognition may reside. Like the stylus of Antiquity, the brush tears into the continuity where its marks are made, breaking open the smooth and waxy surface of presence: where perception had been bathed in air and light, the trace of the brush knows only matter and opacity; and where perception had glimpsed the world on the wing, in the split-second and infinitely fresh disclosure of the now, the trace takes hold of that movement and articulates it through the network of signs. The sign is also on the wing: for it, too, there is motion, as the glance scans from point to point and generates the flow of recognition and of meaning. But its motions are those of the signifier, not of original perception, and to this dynamic of the trace perception must yield, passing from the lived horizon into the sign which surpasses it and absorbs it, back into the inescapable web of tradition and the past.

IV

The *impossibility* of presence is all the more apparent in the art of the West because its Zeuxian ambition is expressed with such vehemence. Outside the West, for example in the scroll attributed to Kuo Hsi called *Clearing Autumn Skies over Mountains and Valleys* (illustration 10), we can see that quite different aims are being realised: the trace here makes no attempt to stand in for presence.[27] There is hardly a mark on its surface in which we do not feel the approach of the brush towards the silk, the bending of individual hairs as the first contact is made, the squeezing out of ink as further pressure is brought to bear. It is impossible to conceive of the image as separate from the means of its production, and the image recognises that the trace does not itself convey any presence; it accepts that no stroke can define in itself, but only in relation to *another* stroke; its full and exuberant acceptance of the symbolic register is exactly what the painting dramatises.

Yet the contest here is for self-presence in the making of the image, not for presence within it; it is waged in the muscles of the painter's hand. In the West presence is a greater prize, and its pursuit is consequently far more intense. Let us take an emblematic moment: the great leap of Bacchus in Titian's *Bacchus and Ariadne* (illustration 11). Mastery of the stroke consists here in its own self-effacement, and all strokes fuse in a moment of the gaze from which their own distraction has been banished. Not one of the participants in the encounter can see the scene as sharply as the viewer. The image captures movement at a point of immobilisation which normal vision does not and cannot experience; it sheds the incomplete and fragmentary vision of its figures, exchanging the shattered or Dionysian vision for a gaze in which all flux is petrified. To arrest Bacchus and to convert his emergence, his destructive suddenness, into the outline and stasis of a frieze, is to raise vision to a superhuman level where it transcends material limitation.

If he is to succeed in possessing the image, Titian, like Kuo Hsi, must engage in combat with the executive schemata which work to prevent authentic expression, yet unlike Kuo Hsi, Titian also undertakes to surpass the viewer, and to go beyond him into a dimension of inaugural vision which begins where normal perception ends: to reach presence the image must dislodge the inert repetitions not only of painting, but of seeing. Pressure of tradition weighs not only on the painter, in his private struggle

10 Attributed to Kuo Hsi, *Clearing Autumn Skies over Mountains and Valleys*

with the precursors, but on the viewer, and on the viewer in the painter. It embraces the whole circuit of visuality. Western or Zeuxian painting is thus in permanent and necessary conflict with the past. The logic of recognition entails that no vernal or primal vision can be represented, yet the pursuit of presence involves endless struggle against repetition, and if the image is to persuade the viewer that it is presence, not representation, then it must constantly conceal its debt to history and deny its origin in the system of signs. Zeuxian painting is condemned always to combat belatedness, and this remains true whether its style is Renaissance, or Baroque, or Rococo, or Neo-classical: if the painter fails in his fight against repetition, presence will elude his image, and tradition will expropriate or annexe his work.

Though all the styles are arenas for tradition's agon, none is therefore as dangerous as Neo-classicism, since what Neo-classicism proposes, the conscious restoration of the alleged origins of the tradition, negates the right to war with tradition at all.

Where Realism, or Zeuxism, issues a mandate of transgressions

11   Titian, *Bacchus and Ariadne*

('where it, the tradition, was, there shall I be'), Neo-classicism issues a mandate of repetitions which blocks the painter's self-individuation against the tradition's background, and threatens him directly with his own death as artist ('where you might have been, there it, the tradition, shall be'). A style which defines itself by restoration, Neo-classicism perceives acutely its latecoming in time: 'We come after, the era of the titans is past, and to absolve ourselves from our late arrival we will move back in time, so that the past is made contemporary with ourselves, and again we may begin.' Yet the solution to belatedness offered in the restorationist project places the painter in a double-bind: to begin, he must turn back into the past, yet in turning back he has yielded to the expropriative force that will take away all beginnings. Neo-classical style constantly risks the loss of inaugural power, and from the first its productions reveal the invasion of the ancestors, not as superego, but as id: in taking away the right to censor or mask the predecessors' work through creative deformation, Neo-classicism erases the boundary between the classical impersonality it seeks and the automatism of serial or repeated forms which in practice it sets in motion.

We need only look at the results. If we consider Mengs' pioneering design in the Villa Albani in Rome, we can see just how disastrously tradition can flood: hardly a trace of personality remains (illustration 12). The same is true of what is probably the most precocious work in English Neo-classicism, Benjamin West's *Agrippina with the Ashes of Germanicus* (illustration 13). West has taken immense pains to reconstruct the moment, in AD 19, when Agrippina, companion in Germanicus' disastrous Eastern campaign, landed at Brundisium together with her children, and

12 Anton Raffael Mengs, *Parnassus*

bearing her husband's ashes; yet despite the studiousness of its reconstruction and the accuracy of its archaeology the painting cannot reinvent a present in which figures are alive: with draperies which look as though they have been carved in terracotta, with skin like enamel and flesh that seems made of cast iron, the people in the painting remain inanimate objects, husks. And in Gavin Hamilton we find the same configuration: the figures in *Andromache Bewailing the Death of Hector* (illustration 14) remain statues, simulacra, and the only vitality that enters their frozen, cryogenic forms comes when Hamilton breaks the circle of repetitions and allows himself to transform the work of his predecessor, Poussin.

Neo-classicism is a deadly style: it has a *lethal* quality, and nearly all of its productions bear, somewhere on their surface, the marks of death. Surveying the masters of his literary tradition, Edward Young observed that 'they *engross* our attention, and prevent a due inspection of ourselves; they *prejudice* our judgement in favour of their abilities, and so lessen the sense of our own; and they *intimidate* us, with this splendour of their renown.'[28] Every word of Young's assessment can be amplified in the case of Neo-classical painting, for unlike literature, painting lacks an immediate 'outside', an opening out on to the verbal discourses that flow through society

13   Benjamin West, *Agrippina with the Ashes of Germanicus*

like a bloodstream; its advance must always involve the breaking
and refiguring of its own bounded past. Looking at these
pioneering works by Mengs, West and Hamilton, we can restate
Young's indictment in even stronger terms: the work of tradition
will mesmerise, unless by repression a space is cleared where the
visions that come from ourselves may be safeguarded and
nurtured; it will debilitate, unless its constrictions can be overcome
by a redirection of the weight of the past against itself; it will blind,
unless its splendours can be dimmed by a willed forgetting. To
succeed, Neo-classicism must find stratagems with which to
outmanœuvre its own premises: beneath the guise of restoration
the tradition must be secretly voided. Its painters must possess a
genius for rationalisation and for subterfuge; which brings us to
David.

14 Gavin Hamilton, *Andromache
Bewailing the Death of Hector*;
engraving by D. Cunego

2 *David and the problem of inheritance*

Antiquity will not seduce me   Jacques-Louis David

I

DAVID'S RELATION to the art of the past, and in particular to the art of Antiquity, is a dark and complicated affair. Embedded within the relation are to be found some of his deepest insights into human vision, yet to this profound dimension of his art 'classical' source analysis – one of the cardinal practices of 'normal' art history (with the force this word has in 'normal' science'[1]) – has chosen to remain blind; not because of the insensitivity or obtuseness of individual art historians, but because the collective assumptions of art historical practice leave so many possibilities in the understanding of what a source is, and the effects it may have, so largely unexplored.

Perhaps the most disabling notion of the source with which to approach David is that, for the painter, sources are simply and neutrally *there*, in the manner of natural substances, or pigments to be mixed. It is a view implicit in what I have elsewhere called the Perceptualist account of painting's function, and evolution – the account, rooted in Antiquity, that proposes as the goal of painting the increasingly accurate registration of visual experience;[2] for if that goal is accepted as explaining the specific orientation of European painting, and its pursuit as providing the basis for a 'progressive' history of painting, then every source will be seen as useful in proportion as it furthers that ambition, just as every source may be seen as discountable or discardable by the painter in as much as it is found not to further (or actually to impede) the reduplicative project. The source is ascribed a primarily instrumental value; it is a tool or mechanism, and accordingly there is no more reason for us to consider the painter's attitude towards his sources, or towards the schemata he has deployed in his work, than there would be for us to consider a carpenter's attitude towards his lathe, his chisel, or his workbench. Instrumental value is timeless: if a tool does the job, there seems no point in asking questions about when it was first devised, or what its original purpose may have been. When they are found still to function efficiently, the schemata are outside history, and only *enter* history when they are discovered to have grown obsolete.

Equally reductive is the related notion, that for the viewer a 32 knowledge of sources is essential for the accurate 'decoding' of representations, where the production and recognition of representations is assumed to follow the model of 'code' and 'message'.[3] The basis for the famous joke-drawing that begins Gombrich's *Art and Illusion* (an ancient Egyptian life-class, where the students accurately copy a hieratically stiff, rigid-limbed model) is that unless we know what are the appropriate conventions governing a particular representation, we will 'decode' the representation in the wrong way (and assume that the Egyptians really *looked* stiff and hieratic).[4] A joke harmless enough – but not if the implication is that the 'conventions' of representation which we learn about by studying the sources and the provenance of a given work are always and only *preconditions* for understanding the work; that such a code 'contains' or 'subsumes' the work, as a set of transformations operating upon the work from the *outside*. What must tend to be overlooked, in such a view, is that in a tradition, and particularly in a tradition of the longevity of European representational art, it cannot be assumed that only one kind of code governs a representation; certainly it cannot be ruled out that a painting will mobilise more than one such set or code. The *play* of styles is what is in danger of being lost here, in the enquiry into the conditions of recognition in the image, since if the model of 'message' and 'code' is accepted it becomes difficult to imagine a painter *working* styles (as one can say that Flaubert works literary and linguistic styles); just as it becomes difficult to imagine an ironic use of style, or a use that defamiliarises or dissents from a style. At risk is the whole range of what might be called the 'tonality' of style, along with every aspect of style as *part* of the image (rather than a code or cognitive framework standing outside it). When the model which asserts the *external* relationship of 'code' to 'message' is rigidly followed, the painter is denied one of the richest and most vital parameters of his art, for he is in effect reduced to an agent of visual reproductions for whom the art of the past is little else than a set of more or less adequate work-tools, to be set aside when found unequal to the task. But the styles are not only instruments, or schemata: in the case of representational art, at least, they are also fields of the sign and of discourse; and concerning these we have every reason to expect from the painter, an operator of discourse as well as of design, the most complex attitudes.

II

Let us take two early works of David, *The Combat of Mars and Minerva* of 1771 (illustration 15), and the *Antiochus and Stratonice* of 1774 (illustration 20).[5] Both are so heavily dependent on sources that if we take their measure in terms of 'originality', where this is defined by a formalist comparison, then neither will seem to amount to any kind of impressive achievement: if we were to blot over those areas of the two images that are clearly derived from David's precursors, the remainder would in each case amount to only a fraction of the whole. The figure of Mars, in the first painting, is probably taken from Doyen, perhaps from the *Juno and Aeolus* of 1753; the figure of Minerva, which recalls similar goddesses by Carle van Loo, moves further back in time; the defeated warrior to the right of the painting seems to come from Fragonard; the aerial platform supporting Venus, made of a mysterious filler-substance that looks like cloud yet acts like cushioning, takes us into the vaporous and tinted world of Boucher; while the oddly rearranged anatomy of Venus, leaning over to look at Mars, yet with breasts which rise up to point directly at the viewer, belongs to the even older tradition of Natoire. David's painting of 1771 is almost wholly accountable to the past. And *Antiochus and Stratonice* is much the same. Every aspect of Antiochus' pose, together with the prominent post of his bed, the toothed crowns, the physician's outstretched hand, that slightly nervous gesture of Stratonice – even the overhanging drape, and the idea of a view extending behind the figures to the right; these details are imported directly from Pietro da Cortona (illustration 21).[6] Stratonice has perhaps been further modified by

15 Jacques-Louis David, *The Combat of Mars and Minerva*

the more restrained figures of Neo-classicism, such as the Andromache in Gavin Hamilton's *Death of Hector* (illustration 14): the body

is tall and columnar, the feet are clearly articulated with the floor,
and the head is in profile; while the figure behind Stratonice, the
servant at the lower right of the painting, comes from a rather
different provenance – kneeling, humble, and saturated with
markers connoting 'surprised realisation', Stratonice's handmaid
echoes the various kneeling women in LeBrun's *The Queens of
Persia at the Feet of Alexander*.[7]

Normal source analysis might well end here, on a note of
disappointment at the impoverished state of David's imagination
in the 1770s. What I would rather suggest is that source analysis has
not yet properly begun. It would be wrong to imagine, in the case
of *Mars and Minerva*, that David is simply at the mercy of his
precursors' visions: accountable to the precursors though the
image may seem, what fails to emerge in the customary scansion of
influence is *how* David mobilises the images of the past; and
essentially what *Mars and Minerva* does is deliberately to open itself
to the whole course of French painting styles since Natoire. The
painting doesn't so much continue their advance from the point
the evolution of styles had reached in 1771, as end that advance by
going back to the origin of the French rococo styles; and having
moved back as far as Natoire, it then retraces the stylistic evolution
that runs, in distinct and successive stages, through to Doyen. *Mars
and Minerva* places itself in tradition by throwing a cordon round a
certain consistent and self-enclosed corpus of precursive work,
thereby defining an epoch of styles, to which it offers itself up as
containing vessel, or palimpsest. Such recapitulation is acutely
conscious of style as historically emergent and historically bounded
– there is no question that David is accepting the formulae and
schemata of the past uncritically, or treating them as though their
temporal position were within the present time of craft. On the
contrary, the styles are so juxtaposed that the usually invisible
'conventions of representation' – the code or metalanguage not
normally detectable when a work by Natoire or Boucher or
Doyen is viewed on its own – are conspicuously foregrounded; the
painting includes *as content* both the precursive 'message' *and* its
'code'.

In rhetorical or discursive terms, the painting's apprehension of
its precursors unfolds through a figure of irony, by which one does
not necessarily mean that the precursors are mocked; only that
their productions are suspended within a logically higher set,
within an image which presents itself (at the extreme level of
refinement embodied in this painting) as a container of other
images, rather than as an independent content. Of course there *is* a
content – this new scene of Mars and Minerva. But that is not the
image's *raison d'être*, and, if we think it is, our approach is little short
of rustic. The label is worn deservedly, if a Perceptualist theory

tells us that knowledge of the work of Natoire, Boucher, van Loo and Doyen 'helps us to recognise' the scene, providing us with the key that will decode the message, 'Mars fights with Minerva'. But what one recognises is not merely this mythological subject, this pretext for the painting: but a figure as familiar in the study of discourse as it is impossible in the Perceptualist account, ironic contextualisation. Two terms are created: the present image, and images from the past ('sources'); and the effect, in this particular case, lies entirely in the uneasy relation between those terms. From one point of view, the present image is curiously self-effacing, and in a sense invisible (it is *all* context, no content; it banishes as embarrassment the contamination of content): it nuances the images of the past, but it does not allow itself to come into view alongside those images (as though that, too, would be a lapse of taste). And since no urgently new image is forthcoming, against which to measure the cited or quoted imagery, here one is dealing with irony in the virtually pure form, of inflection. The precursors' images are inflected but not challenged; modified from some external position, yet that position is stated *only* through inflection. We might most vividly characterise the inflection as *vocal*: it is a matter of how the existing fields of discourse are organised and rearranged, of redistribution rather than inauguration.

The location of the logically higher or 'containing' set is therefore indeterminate: we cannot state with certainty that its address to the quoted styles is one of reverence or irreverence, only that it has cultivated an 'unspecified' form of ironic interval. Features which might point towards admiration would include the deftness with which the series of styles is blended into coherence of colour and touch – a blending which neither falls into mimicry nor yokes together by violence; yet against this one must set the bathos which inevitably results when a long evolutionary process is seen under conditions of compression or abbreviation ('speeded up'). David goes *behind* Doyen and behind Carle van Loo to the high rococo of Boucher and Fragonard against whose background their achievement had emerged, and behind high rococo to rococo's own key source or precursor, Natoire; and this successive placing of the past against the past acts as a counter to the self-effacement (the comparative invisibility) of *Mars and Minerva* as an independent image, for what it amounts to is a subduing of the force of the past by recapitulative irony. David, coming later than all these artists, is subject to a pressure of belatedness far greater than the pressure they themselves had individually experienced. Where the precursors, according to this image, had been able to swim in their tradition without perceiving it *as* tradition, David perceives it exactly as that: he measures the extent of an entire school and, so to speak, takes it on (and we should remember that although for us 'rococo' is a term ready-made, David is creating that term, watching the condensation of a vernacular idiom into a historical style, discovering a discursive boundary). But by accepting the belatedness in which he finds himself exactly at the moment he defines the tradition, he turns the pressure of the tradition round, so that he, the latecomer, is seen to know more than any of his predecessors could have known. By taking each of the precursors in turn, and by pitting each painter against that painter's own precursor, David playfully *diminishes* both sides; each artist is depotentiated by making visible the predecessor he had worked to overcome; while the earlier artist is weakened by citation of the successor who displaced him.

What David is not doing, is simply continuing a tradition: if he were, we should have, in addition to the allusions to the art of the past, a clear innovative statement from David; and this is exactly unforthcoming. Normal analysis of sources cannot easily penetrate this subtle terrain, for in its attachment to the idea that a source is simply a block of imagery transported from image *x* into image *y*, it is unable to comprehend a deployment of sources where there *is* no clear image *y*, and where the painter's work on sources has been carried out in terms of configuration, rather than straight importation. *Mars and Minerva* is essentially a patterning, a re-ordering, a *turning* of sources; and perhaps the most accurate word to describe this activity is the rhetorical term *trope*, from the Greek *tropos*, to turn. Within an ironic suspension, *Mars and Minerva* tropes tradition in the first place by gathering it together through synecdoche or totality – David's palimpsest recapitulates a dynasty of styles, from Natoire to Doyen; and it tropes tradition in the next place by fragmentation or bathos – each component style is defined and diminished by bringing forward from the past the earlier style it had laboured to replace, and at the same time by presenting from the future the later style which rendered it obsolete.

Mars and Minerva is an impressive piece of what we might now think of as graduate painting: under the guise of homage, David turns or tropes tradition in such a way that his own painting – through its tropes, not its content – achieves a kind of panoptic elevation above tradition, a detachment or equidistance from styles which might otherwise, and taken in such massive doses, tend to engulf. It is a painting which acts out the fall from stylistic innocence which will so trouble David's career, as it will trouble Ingres and Delacroix, for the question of tradition is now far from simple. It may have been possible for Boucher to relax in the support given to his work by Natoire – and by merging the early styles with their later offspring, David establishes with each fusing stroke a myth of continuum and dynastic confidence; but it is a confidence that David declares he cannot easily share. Continuous with no particular predecessor, and apparently no closer to the painters of the recent generation than to Boucher and Natoire, David presents himself as the heir to a generalised, but distant inheritance. His precursors might relax in tradition, their relaxation the result of perceiving the style in which they swam as a vernacular, a natural idiom; but for David that vernacular idiom is perceived as a *tradition*, and the implication is that this painter who presents himself in such refined disengagement from the predecessors he invokes is altogether tougher-minded and more experienced than they had been: where they had been innocent, he is disabused; and although David's mastery of technique is more than equal to the tradition he describes, the strongest single emotion that emanates from the painting is, curiously, not the delight in virtuosity which one might expect, but rather an unfocussed melancholy; David knows (he states) that his work comes at the tradition's end, at the point where a transparent vernacular clouds over, grows opaque, and becomes – exactly – a tradition; as he knows that the troping of tradition by which he makes the painting his own entails a sorrowful termination of others' continuities.

III

Yet it does a disservice to the stylistic complexity in early David if we think of *Mars and Minerva* simply as an *envoi* to rococo. On the contrary, what is striking about David's career in the 1770s is the persistence of his interest in rococo at a time when 'progressive' tendencies at the Académie were moving rapidly towards a new, neo-Poussinist orthodoxy.[8] The rising star of severity was not in fact David, but David's now underestimated rival Peyron; and to understand the stylistic intricacies of David's *Antiochus and Stratonice* of 1774 (illustration 20) we must first grasp what stylistically is at stake in the competition that takes place between David and Peyron for the *Prix de Rome* in 1773. David's submission *The Death of Seneca* (illustration 16) persists in its rococo echoes: refusing to yield before ascendant neo-Poussinism, David fills his canvas with allusions to Tiepolo and Fragonard. By contrast, Peyron's corresponding submission *The Death of Seneca* (illustration 17) is, on the face of it, an exercise in the shedding of such *retardataire* allusions, where swooning, operatic figures give way to figures now motionless and restrained; the use of indefinite ground-plan, and the tendency to treat architecture as a backdrop, give way to the systematic integration of figure with architecture, in a space rationalised by an explicit and coherent ground-plan. In this appeal to Poussin as the saviour of French painting from rococo indulgence and excess, Peyron's behaviour is irreproachable: the return to Poussin had long been advocated by the critics; the first post-rococo works of Vien had already received their critical acclaim; and so far from being daring, Peyron's revival of Poussin could safely anticipate official approval. It was his version of *The Death of Seneca*, not David's, which predictably took the Rome Prize.

Yet Peyron's painting is actually subtler than its official approbation might suggest. Peyron's more secretive and dangerous appeal is, in fact, to Caravaggio, whose starkness of lighting, isolation of figures and interruptions of narrative focus, already evident here, will eventually come to dominate his dark and mysterious canvas *Cymon and Miltiades* (illustration 18). Peyron had discovered the possibility of manipulating tradition in such a way that homage to an approved master could both conceal and legitimate the return to a less sanctioned source: Poussin *masks* Caravaggio. One is dealing here again with the kind of trope or turning within tradition which classical source analysis is unlikely to detect (what it will tend to do is inventorise); though to be insensitive to such effects is to risk not perceiving what is actually going on in the extraordinary and subtle shifts of source and style in this period, and above all in the Académie's competitions.

Antiochus and Stratonice (illustration 20) owes much to Peyron's severe manner and to the gathering force of neo-Poussinism at the Académie, but it owes perhaps more to Peyron's devious and relatively invisible troping of tradition (one cannot *see* a trope, in the same evident way that one 'sees' a source). David's and Peyron's innovations will show up in formalist analysis at the level of design, but their innovations within the discourse of paintings, their *rhetoric*, will not. Both David and Peyron exist in an artistic

16   David, *The Death of Seneca*

and institutional climate where the way in which sources are used is a matter to be judged certainly as carefully as composition, perspective, anatomical accuracy, and the other aspects of *métier* which, by the time a painter is competing for the Rome Prize, may be taken for granted in the serious candidates; and in looking at their work, our own sensitivity to the deployment of sources is of the essence, if we are to understand them in the terms within which they were created. David's *Antiochus and Stratonice* duly won the Prix de Rome for 1774, and if one refers it back to his *Death of Seneca*, the painting which failed to win the palm in 1773, one is tempted to view it as a work of recantation. The aspects of opera, of large gestures and of direct address to the spectator, have been successfully purged, notably in the figure of Stratonice; the undulant and baroque pose that is hers in Pietro da Cortona yields, perhaps by way of Gavin Hamilton, to columnar elegance and rectitude. Apparently bowing to official taste, David takes from Poussin/Peyron an architectural setting which stresses highlighted columns, cornices seen in silhouette, and recessions into tall arcades; wall surfaces are placed, true to form, in parallel with the picture plane, and ranged into large rectilinear masses.

Yet what really counts is that David allows the references to

17　After Jean-François-Pierre Peyron, engraving of *The Death of Seneca*

Poussin and Peyron to go no further than this, and that at the right of the painting he invents an alternative architecture which opens on to spaces which are precisely *not* in parallel with the picture plane, nor indeed particularly coherent with the architectural masses on the left which do stand in that plane. The plunge to the right down arcaded space may echo similar views in Poussin, for example the vista at the left of *The Death of Germanicus* (illustration 19); but its final twist into a vaulted space from which vision is excluded behaves in a manner that exactly contradicts the classic Poussinist 'plunge'. We can say that space in *The Death of Germanicus* is charged with the idea of an enclosed visibility: as in French classical theatre, unity of action is matched by unity of place, and the spectacular definition of moral action matched by an architecture that is fully coherent before the spectator's viewpoint – so coherent, in fact, that the viewer can actually reconstruct a ground-plan for spaces that are not physically presented, but only implied. Peyron, for his part, repeats the general features of this emotionally and semantically charged architecture, while reducing or simplifying it into a more formulaic pattern (figures stapled against masonry) whose main function is to stand as a marker for Poussin himself: Peyron needs the full force of the identification 'Poussin' if he is to carry out his more secret innovations under the Poussinist mask.

David breaks with both precedents. The central space of

18 Peyron, *Cymon and Miltiades*

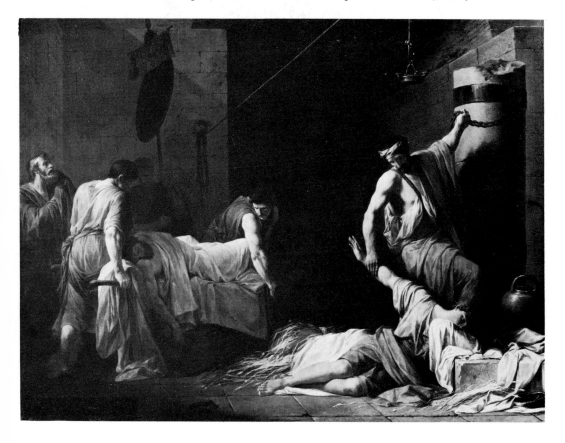

Antiochus and Stratonice (illustration 20) 'identifies' Poussin, but everything else then breaks the coherence of Poussin's visible enclosures. The two parallel wall surfaces invoke the master, but after that their mutual articulation is obscure – the first surface stands in front of the second, is superimposed upon it, but neither the distance between the two surfaces, nor the overhead construction that might unite them, is explained. One key to Poussinist principle, planarity, is used in such a way that it counters another Poussinist principle, the cubic intelligibility of space. The distant vault, from which no ground-plan can be inferred (though certainly one is needed) carries the disjunction of space one move further; a disjunction that becomes even more striking when we note the vault's stress on aerial perspective, the *milkiness* of its light, with its suggestion of an immensity of unknown spaces. Features such as these are not easily compatible with the linear perspective, the stark illumination, the high-contrast tonality which define the central 'Poussinist' space; in fact they are at odds with Poussin, and their effect is to turn one part of tradition, the baroque, against another part, Poussin's *grande manière*, in what amounts to a negative inflection of an *almost* dominant discourse.

These are remarkable marginalisations: Peyron, the strong contemporary, and Poussin, his powerful protector, are associated

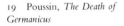

19   Poussin, *The Death of Germanicus*

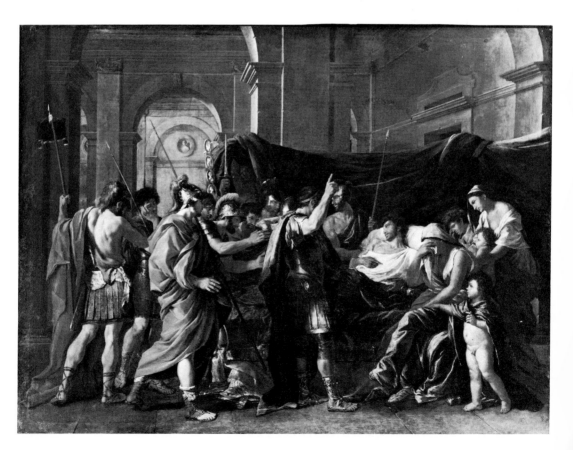

with what is of limited importance in *Antiochus and Stratonice* (illustration 20) – the architectural surround; associated, then challenged by a space and an architecture of baroque. On his own perhaps not even David, who though mutinous in the 1770s has still to make his reputation, could have taken such risks; and it is here that we can begin to explain the intensity with which the painting addresses Pietro da Cortona (illustration 21), calling on him in detail, in the explicit reworkings of Antiochus' body, the hand gestures, the bed, the jagged coronets: to dislodge the combined weight of Peyron and of Poussin, David incorporates into himself the whole force of Pietro's painting, and speaks in Pietro's own name. Working from his own weak and belated position at the end (as he sees it) of the rococo age, David does not yet command the resources he needs if he is to intervene directly in tradition, as he will with *The Oath of the Horatii*; he is still primarily troping on the surface of tradition, and neither here nor in *Mars and Minerva* does he produce a vigorously independent image. Instead, he plays one segment of tradition against another, Pietro against Poussin, the Italian against the French. The risk is that by moving Pietro against Poussin, David will side too far with Pietro, will become identified with him, and lose the protective distance on tradition which he seeks (the distance so evident in *Mars and*

20 David, *Antiochus and Stratonice*

Minerva); a risk which is neutralised by taking from Pietro a single work, enabling David to speak in its name without engulfment by Pietro da Cortona's style as a whole. *Antiochus and Stratonice* displays, in other words, the same ruse of self-effacement and self-opening before tradition that we saw in *Mars and Minerva*, but through removal into the seventeenth century David can overcome the sense of latecoming and stylistic placelessness by which *Mars and Minerva* had been suffused. Once repositioned in the seicento, David can enjoy a commanding view: the whole of rococo, the style from which *Mars and Minerva* had worked to dissociate itself, can be perceived as subsequent and belated; Poussin, now a contemporary, can be countered by his own near-exact contemporary, Pietro; while Peyron, who a year before had inflicted on David a resounding defeat, can be seen as a remote future satellite.

One might call the trope on tradition in *Antiochus and Stratonice* by the name of *aegis*, after Athene's shield. It is a trope of some subtlety. In practical terms it enables the painter who is uncertain about his own intervention within tradition to defer the problem. There may be a price to pay – the trope pushes the painter dangerously close to mimicry, a strategy no painter can afford to pursue for long, since the self-effacement the trope entails threatens him with entrapment in an ironic separation *above* images, and this makes innovation in visual (rather than tropological) terms increasingly difficult. Yet not the least of the trope's advantages is that it allows its operator to innovate under the cover of the aegis and at the margins of the imitation, in the secure knowledge that

21 After Pietro da Cortona, engraving of *Antiochus and Stratonice*

such innovation will still enjoy strong protection. The inventive-
ness of *Antiochus and Stratonice* hardly shows up in an analysis
which measures originality 'by area' for the reason that in this
painting, as in *Mars and Minerva*, David is still thinking primarily
in tropes of style (and it is precisely the trope, the turning of
tradition, that classical analysis of 'influence' screens out): his
deployment of sources is unusually literal and reduplicative.
Pietro's *Antiochus*, Hamilton's *Death of Hector* and David's own
Death of Seneca, these are surfaces to which his consciousness, so to
speak, adheres. He is certainly able to manipulate the surfaces by
means of his chosen trope, and his dexterity in the condensation
and displacement of images is remarkable; yet basically he is
thinking in planes, as though his mind were itself a canvas,
bounded by the four sides of the frame. But in one respect, David is
beginning to move away from the surfaces that hold him captive.
This is in his handling of an aspect of the image which, again, is
unlikely to be noticed in formalist analysis; yet it is a crucial
element not only in David's general evolution, but in his
development into a radical and a profound painter. At a local and
technical level, it concerns how David arranges *eye-lines*; more
deeply, it concerns the structures David invents to describe what I
will be calling 'visuality' – a term larger than 'vision', and one
intended to represent the construction of vision under conditions
of society and discourse, into a visuality as it unfolds within the
human subject.

IV

In order to commence the definition of 'visuality', and to indicate
its difference from 'vision', I would like to turn to the interpretation of visual subjectivity advanced in a book I greatly respect,
yet also disagree with: Michael Fried's admirable *Absorption and
Theatricality*.[9] In the course of his investigation of French eighteenth-
century painting Fried demonstrates that at certain key moments
in the tradition various attempts are made to overcome what he
terms the 'theatricalizing consequences' of the viewer's beholding
of a painting; the particular solution he explores is the mid-
century's portrayal of figures presented in 'states of absorption'.
   Where figures seem fully aware of the viewer's address, where
they seem posed advertently (as in the more spectacular of the
rococo mythologies), the image as a whole may generate a number
of negative repercussions. Its temporality becomes asymmetrical
with the temporality of viewing: the figures of spectacle are seen to
exist in an incremental moment at which they reveal all of their
beauty, power, or suffering, whereas the viewer exists in a time
that is prolonged, extended, his eye probing slowly, unhurriedly,
ruminatively; and the painting which allows too great a disparity

to arise between these two kinds of temporality risks cleavage – it will be found too hot, too explosive. A dimension of tact now opens up, for if painting instead cultivates union of the two kinds of temporality, the viewer who was excluded, or thrust out of the painting, may again be ushered in: if the activity chosen to be represented in the painting is also prolonged, extended, unhurried, then the figures within the frame come to share a temporality continuous with that of the viewer; if they cease to turn, advertently, towards the external viewing space, but instead focus their attention within the internal space of their surroundings, then the viewer may watch them in the manner of an unseen observer. An apparent exclusion of the viewer – no one turns to face his space, the attention of the figures is detained elsewhere, in their tasks, their meditations, their inwardness – in fact serves to admit the viewer into the pictured world.

Fried's mode of argument is remarkable in that it enables him to describe change in presentation of the image – the difference, for example, between Boucher and Chardin – in *non*-formalist terms: the features he analyses are not those of design considered as a configuration of shapes in two dimensions, design as it manifests to the formalist *ascesis*, but rather structures of narrative. These are of enormous importance in the description of discursive, that is representational, art; and Fried's approach marks, I believe, an important change of orientation in art history itself.[10] Its limitation, nevertheless, is that it confines itself to a definition of the viewing subject narrowly concerned with the issue of the admission and the exclusion of the observer: the viewing subject is variously kept out or ushered in, but either way he remains an agent who simply sees, a viewing substance invited into the sphere of perceptions. Fried's subject is the same subject that is posited in the phenomenological reduction: monadic and self-enclosed, the subject sees the world from the world's centre and in unitary prospect. Fried's 'absorption' is the positive pole, as his 'theatricality' is the negative, of a subjectivity proposed in terms of inward repletion, of self-contemplation, of the completed essence. The account therefore precludes any subject in vision that is not also a subject in visual presence: the only trouble in vision here is at the 'negative' pole, where the theatricality of a particular painting prevents or interferes with its apprehension by a vision that is self-absorbed and self-containing; while at the 'positive' pole, the absorptive painting and its absorbed viewer meet in the fullness of 'subjective' vision. This leaves (at least) two things out: the presence of the other in vision which makes of *human* visuality (as opposed to the vision of the camera) a divided visuality, divided because the subject is not alone in his perceptual horizon, but surrounded by the visualities of others with which it must interact; and secondly (a corollary of this) the permanent division of visual subjectivity in the visual *sign*.

Of this I shall have more to say later, but I want for the moment actually to pursue Fried's line of enquiry, since clearly *Antiochus and Stratonice* establishes an address to the spectator which is quite different from that established by David's earlier *Death of Seneca* (illustration 16). In Fried's terms: if *The Death of Seneca* is an image in theatricality, *Antiochus and Stratonice* is an image in absorption. Both Seneca and the female figure twist in contrapposto against their line of vision towards and into the space of viewing; in *Antiochus and Stratonice* the figures turn only towards one another. The extraverted or theatrical orientation of *The Death of Seneca* is confirmed by numerous details: from the conspicuous emphasis on the nape of the handmaid's neck (an emphasis responsible for much local distortion), to the rococo breasts whose destined impact is not at all within the orbit of the drama, to the *panache* of the standing soldier – an apex which reorganises the composition into a triangle intelligible only from the *viewer*'s point of observation. In *Antiochus and Stratonice*, by contrast, the viewer's point of observation is addressed only by the architecture, not by the figures, whether individually or in their grouping. In Fried's terms, *The Death of Seneca* builds a proscenic barrier between the active figures on the stage and the passive spectator in the audience, whereas *Antiochus* works to break that barrier down, so that the space in which the spectator sees and the space in which the figures see become continuous: the two elide. This is certainly part of the case, but what counts rather more than the elision, and what escapes detection in Fried's scheme, is the next stage – David's characterisation of the space of visuality.

In the narrative of *Antiochus and Stratonice*, each of the figures is defined in terms of *troubled or distorted sight* (illustration 22). The look Antiochus casts on Stratonice is that of a Racinian protagonist transfixed by an erotic impulse which, originating in vision, must remain confined there: Antiochus must betray no signs of the passion he harbours for his father's wife.[11] The secrecy of his emotion, and the constant provocation to desire whenever Stratonice appears, function like a chiasmic transformation of *Phèdre*, with Phèdre and Hippolyte in changed places. For Antiochus, Stratonice can *only* exist as an image, and the distance that separates him from the object of his desire is the optical interval itself: the prince may look upon Stratonice, but only in transgression, for his looking is subject, even when the king is not present, to the law of the father, and its menacing and introjected gaze upon his own. With complete insight into the dramatic logic of the situation, David fills the interval with the *silhouette* of the king. The look of the physician is of a different order: if, for Antiochus, vision and the body exist in opposition, if they have been sundered by the paternal interdiction, it is the physician who reunites them; not by looking at Antiochus, for the latter's malady is invisible, but by feeling his pulse, and its quickening at

Stratonice's approach. The pointing hand of the physician rejoins the body and the visual field whose dissociation *is* Antiochus' affliction. The physician's arm, dark against the pale skin of the prince's chest, and by far the most powerfully physical and exactly transcribed area of the painting, stands in opposition to the regal and paternal ban: where the king *breaks* vision and body, and fills the space of the ban with his own shadowy presence, the physician's arm reconnects body to vision, not only in the work of diagnosis, but in the virile thrust which challenges the interdiction, and which promises to heal Antiochus' mysterious debility. To this quartet of concealments and disclosures, the kneeling servant is a lesser witness, and her gaze is the only one that could be dispensed with by the narrative; but the servant, in this eminently Racinian painting, is also Stratonice's confidante. Her mistress cannot move. Even if Stratonice felt nothing for Antiochus (though her right hand, placed over presumably still more unseen palpitations, suggests otherwise) decorum forbids her to meet this illicit gaze: it is her servant who moves where she is paralysed, and conveys surprise and even welcome, where her mistress must remain impassive.

It is not enough to say the figures are absorbed, or that their

22   David, *Antiochus and Stratonice*

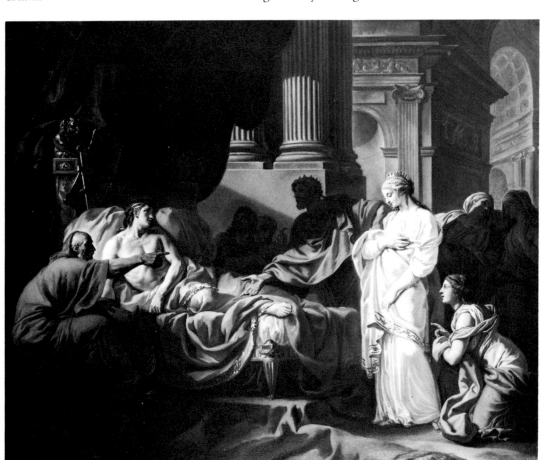

absorption admits the presence of the spectator where the comparative theatricality of *The Death of Seneca* had worked towards the spectator's exclusion. The vision of the spectator and that of the figures are made congruent, or a move is made in the direction of their congruence, but the visual world into which the spectator is ushered, through dissolution of the proscenic barrier, is one of disturbance and dispossession in sight. Stratonice is defined from the outside, as spectacle; decorum prevents her from meeting Antiochus' look with her own; interdiction holds her in place as image. Antiochus' situation is just the reverse. The king sunders what is within, from what manifests without as the visible: withdrawn almost fatally into the interior space of his desire, Antiochus is prevented by interdiction from allowing that desire to become spectacle; it is left to the physician to rejoin the two, vision and body, together. What is *not* represented anywhere in the painting is vision in self-possession, or self-presence – the kind of visual subjectivity which Fried proposes: the characters are torn between how they are, and how they appear before the gaze of others. The terms 'theatricality' and 'absorption' are useful, in that they draw attention to the inwardness of the drama portrayed by the painting, an inwardness more or less excluded by the theatrical conventions still active in David's *Death of Seneca*. But they amount in effect to terms of *measurement*: theatrical painting excludes, as absorptive painting includes, a subjectivity that is to be quantified, not analysed, for it is assumed as a unitary essence. Whereas what we have in *Antiochus and Stratonice* is rather a statement of the difficulties, the vicissitudes, of vision. The subjects represented as caught in the world of sight are divided, broken, in their habitation there: they see and they are seen, and how they see is distorted, violated, by how they are seen. Partly they see from the viewpoint of self-possession and self-enclosure, but their vision is cut across by darkness, by the installation *into* their vision, of the viewpoint of the other. Their sight is held in the gazes of others, and it is this hold that David is exploring.

In *Antiochus and Stratonice* the exploration is still conducted largely at the level of content, in that the style of the painting is less insistently problematic than it is in *Mars and Minerva*, and less than it will be in *The Oath of the Horatii*. But what nevertheless must be remarked is the way that the preoccupation with finding an authentic style, David's posture of adjudication among the competing authorities of different styles, is *beginning* to merge with a preoccupation with authentic vision, and with what can only be termed the alienation of sight by some principle of alterity operating *in* sight. Stylistically, *Antiochus and Stratonice* is a game of masks and impersonations (and also of detections, of revelations): in the register of style, Peyron, who put on the mask of Poussin, is unmasked by a David who wears the mask of Pietro; in the register of narrative, Antiochus is unmasked by the physician before a

Stratonice who is pure mask, pure image. The registers of style and of narrative are, to be sure, not yet fully interlinked; but the connections are beginning to form. For the characters in the drama, vision must painfully traverse a span which runs from externality-without-inwardness to its opposite, inwardness-without-externality; from Stratonice across to Antiochus, through the various intermediate positions marked by the physician, the servant, the king. The viewing subject is *crossed* by a viewpoint he or she cannot occupy: a blindness *in* the world of sight, a gaze of the other that *clutches* the gaze of the self. And for David, his own image is held in the gaze of the precursor, Pietro; as Peyron's gaze had been held in that of Poussin. A series of expropriations or occlusions in vision is beginning to extend from the figures out to the spectator, and also from the painter out into tradition. The ways in which visuality is experienced by the figures within the painting is coming to articulate with the tropes by which the painter organises his inheritance. The full implications of this articulation will emerge only after 1784; but let us turn to a less familiar work, the *St Roch* of 1780 (illustration 23).[12]

V

This has always been sensed as an aberrant or unorthodox painting, though viewers have usually been seduced by the similarity between its plague-stricken giant in the foreground, and certain figures in Gros' *Plague-hospital at Jaffa*. While it is certain that David's victim of pestilence was to become a potent source for the Romantics, it would nevertheless be a mistake to view David's painting only from its future: essentially it is a revisionary elaboration of Poussin's *The Virgin Appearing to St James the Great* (illustration 24). The composition's diagonal descent is almost exactly repeated; the Virgin points down from the same cloudy and elevated platform; the two most prominent of her worshippers are simply fused together and turned through space. Quotation is massive and explicit enough to amount once more to the trope of aegis: the later work neither simply alludes to nor raids its predecessor, but rather asks to be read against it and placed under its protection. It is a trope which urgently raises the question of authority over vision, since its effect is to polarise the later image between conformity and transgression: through an act of bisection, it divides the image into elements of repetition and elements of deviation, where both sets augment the sense of the later image's dispossession of its own vision. The trope's essential action is therefore to locate an absent gaze in which the present gaze, upon the new image, is held, to hollow out or darken vision by installing a viewpoint the later painting cannot occupy, but by which it is nevertheless authorised and mastered.

These considerations, already evident in *Antiochus and Stratonice*, are carried much further by *St Roch*. If we refer back to the Poussin (illustration 24) we find the image of *an apparition that looks back*: the Virgin and Child irrupt into the natural world where they see, and where in turn they are seen, by all the figures in the painting. The natural and supernatural harmoniously interpenetrate, through the miracle of an Incarnation at once human and divine. The premise of Poussin's painting bases itself firmly on the capacity of human vision to encompass, and of representation to hold, real and transcendental worlds, but the premises of David's *St Roch* are otherwise. By changing the mutual positions of the Virgin and of the Child, David closes the supernatural figures in on each other and cuts them off from their surroundings; through alteration of the mutual scale of the Virgin's hands and those of St Roch, he places the real and the transcendental in almost discontinuous

23   David, *St Roch Interceding for Plague-stricken*

spaces; and by making it seem as though the Virgin does not see St Roch, he creates two private and incommensurable spheres of vision. The Virgin, pointing less directly than obliquely at the Saint, and looking only at the child, becomes a distant intercessor who may exist only in the devotional consciousness of her supplicant. If this is so, then vision does not so much encompass, as in Poussin, the real and the transcendental, as separate them: we are shown a vision which might not or does not exist in substance, and this in a representation which alleges, through the trope of aegis, that *its* vision may be here but may also be elsewhere: in Poussin.

The theme of disconnection of inward vision from outer world is taken up in the other figures. The boy, whose gaping look suggests either hallucination or epilepsy, is on either count blind to the world (and again, is a vision from elsewhere, from the Raphael *Transfiguration*); the woman he clasps is in the throes of such pain, of such grief, that she seems not to notice even the tight grip on her forearm: while these repeated statements of self-absorption leading

24 Poussin, *The Virgin Appearing to St James the Great*

to non-seeing (the Virgin, St Roch, the boy, the woman)
culminate in the most daring innovation in the painting, the reclining plague-victim's stare at those who view him. Here the series of figures caught up in disturbed or troubled vision begins to include the spectator directly, for the victim's stare is both addressed to the viewer (is a counterpart to the viewer's gaze); and looks out on nothing, addresses a void. As in *Antiochus*, visuality is broken across two terms: certain figures – the Virgin, and the Child – are pure image, spectacle, exteriority-without-inwardness; others are just the opposite – pure beholding, interiority, withdrawal from the world – the Saint, the hallucinating or convulsive boy, the moaning woman; while in the key figure, the foreground giant, spectacle (the heroic and ruined body) and vision (his retreating, evacuating stare) are split apart and pushed to opposite extremes. Dying, the transformation of subject into object, like ageing, the disintegration of the ego's imaginary and heroic theatre, provide uniquely charged themes for, respectively, David's history painting and his portraiture; and in both what is at stake is a dissociation in visuality, between what can be crudely called 'seen' and 'seeing' elements. Balance between them is not to be found – David says it again and again. Either there is an excess of the exterior, so that the subject exists as an image for others (decorous, devotional, heroic), exists in the demand and desire of others (lover, worshipper, adulator). Or there is an excess of the interior, so that what is within cannot manifest itself in the world, and remains in hiding, driven under cover by interdiction on what is to be seen, or withdrawn autistically into hallucination and reverie.

As in *Antiochus and Stratonice*, in *St Roch* David is not content simply to formulate this theme at the level of content. He traces its implications for his own case, for he too exists to see, to discover new images, in the insight of painterly invention; but that insight is crossed, traversed, by the visions of others housed in tradition. He too is bisected between vision that is to be elicited or won from within, the endogenous and 'hallucinatory' creation of new visual forms and scenes; between that, and vision that seizes him from the outside, expropriates what is his and makes it other, in captivity to tradition's gaze. The trope of aegis pulls in both these directions: towards an excess of invention and original vision, excessive because it always transgresses – goes beyond – the given; and towards the capitulation of one's own vision, surrender before what the precursors saw. The giant inhabits a *stricken* visuality, where his looking has to it an almost contentless purity – no known object fills the vacancy of his stare; while at the same time his body turns into an alien image, reified, not self but thing. And for David, in the trope of aegis, visuality operates across a similar tear or fracture: he must see from within, create unprecedented images, if he is to survive as artist, but his vision is pre-empted or evacuated by what, for the artist, is the only gaze of the other that matters, the tradition in which the predecessors' visions are stored.

VI

That David's exploration of the structures of visual subjectivity overrides the divisons of genre is proved by the appearance, a year after the *St Roch* altarpiece, of his history painting *Belisarius Begging Alms*, of 1781 (illustration 25).[13] Like *St Roch* it is based on conspicuous derivations, though David does not activate the trope of aegis, or place his painting under the sign of one especially powerful protector. The interest now is in stylistic fusions, or clashes, between two remote provenances: the neo-Poussinist and Neo-classical 'severe manner' advocated and practised, with the sanction of the Académie, by Vien and by Peyron; and the *drame bourgeois* of Greuze. Since the débâcle of 1769, when the unfortunate Greuze, having failed to be upgraded by the Académie,

25   David, *Belisarius Begging Alms*

set up as an independent, Greuze himself had begun to make tentative advances towards a new severity himself; but essentially the manner of Greuze and that of academic history painting remained distinct and institutionally separate branches of French painting. What strikes one in the *Belisarius* are the complex elisions and collisions between the two styles, which between them account for, and claim, the greater part of the painting's surface. The distant view of temple, obelisk, hill and sky so directly translates such landscapes of Poussin as the *Landscape with the Ashes of Phocion* as to seem almost an indented quotation, or painting within a painting (illustration 26); the graven inscription beside Belisarius directly invokes such counterparts in Poussin as the *Et in Arcadia ego*; while the figure of Belisarius requisitions the *Seated Philosopher* in the Villa Borghese. Concurrent with this academic orthodoxy is a separate cluster of allusions to Greuze: though the inverted helmet held out by the child is clearly borrowed from Vincent, the atmosphere of salvific charity that permeates the painting comes directly from such Greuzian homilies as *La Dame de Charité* (illustration 27), while the figure of the distressed female donor extending her hands is essentially a transformation of the mother in Greuze's painting *The Drunkard's Return* (illustration 28). While classical source analysis is unlikely at this point to do more than list these derivations, what it would thereby overlook is the incongruity of the juxtapositions: a transaction of a personal and even intimate nature, associated through Greuze with domes-

26 Poussin, *Landscape with the Ashes of Phocion Collected by his Widow*

tic and interior space, a space where individuals are defined through private virtue (charity), this narrative of the interior or *drame bourgeois* is placed in a setting that could hardly be more pre-eminently public (road, arch, temple, obelisk), placed in other words in the full architectural panoply of the state.

The juxtaposition of public and private in the narrative register occurs again, and emphatically, in the register of style: the *drame bourgeois* invokes a lower genre, painting to be viewed by private persons, or (more particularly in the case of Greuze, whose patrons included Gustav III of Sweden, the Emperor Joseph II, and Catherine of Russia) by public figures in their capacity as private persons; while the architecture of state invokes the highest of the genres, the *tableau d'histoire*, painting to be viewed by the public *as* public, or by private persons in public role, as citizens. *Belisarius* joins together contradictory visual discourses through the trope known to rhetoric as catachresis, or wrenched conjunction. The trope had, in fact, been used before, notoriously, in Greuze's *Severus and Caracalla* of 1769 (illustration 29), where in a similar fashion the architecture and the narrative of state had been redefined in terms of privacy and seclusion, as a domestic drama of fathers and sons, and where the conjunction of public and private had also been portrayed in an image that joined together the style

27 Jean-Baptiste Greuze, *La Dame de Charité*

of private or *genre* painting, with that of the *tableau d'histoire*. The result, for Greuze, had been unmitigated disaster: his image, derided on all sides, was found to conjoin branches of painting whose separation provided the basis of the Académie's hierarchy; it was declared that 'Greuze est sorti de son genre'; the painting was criticised, and in the severest terms, even by the champion of stylistic progress, Diderot; and after the catastrophe of 1769 such dangerous fusions were not again attempted in the Académie.[14]

No such scandal greeted *Belisarius*, partly because its severe Neo-classicism now coincided (as Greuze's had not) with reigning orthodoxies, partly because David's position within the Académie was far more secure than Greuze's had ever been, and partly because the problem posed to the Académie in 1769 by the meteoric rise of Greuze's bourgeois painting no longer existed. But *Belisarius* is nonetheless a direct descendant of *Severus and Caracalla*, a generic cross or catachresis between history painting and *genre* painting, between public and private art, between classical history and *drame bourgeois*. The cross of styles is matched at every point by the events of the narrative: Belisarius is both the general who saved the state, and the ruined private person; the soldier reacts to him in part as to a commanding officer, in part as to an outcast without

28   Greuze, *The Drunkard's Return*

social space – it is the duality which provokes his consternation; and the woman's charity is half that of the citizen, acting towards Belisarius in social role and in fully public space, and half that of mother, helping the child, in her private and maternal capacity. David's articulation of stylistic and narrative levels is, in this painting, notably thorough; but what still remains to be said is that both the stylistic and narrative registers are organised around the specific structure of visuality we have seen emerging in *Antiochus and Stratonice* and in *St Roch*: a structure that traverses *all* of the painting – the narrative, the styles entering into the image from tradition, and the painter's stance towards that tradition. Such a structure is not at all a matter of design and will not appear to formalist analysis: it is trope, what one might call a Grand Trope, since it subsumes into itself all other structures, including the lesser trope of catachresis. The tropes are agents of organisation rather than the visible shapes or forms known to formalism – but the discovery of this trope is still what makes David, David. And if a name is to be found for this grand trope which runs from *Antiochus* to the *Oath* and beyond, it might be called the trope of the gaze: not a transcendent gaze, or visual equivalent to the gaze of the *cogito*; but the opposite, a decentering gaze, the Gaze of the Other.

29   Greuze, *Severus and Caracalla*

In *Belisarius* the articulation of style with narrative is unusually sustained, yet it would be wrong to end discussion there, in merely stating a unity of 'form' with 'content', or in proposing such unity as a criterion of value in the work of art. What propels description further is David's now characteristic portrayal of vision as distorted and disturbed in its negotiation of self with world. As in *St Roch*, the dramatis personae are defined by the ways in which they both *see and are seen*, and by a dissociation between these two aspects of vision, which David is beginning to sense as the pain, the fundamental pain, of human visuality.

For none of the figures in *Belisarius* does there exist any firm congruence or balance between the worlds of their internal vision, and their manifestation to others, as image: visuality for them is exactly the splitting of the self across the term of sight. In the case of Belisarius and the child, an invisible inner state of want and need can only be relieved by transmitting into the world a certain image that will forcibly enter the vision of others. They must attempt to link what is internal and unseen, yet to them omnipresent, with what is external and visible, through the projection of *pitiable* images. We can say that in the act of begging the essential terms are the hidden (hunger) and the theatrical (the image of pathos); just as in the sister act, charity, the essential terms are the discomfort of *concealment* (of money, of guilt, of sympathy) and a *conspicuous* act which relieves that discomfort (donation). Even when the need is real and not feigned, need must be exaggerated, presented to the world with a force that will make the world act: to appease the hunger the world cannot see, the hungry must convert their hidden lack into the patency of spectacle. The theme of begging joins here with the theme of the triumphal arch, and not only as ironic reversal: both triumph and ruin are intrinsically spectacular states, as Belisarius and the child, in selecting their pitch, well understand. Belisarius' begging for alms, his conversion of invisible lack into outwardly visible imagery, is therefore cognate with his blindness, where the inner experience (of unseeing) and the outward spectacle (of looking blind) are again broken in two. It is not just that both are misfortunes: both are forms of dissociation between inward and projected states. In his blindness Belisarius experiences his being as altogether lacking a visual dimension; he cannot *know* what he looks like, and even to beg he must rely on the child to project his image for him into the sighted world. In the subjective experience of blindness, it is less the case that the world is without imagery, than that there is no natural alliance or continuity between the self and the image it cannot help sending out into the world: the self cannot locate itself as image, while at the same time the world sees the blind only *as* image, the inner experience of the blind remaining literally unimaginable to even the most empathetic observer.

The dissociation between the self-as-seer and the self-as-seen is, in the case of Belisarius and the child, extreme, but their condition is shared, to a lesser degree, by the other principal figures. For the soldier also, the normal or the ideal climate of vision is one of congruence between image and strength, and it is that congruence which Belisarius' blindness threatens. Both the command structure of military life and actual combat demand the projection of deeply potent self-imagery, just as military deterrence consists in the credibility of the projected image as evincing more power than that of the adversary. Warfare and military hierarchy are, like begging and like charity, theatres of the imaginary, where the possible separation of inward state (fear) from outward projection (valour) must be countered by the heroic, the heraldic spectacle. In seeing his former commander as a blind beggar, the soldier is faced with the breakdown of this system of signs and images allegedly backed by strength: as much by his blindness as by his penury Belisarius disturbs the necessary theatre of power, and although the blindness is not itself contagious, the split it represents challenges the whole principle of suture between subject and self-imagery on which military organisation must depend.

A similar threat to, and demonstration of, the assumptions of normal visuality is evident in the case of the donor. The visual economy of gender proposes an intrinsic division of the sexes between active (= male) and passive (= female) principles: woman as Image, man as Bearer of the Look. The transaction between the donor and Belisarius is a reversal of their gendered roles: the woman cannot become an image to this man who cannot see; Belisarius, blind and depotentiated, cannot be the bearer of any look. An aspect of confusion surrounds both the donor's perception of the scene, and her reaction to it: we cannot tell which piteous image provokes her response, that of Belisarius, or that of the child. Of course it is both, but her generosity is not open or confident, as we might expect when there are two good reasons for it: she seems to experience instead the nervousness the sighted sometimes feel in the presence of the blind, and she places her coins in the helmet cagily, with suspicion on her face. Where in Greuze the act of charity stems from an abundance of goods and of virtue, and joins together in the moment of donation all the ages, estates and conditions of man, David's act of charity is divided and tense: the woman finds herself caught, caught *out*, between different images coming *to* her (general, beggar, child), which require different images or self-presentation *from* her – as citizen, as patron, as mother; while Belisarius' blindness undercuts all these images, leaving her existence as woman and as image consequently stranded, exposed, in *naked* visibility before a look of absolute otherness, the gaze of blindness.

Belisarius Begging Alms is a work in which the vision of its characters and that of its creator begin to form complex harmonies. The juxtaposition of a 'high' academic manner, replete with classical and Poussinesque allusions, against the lower and unacademic manner of Greuze and the Greuzian *drame bourgeois* may not create the kind of dissonance that so perplexed the viewers of *Severus and Caracalla*; on the contrary, where Greuze's attempt at crossing the boundaries of the genres produced a kind of hybrid or sport, *Belisarius* is relatively decorous, a gracious merger of public and private visual discourses. But what David's subtlety of generic fusion draws attention to, by its very deftness, is the fact that the two formerly separate and mutually exclusive kinds of representation now exist side by side in the same image. David's success highlights the styles within which he is working. That neo-Poussinism and the *drame bourgeois* can, surprisingly, be made to coexist in the same frame has the effect of 'foregrounding' both styles, so that although the viewer is shown a scene of intrinsic interest, where the visual language performs a clear referential function, he is shown that scene in such a way that the visual language draws attention to itself, makes itself visible *as* a system of signs.

Obviously the term 'foregrounding', as applied to painting style, is one of widespread applicability in discussion of the image: one could say that certain kinds of painting, for example Northern still-life, seem to have a minimum of stylistic foreground, the representational language directing itself insistently towards its referents; while other kinds, and certainly the tradition discussed in this book, are heavily foregrounded, forcing the viewer into awareness of the painting's relation not so much to its referents or its represented content, as to other paintings and to the tradition from which the present painting has emerged. The point to be made here, however, is not just that the play of styles in *Belisarius* foregrounds its representational means, but that the foregrounding restates in the register of representation what is stated also in the narrative: that just as, for the figures in *Belisarius*, visuality spans two poles, from a pure inwardness disconnected from the exterior (blindness) to an exteriority which only uneasily connects with inwardness (spectacle), so for David the image spans two extremes – it is a *scene*, a freshly created image issuing from the painter's inward imagination, uniquely possessed and authorised by its unique creator; and yet it is also a work *in tradition*, a work that dramatises its prior authorisation by the visions of the precursors (Poussin, Greuze). Although it is possible to imagine that a viewer unfamiliar with Poussin or with Greuze, and coming to the work for the first time, will recognise the scenic aspect of the painting, what such a viewer would necessarily miss is the dimension of foregrounding which casts him, the viewer, into the same condition of belatedness as the painter. Fully to understand (to *recognise*) the painting, the viewer must refer it to his previous experience of the images in tradition: just as David *portrays* his imaginary vision as held in the gaze of the precursors, so his painting *places* the look of the viewer under the gaze of tradition, of Poussin and of Greuze; and this is as true of *Mars and Minerva*, *Antiochus and Stratonice*, *St Roch*, and the rest of David's production up to 1784, as it is of *Belisarius*. The viewer can no more be the sole possessor of what he surveys, than can David be the sole possessor of the vision he paints. The *play* of styles, which on a superficial level may seem only an effete or a recondite game, extends the series of alienations or expropriations in vision one stage further. The figures in the image, and the painter and the viewer who stand *outside* it, are in different ways all subject to the 'othering' of what they see: to the troping or turning away of vision itself; in a *circuit of visualities* that is quite unlike the consoling picture of the *channel of transmissions* (from A to B: from painter to viewer) which painting might sometimes seem, and perhaps always promises, to be.

Mortal sight: The Oath of the Horatii

A Marat, David. L'an deux   signature to Marat assassiné

I

IT IS PERHAPS inevitable that the origins of *The Oath of the Horatii* should, by now, have been fairly exhaustively researched.[1] Yet given the premise on which investigation has usually rested, that the mode in which the images of the past present themselves to their future is primarily as formal and bi-dimensional design, it is perhaps no less inevitable that, all the previous visual designs with any persuasive similarity to the *Oath* having been unearthed and compared, classical source analysis at last reaches a point at which the *Oath* is found finally more to differ from its predecessors than it is found to resemble them; a point when that analysis admits its own defeat and presses the escape button marked Genius.

That the *Oath* is a work of genius, no one who actually sees the original is likely to deny. But it is a work whose genius is peculiarly undemonstrable in the traditional enumeration of sources. The paintings that best interpret the *Oath*, *The Combat of Mars and Minerva*, *Antiochus and Stratonice*, and *Belisarius Begging Alms*, hardly resemble it as design at all; yet it is on design that the traditional analysis, with its tendency towards identikit working methods, remains fixated.

Part of the significance of David's relation to tradition, from *Mars and Minerva* through to *Belisarius* is precisely that he is gradually acquiring, through the strategies I have been calling tropes, the means to locate his imagery within tradition in ways that exactly break the thraldom of thinking in simple montage, or superposed planes; yet classical source analysis itself proceeds largely by the super-positioning of planar surfaces: it depends on a method which David's whole development as a painter has worked to overcome. No less serious than the structural in-adequacy of the method is that method's set of tacit assumptions concerning what human visuality consists in, and how it works; for underpinning the practice of planar analysis, as it underpins the ascesis of formalist descriptions of the image, is a conception of sight as geometral, punctual, and as fully absorbed in vision, which in turn entails a model of visuality as the expression, in the visual, of the human subject's self-presence. Analysis 'in planes' proposes and assumes vision as the consequence of light entering the pupil and forming an image on the screen at the back of the eye; the   63 painter has special skills of recording the 'impression' thus formed; and with greater or lesser success, and with some degree of accommodation to the 'influence' of previous images and impressions similarly formed, he re-presents it.

II

It is at this point that I would like to make an excursion which, while necessary as a preliminary to discussion of the *Oath*, must to some degree go beyond its context. One reason that 'influence' is a vital object of enquiry is exactly that the prevailing picture of influence restates assumptions concerning vision which are so deep-rooted and multi-determined, that to discuss influence in any adequate fashion inevitably requires going behind it, to adumbrate the larger questions with which conceptions of influence have become entangled. In so far as the assumptions propose an apparently 'natural' description of vision, they oblige us directly to confront certain deeply influential Western myths of seeing, in which one finds inscribed the most complex cultural archaeology. Its levels and striations still await their historian, and nothing more than a prolegomenon can be attempted here. That the 'natural' account of vision is a specifically European cultural construction is apparent as soon as one tries to embrace within it the art of the Far East, yet so deeply tenacious is its hold on the way vision is thought about that at the same time it seems virtually impossible to discard. Imbricated within it one will find the whole complex of scholastic reasoning that finds in vision the principal mode of deriving from material singulars their immaterial form, and finds the highest mode of vision in a divine mind that perceives only connatural form;[2] just as one will find the continuity between the assumptions of the gothic image and the development of perspective,[3] with its richly elaborated practices which, nevertheless, reinforce what is always a simple diagram of visual knowledge and visual representation, a diagram perhaps nowhere stated so succinctly as in Leonardo (illustration 30). Embedded close by, one will find the panoply of the Cartesian *cogito*, with its assumption of a subject housed in privileged separation 'behind' the retina, physically located in the pineal gland, metaphysically located in masterful overview of a flat, retinal prospect, a prospect which the unitary subject, by applying its stock of ideas, organises into representations; representations which, by virtue of that work of organisation, belong or are *proper* to the subject. Nor is the reign of the *cogito* ended. In a transformation of the *cogito* conducted in our own century, we will find also the reduction or *époché* of Continental phenomenology, which switches the current but leaves the circuit intact. While stating with extraordinary emphasis that I see *outside*, that perception is not *in* the subject in the way the original *cogito* had maintained, but *on* the objects which perception apprehends: while arguing that vision comes not *from* the body but *towards* it, from what Merleau-Ponty calls 'the flesh of the world',[4] and that from that iridescent flesh I extract myself, I emerge as eye: while rising into heights of lyricism where Merleau-Ponty and Messiaen seem twin messengers of the *Vingt Regards* of the Incarnation; nevertheless phenomenology remains within the orbit of the ancient, the atavistic visuality of Europe, where whatever concessions are made to the role of the world in fashioning sight, the result still culminates in a bi-polar relation between *I* and *world*, and between these terms everything to do with vision can be placed, as I constitute the world in my vision of it, or (more sacramentally) the flesh of the world constitutes its sight in me.

Of these archaeological layers it is certainly the last, phenomenology, that possesses the greatest maturity, and does most justice to the *human* dimension of visuality, just as Leonardo's sketch of monocular perspective tends towards elimination of 'the subject' as a necessary component in the account of human vision. That omission intrinsically depresses the level of our discussion of, and our thinking about, the image; we are not like cameras, or visual computers (though we will certainly have to address the discursive face of the image as soon as we start to build discourse-analysis, and visual recognition, into our computer systems). Human beings do not simply register light, in the manner of photosensitive cells: our awareness attends not only to the figuration, but to the sociality of vision; not only to the images we receive from the visual field, but the images through which we present ourselves to that visual field; to who is watching us, the number, intensity and intention of their gaze; to what are the rules which govern the manipulation of the images we project into the world, and to what latitude they allow; to the introjection of the gaze of others in the form of a consciousness surveying consciousness from the outside ('self'-consciousness); in short, to the whole nexus of formations that can be summed up in the sentence, or the narrative: 'I see myself seeing myself.'

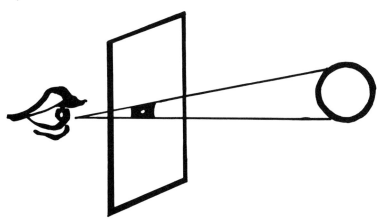

30 After Leonardo, *Diagram of monocular perspective*

The point is that the classical model of vision, the essence of which is contained in Leonardo's sketch, assumes a quite different structure of vision: the equivalent sentences there are, 'I see the world', and 'I am one within my seeing of the world.' And if things really were as simple as that (among other things) one would have no quarrel with art history's procedures of source analysis. For it if is presumed that the painter receives *impressions*, from the world and from other paintings, and that these impressions are then represented by the painter; if it is proposed, as in Gombrich, that the impressions received from other paintings support and modify the way the painter's impressions are re-presented, then certainly it is the legitimate business of source analysis to trace the various paths of support and modification that converge in a particular image. But the word 'impression' here makes the massive, highly questionable, and unchallenged assumption of bi-polar, dyadic vision, vision in two terms: the world is here, and the painter's eye is there – the problem lies only in making the image adequate to the painter's impression of the world; in discarding schemata found obstructive, in forging schemata that will facilitate transcription of the impression. That is: the problem lies in the extent and the magnitude of the task (to paint the world) – not in the means by which the task is to be performed. Representation poses no difficulties here except those of an *executive* order. It is to channel impressions from one individual to another, and where it fails in this, it is because the means of representation have emerged in the channel as 'noise': where, ideally, the means of representation are limpid, crystalline, lustral; like the lens of the eye itself. This is to deny the enormous complexity of negotiation that exists in vision not only between the self and the world, but between the self and others; it denies the social, the interpersonal nature of vision; and, most crucially, it denies the intervention into bi-polar or dyadic vision, of the third term by which the socialisation of vision is effected, *the sign*; and of the agency which consummates the diverse activities of the sign in human society – language.

We can never directly experience the visual field of another human being – that much is certain: the only knowledge of another visual field, which we are able to acquire, is that which comes to us through *description*. Such description proves that others also see what we see, but the definition of what *is* seen originates, therefore, not in the visual field itself, but in language: originates outside sight, in the signs of the description which, though they may be in referential relation to light, in themselves possess no luminosity of their own. For human beings collectively to orchestrate their visual experience, each must submit the field of vision to appropriation by the sign; vision must be through-penetrated by a symbolic register that will ensure the collective coherence of visuality in the social organism. Access to the terms in which the description of vision are held marks the annexation of the individual's sight by the society he or she inhabits: henceforth, all statements that are made concerning the individual's field of vision must conform with a collective visuality, from which deviations or non-congruent statements can be measured, variously, as hallucination, misidentification, or 'visual disturbance'.[5] From that point onwards, to speak of the visual field of the 'individual' is to use a misnomer, since what can only be named as a division, a separation of the undivided, has now taken place: the individual becomes a subject in (others') vision. Annexation of the subject in his or her sight is only one aspect, yet it is a crucial aspect, of a process of socialisation that will continue throughout the subject's life; though the intrusive or irruptive character of socialisation is rarely as pronounced or as unmistakable as it is in the sphere of sight.

The engagement between the eye and its visual field seems altogether dyadic – the eye is, after all, a sensory organ which, like other such organs, seems to know only two sides: outer stimulus, and inner response; and if we think of the back of the eye as a specialised kind of dermis, or if we are called upon to depict the sensations of the eye in the form of a sketch, our account of vision is likely to structure itself, like Leonardo's perspective diagram, around only two terms: the retina, and light. Yet this apparent dyad, of retina and its perceived world, is interrupted at the acquisition of language (globally conceived) by a *third* term, the term of the sign. After the acquisition of language, the visual field is orchestrated from outside the dyad, and by a force that is not in itself visual (prior to literacy it is, rather, acoustic). The socialisation of vision can be pictured as the insertion into the dyad of a *screen* of signification, language, which, cutting across the dyad, subjects vision to the internal movement of the signs (from signifier to signifier): one might call this irruption, or cutting-across, the primal break or *Spaltung* of vision (illustration 31).

From this original cutting into vision, whereby the individual emerges as the subject in vision, many consequences proceed, two at least of which become particularly urgent in discussion of visual representation: the issue of *space*, and as a corollary of that, the issue of the images to be projected by the subject *into* the space.

The irruption into vision of descriptions coming to it from the outside requires of vision a decentering in which the *idea* of space becomes for the first time a complex notion. One can perhaps conceive of the decentering as follows. In a perfectly dyadic vision, the world moves 'with' the movements of the body. The essence of that centering of vision in and around the body is clearly stated in the famous sentence recorded by Piaget, when the child says 'I run, and the sun follows me';[6] though it is not so much the childish or naive aspect of the sentence that I want here to stress, but rather the exclusively *optical* reference it makes to the world. The world and the self are fully and mutually absorbed in vision, in the sense that the 'I run, and the sun follows me' describes the way things actually appear to the eye (whether it is the eye of the child *or* the eye of the adult), *and only* that appearance.

To invoke Piaget is perhaps to imply that it is only at some archaic stage of development that the world appears to the eye in this fashion; and that implication suggests further that 'I run, and the sun follows me' represents a disturbance of vision that is cleared up in the process of maturing. The sense I wish to take from the sentence is, however, not that this mode of vision is peculiar to the child, but that it is intrinsic to the eye's dermic relation to light: it subsists in the organism *whatever* the individual's degree of 'maturity'. Now consider the perception of a cube. Perception, if one can put it like this, takes the object as it finds it: perception finds the cube – yet from every point of view the cube appears as a parallelogram; from no point of view can the subject obtain a view of *the cube*.[7]

It is in the way that our perception, despite appearance, is nevertheless perception of *a cube*, that we can sense the rupture of space consequent upon our recognition of cubes, chairs, tables, of every entity named by the language in which such terms as cubes, chairs, and tables, are recognised; recognition which is irruptive in this way not only the first time it happens, or at an archaic stage of development, but irruptive in an ongoing and permanent fashion, in the collisions between the intrinsically dyadic relation of the dermis to the light which stimulates it, and the third term or vector (the sign) that is introduced by the social codes of recognition. The cube is situated in a space that is not in its essence visual: it belongs in another space than the space given by optical experience, or rather it belongs in the disruption of space that is precipitated by the movement of the signs (from signifier to signifier). The individual's continuous operation of the codes of recognition *tears* optical space by annexing the latter in such a way that what is physically and literally seen, as a companionable continuum

31 Diagram of the *Spaltung* of vision

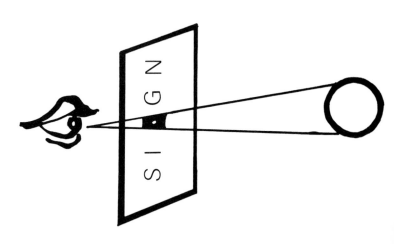

around the self, this envelope of light in which I am bathed and contained, is disrupted by demand to see according to the description of others, through their signs that break up the continuum into differentiated mobility: a mosaic that moves.

At the same time, the social description names me as a visible entity recognised by the description, and it is to this description that my vision, in order to become and to remain socialised, must conform. The description locates me in a language and a vision where all the terms become reversible: what is 'left' for me is 'right' to the description; what is 'here', to the description is 'there'. Mastery of laterality requires that I learn not only to insert the register of signifiers into my optical experience, but that I understand the terms to imply my own visibility *from* a point of view I am unable to inhabit, yet *to* which my own optical field must constantly be referred.[8] Where we are speaking of one kind of crisis when we consider the insertion of the screen of signifiers into the continuum of retinal or dermic experience (a crisis of the interior), we are speaking of another kind of crisis when we consider the visibility of the subject before the codes of recognition (a crisis of relation to the exterior): the first occurs when the codes of recognition provoke a disruption of optical space in order to find, for example, the cube; the second when I find myself named by and located within the codes of recognition coming to me from the outside.

Yet these distinctions are only emphases, because the essential point is that the terms 'inside' and 'outside', the bi-polarity of dermic reaction, can precisely no longer obtain. 'Inside' and 'outside', the dyad of sensation, must accommodate to a third term; the sign *constantly* disrupts the dyad, but for as long as there actually is organic sight, the sense of the dyad with equal constancy remains. The dominant command of sociality is that I orchestrate my retinal experience with the discourses of recognition, that I *renounce* optical experience: on the one hand that I subordinate the retinal continuum to the mobile mosaic of signifiers; and on the other that I make my viewpoint reversible with that of others, even though I cannot *know* those others' viewpoint. In the description of vision coming to the subject, the subject is located as an image; so that *concurrently* with the reorganisation of internal vision around the signs, and as a further consequence of the same splitting of vision under the impact of the sign, there begins the process by which the subject is made to organise the images projected out into the world (towards others) according to collectively legitimated prescriptions.

Ultimately these involve, in adult life, the whole complexity of posture, comportment, address, demeanour, expression, gesture, dress and so forth, that makes up the intelligible and nuanced presentation of the self in the social world. Of prime importance among the images through which the individual subject learns its *ethos* or mode of self-projection towards the social world are those of gender, since *from the first* the subject must fashion its self-imagery in congruence with the images of male and female. These are connotations which in adult life reach, and in every culture, the most elaborate levels of inflection. But while both genders are destined to a life-long work of elaboration of those gendered images, in the dispensation patriarchy (at least) a crucial asymmetry is introduced into the subject's relation to the gaze of the other, to the social *description* of vision. Both genders must locate themselves within the description, but *possession of the Description* – I capitalise the term to indicate its status as the *whole* construction of social vision – is a correlate of social power. The Description embodies within itself the codes that go to make up the collective visuality of the society, but this knowledge, the result and deposit of centuries of collective endeavour, is not to be understood as suspended in a void, as mere information, accessible to all, but as backed by the full force of social practices; and in terms of those practices, while both genders must submit to visibility before the Description as part of their normal enculturation, it is in the *concentration* of power (in effect, in the males) that the Description is inhabited from the inside, as the power to operate the codes of visuality, as power to *see*; while it is in the lesser concentration of power (in the females) that the Description operates as though on to an outside, to produce an image for that seeing.[9]

III

These remarks are not offered by way of excursion away from painting into exotic or extravagant terrain: in fact they are centred firmly upon *The Oath of the Horatii* (illustration 32). It is not that such concepts, and the provenances from which they derive, can *explain* the painting: the moment we invoke causal explanation, the *Oath* becomes an *illustration* of concepts and processes that are fully stated elsewhere; the painting is effectively demoted. All that such concepts can provide is an orientation that may help in the understanding of the painting; and, in this case, I am certain that both David's painting and psychoanalysis are investigating the same area. The *Oath* is an exact image of visuality for the subject living under patriarchy. The females, denied political authority by the patriarchal mandate, are consigned to silence, to the interior, to reproduction; while simultaneously the males are inserted into the equally destructive registers of language and of power convergent in the oath (or, in the case of *Brutus*, the death sentence: illustration 33). The visual space of the males is filled with objects caught in the transfer, from sign to sign, of the patriarch's power. It originates in a body that can no longer sustain the weight of power: the patriarch is now weaker than his sons, his debility stressed by

David in the instability of his pose, arms and legs bent where the legs and arms of the sons are straight, the left foot uncertainly placed, while the feet of the sons are square with the ground. From this source the charge moves to the first of its relays, the swords, to the second, the taut and outstretched arms, and on to invest the bodies of the sons with every mark of virile possession, from the spear, to the stiffly erect crest of their helmets, to the dilated veins of their arms; it energises the oath they swear, re-dedicating the body to the description coming to it from the outside and re-consecrating that description through the flesh; it travels within an enclosed circuit of substitutions in which the sons, losing their individual contour, merge into one another in the spatial plane cut by the father's sword and hand.

The image exactly traces the negative consequences of the subject's insertion into language and gender, for the visuality of the males is now dominated by the outward projection of heroically gendered self-imagery, moving forward to meet the description coming from the outside, in the oath itself; while inwardly every object of sight is submitted to the repeated figure of substitution, the sword standing in place of the father whose strength has gone, the bodies of the sons converging in the oath around their weapons

32 David, *The Oath of the Horatii*

and into one another. And the chain, the contagion, of substitutions does not cease here, but will continue to ramify beyond the moment we see. The dispute between Rome and Alba is to be settled by a battle between these three warriors, the Horatii, and their identical counterparts from Alba, the three Curatii. Both teams are synecdoches for the fathers and for the state: the battle that is to take place will be between twin reflections of patriarchy (and the patriarchs will win). At the end, when of these three who merge into one, the one victor will return, he will kill his sister, Camilla, betrothed to one of the Curatian warriors and a final synecdoche or last link in the chain of destructive substitutions. Patriarchy is described in the image as being, for the male, a kind of epidemic of substitutions which begins in the transfer of power from the father to the sword, and which having launched itself there develops a momentum of displacement that cannot be contained: the only force strong enough to defeat this headlong collapse of one sign before the next, is death.

Specifically, the death of Camilla. The males cannot themselves halt the process of heroic projection and destructive substitution: their fury is literally blind, and in the moment when the returning hero puts his sister to the sword, it is clear that the system of displacements, heated by bloodshed, has grown so corrosive and

33 David, *The Lictors Bringing Brutus the Bodies of his Sons*

precipitate that Camilla cannot be seen as herself, or as an independent being, but only as a further link in the chain of substitutions (illustration 34). For the men, signs have eaten vision away; they have blinded sight. Their bodies are made, in the swearing of the oath, coextensive with the images they must manifest before what is unknown and alien: the vision of the enemy. They define themselves exclusively in the images they present towards an absolute otherness and hostility; while internally, vision is engulfed, blacked out, by a plague of signs that makes of every object in vision the emblem of annihilating power.

The women, according to David, do not directly support or participate in this system of metonymies: in both the *Oath* and the *Brutus* they are its victims, the marginalised objects of power and vision, yet featuring in the system and in this particular narrative as the final, the ultimate image, at the end of the chain. Here David's presentation of the story is rather different from that of Corneille. In Corneille's *Horace*, Camille is fully inserted within language and within signs, and the great speech in which she denounces the Roman cult of valour is a troubling climax in the drama: the men may have the sword, but Camille has the Word, and she uses it to full effect, as a weapon directed at the Roman state.

Rome, l'unique objet de mon ressentiment!
Rome, à qui vient ton bras d'immoler mon amant!
Rome, qui t'a vu naître, et que ton cœur adore!

34   David, Drawing for *The Oath of the Horatii*

Rome enfin, que je hais parce qu'elle t'honore! . . .
Puissé-je de mes yeux y voir tomber ce foudre,
Voir ses maisons en cendre, et ses lauriers en poudre,
Voir le dernier Romain à son dernier soupir,
Moi seule en être cause, et mourir de plaisir.

(IV.V.1301–18)

Corneille's Camille, although opposed to what she sees as the barbarity of Roman heroism, is in fact part of the same system as the men: a creature in full command of language and of signs, and capable of projecting what is perhaps the most heroic and defiant image of the play, she belongs to the same world as the male characters, of image and of *récit*: of Cornelian *gloire*. David's Camilla and the women around her are placed *outside* the register of speech, which belongs exclusively to the males: drained, exhausted, hardly capable of sustaining the weight of their own bodies, the women are unable to mobilise any resource of language or image that might challenge the males. Like the donor in *Belisarius*, the women cannot produce an image capable of *acting* within male vision: all they can do is become the site of a male look that apprehends the female as passive before vision, the object of and for the male gaze.

The women in the *Oath* do not speak, and they hardly see: their eyes are all but closed; they themselves are signs, units to be exchanged between the men in their inter-male alliances. Their degraded status, almost of commodity within a circuit of exchange, is made clear in the narrative: to lessen the tension between the two camps of Rome and of Alba, a sister of the Curatii has been traded for a sister of the Horatii; the females are moved around as counters whose value derives only from their relation to the males, as further signs in the enclosed circuit of masculinities. It is because Camilla is first marginalised as image, and finally not even perceived as image, but simply as a sign of Alba, the sign of an enemy male, that she is killed.

The *Oath* is itself an image, yet it is also an image of visuality: an image about how *we* are images, and about the relation between sign and sight. For the males, visuality is dominated and blinded by signs: both as the signs of strength and virile possession they must project outwards, in constant strain, towards the gaze of the adversary, the gaze of alterity; and inwardly, as a corrosion of sight where nothing may appear innocently or as itself, for everything has become the sign of another sign (in the *différance*, the deferral of vision).[10] Theirs is essentially paranoid vision, if we take 'paranoia' in its technical sense, as referring to a representational crisis in subjectivity; a crisis in which material life is invaded, devoured by signs, turned everywhere *into* the sign. For the females, visuality consists in being the blinded object of another's sight: the observed of all observers, the women are to be seen, not to see, and for them equally, visuality is the experience of Being becoming Representation. In David's painting both genders are portrayed as living under affliction, and it is this critical detachment from gender which renders the painting itself problematic.

One perhaps wants to say that it is a description of visuality which itself issues from a neutral position; yet the *Oath* is nevertheless an image, an object which itself exists in visuality. David is not describing the visual in a medium, such as written language, that stands outside the visual, as the description or analysis of a dream, for example, stands outside the dream. *The Oath of the Horatii* must assume a place in a visual order that is no less *exacting* than the visual order it attributes to Rome. And it is here that the *Oath* becomes far more complex, far deeper than the language of any analysis (including this one) of the painting can possibly be: it exceeds *any* account. David is portraying a human visuality, and 'portrayal' seems to require a vantage point, a point of knowledge, outside that which is portrayed: but how can the *image* exit from visuality?

The position from which the *Oath* is painted is, I think, a very precarious one, and in the first place precarious in personal terms for this artist, at this time. There can be little doubt that it is a tragic painting: tragic because it shows a humanity broken in two, across the bar of gender, each fragment living in permanent incompleteness; tragic because even the most noble human action is shown as linked with, perhaps as inseparable from, the opposite of man's nobility – the destructiveness of his group-mentality, the violence of his political institutions, the cruelty of his idealism; tragic also because it shows human visuality, in which both painter and viewer must take their place, as operating as though under a curse, stricken by a principle of alterity which deforms the world of sight, or perhaps reflects back to us an intrinsic deformity, an 'othering' which runs throughout our being, and occurs here locally in the world of sight. In as much as the painting *is* tragic, and presents us with disorder, it seeks by its tragic art a place of contemplation somewhere beyond disorder: in art. And perhaps here one may locate the sanity of the *Oath*: its belief that it can represent disorder is a faith in art's finally redemptive properties.

At the conclusion of the *Oresteia*, the curse of bloodshed that has ruined the house of Atreus is purged by law, legality, by the institution of discourse, in the arena of language; and part of the joyousness of the *Oresteia* is its sense that it, too, is discourse, that it is played out in the arena of language, and in its own being is therefore part of the agency which brings an end to the rule of bloodshed.[11] Similarly the *Oath* can be seen as truly classical, *Ionian* art, where because it is a representation, the representation of disorder dissociates itself from disorder's pain. The drama moves beyond *miasma* by a secession 'away': into representation.

But in the *Oath* this is a secession achieved (if it is achieved at all) under great tension. 'To the small, inarticulate, violent and vulnerable David came this fantasy of strength, calm, power';[12] and while part of *the painting* takes upon itself the role of diagnosis, and attempts to dissociate itself from what it represents, part of *David* recalcitrantly subscribes to the imagery of male heroism: the painter of *The Death of Socrates* will later cry out to Robespierre, at a critical gathering just before Thermidor, 'I too will drink the hemlock with you.'[13] An unmistakable vein of hysteria runs through the *Oath* as it does through that cry; and emotionally, this vein runs counter to, it uncannily compromises, the painting's Ionian detachment. It makes the strain between the two impulses – to diagnose, and to participate – so great that 'sanity' and 'detachment' seem finally words too moderate to describe what is going on. The impulse to identify with heroism casts the diagnostic impulse as its own antagonist, as though detachment required tremendous effort; and the apparent sanity of the painting's wish to escape disorder through art merges here with a Promethean desire, to rise above the natural and the normal and to enter the heroic, by painting *this* masterwork.

Yet it is finally not even David's emotional participation in the image of the *Oath* that threatens its rational or Ionian detachment. We can say that an important premise of classical tragedy is that the representation of disorder can secede from disorder because it is a representation: its art occupies a place outside and above the disorder it shows – the place of representations. But the *Oath* is an image: it exists in the same register of visuality as that of its characters; and where the *Oath* seems to me to break with classicism is in its sense that as an image, as part of visuality, it cannot escape into *any* exterior.

IV

I want to discuss this first in terms of space (and later of style). Every viewer of the painting must be struck by the *Oath*'s return to a rudimentary or fundamental space, to what in the Renaissance had been the *veduta* (illustration 35): the organisation of all lines around a clear and centrally positioned vanishing point. It is a space

35 Piero della Francesca, *Ideal Town*

which can be said uniquely to welcome and accommodate the viewer. The axis running from the viewer's eye to the vanishing point – what Alberti calls the 'centric ray'[14] – proposes a spatial continuity between the space in the painting and the viewing space outside it. In the *veduta*, as in the *Oath*, this message of continuity is taken up and reinforced by the themes of flagstone and wall: the viewer's space is *embraced* by the perspective, and since the space of viewing and that of the painting join together, or at least a fiction of continuity is suggested, the viewer is uniquely incarnated by the *veduta* as a physical presence on the actual stage of the painting. Its space is that of the city or the piazza, a social space that is quite unlike, for example, the space of landscape: it is urban, and the viewer of the *veduta* is proposed and assumed as having a natural political right to this space, which is ordered and organised, in all its lines and perspectives, especially around his inclusion. Where pre-perspectival painting makes few assumptions concerning the *unique* physical existence of the viewer, but addresses the viewer rather as a choric or collective presence, perspective and in particular the intensification of perspective in the *veduta* addresses the viewer as a specific individual: it is a *personal* construction, where the image recognises (more accurately, constructs) the viewer as a unitary subject, master of the prospect, unique possessor of the scene.

Yet the paradox is that the 'centric ray' may also be turned around.[15] At the picture plane (if we follow Alberti's account) two cones intersect: the cone of lines emanating from the viewer's eye; and, within the painting, the other cone of lines that emanates from the vanishing point. In the *veduta* the second cone is greatly emphasised: with every flagstone, wall or cornice, its lines multiply. This second cone, now radiating not from the viewer's eye but from the vanishing point, installs in the perspectival image, and particularly in the *veduta*, a force that contradicts the centering of vision in the viewing eye, for this cone is the opposite of the first: it runs in reverse; it dominates the painting; and it introduces into the image a place, a mark, of 'othering'. The source of the centric ray, twin term to the viewer's monocular site, turns viewer into image, seer into seen. As I look at the vanishing point, I am *surprised* – seized by the outside; all the perspectives, the lines of force, of my world, shift, turn, recentre on a point of nothingness where I cannot exist, except as the visible, as image. This can be said of every *veduta*, but in the *Oath* the vanishing point is occupied not by a point, but by the narrative centre where the hands of the sons take from their father the swords to which they consecrate their being. It is here that all the aspects of the male's capture in structures of power entering in from the outside, concentrate their energy. The viewer's encounter with 'the other', in the space of the *veduta* where everything is made visible, meets the processes of decenter-ing and expropriation by the other which fill the depicted scene:

the two systems, of content and of representation, join here at the painting's *fulcrum* – around the convergent hands, the centric ray – and in a conjunction which brings together vision *in* the image and vision *of* the image. That Ionian distance – the idea that representation of disorder can dissociate itself from disorder *because it is a representation* – collapses. The painting ceases to exist in a channel of transmission (from A to B; from painter to viewer); it positions itself instead in a circuit of visualities where the figures *in* the image, and the painter and the viewer who stand *outside* it, are all subject to the 'alteration', the alienation of what they see.

Although it is perhaps the most dramatic of the painting's spatial structures, the *veduta* nevertheless is not the only organisation of space within the *Oath*, for as we examine the space of the flagstones, the arcade, and the plunging perspective, we find another, a second kind of space that intensifies the *veduta*'s expropriative action. This is the space of the frieze. The Horatian warriors stand in a line parallel to the picture plane, like figures on a stele, or bas-relief. Now, the assumptions underlying the space of the frieze are in many respects the same as those of the *veduta*. Where the *veduta* proposes the absolute visibility in metric space of all the objects contained and containable in the *veduta*, the frieze proposes the absolute legibility of the narrative space contained within its relief. Negating the complex shifts of view presented by sculpture 'in the round' – the plurality of a sculpture whose meanings are distributed in time, as the viewer moves through the sculpture's *neighbourhood* (discursive as well as spatial) – the frieze makes it possible for the viewer to receive the scene all at once and from a single point (or line) in space. We may even say that relief exaggerates and intensifies the instantaneous, the *im Augenblick* character of that place in viewing, since, although the viewer does not actually move around the sculpture, he is given the impression of receiving as much information as he would if he were actually to circumnavigate its forms. The frieze distils into a single plane the implied possibilities of other planes, planes potentially stated by virtue of the *emergent* nature of the forms as they rise above their background, yet finally subsumed and compressed into the master-plane of the relief. Just as the *veduta* promises the full intelligibility of the scene to a viewer placed at the centre of monocular vision, so the frieze promises *its* intelligibility to a viewer moving in binocular vision along a line. The unitary effect of relief ultimately depends on a convention, or agreed fiction, that the viewer disregard the cubic nature of the space he occupies: the views obtained as one approaches the relief obliquely (in the gallery, in public space) are proposed as 'wrong', as illegitimate or outside the code of viewing; more precisely, such oblique or lateral views, inherent in cubic space, are established as preparatory, as approaches, as heralds of the true view of the frieze, which can be found at one place only. The frieze is the essence of *classical* sculpture, where we take that word from its radical, from the *classicum*, the flourish of trumpets that announced the entrance of the Roman Senate. By contrast with sculpture 'in the round' – sculpture that gives equal or multiple validity to all of its points of access – the frieze works by disavowing its plastic nature and by suppressing volumetric space both in itself and in its place of viewing.[16] The convention privileges plane over volume.

Yet the *veduta*'s convention or agreed fiction is exactly the reverse of this. It turns a plane, the picture plane, *into* volume: its organisation of space is such that from a single plane surfaces *re-enter* a virtual cubic space; from this gridwork of perspective lines, this precise ground-plan, one can locate objects in a precisely measured space of three dimensions. To place a frieze inside a *veduta*, which is the *Oath*'s dominant spatial action, is to activate two conventions of representation which stand in fundamental opposition; almost literally 'at right angles' to each other. The *veduta* promises a complete prospect, and proffers it to the eye as though to an individual who is to be its master, proprietor of the scene. It offers two terms of vision, the eye and the world, and the world is apparently organised around and for this masterful eye, as a spectacle designed for precisely this moment, of unique consumption. Yet the *veduta*, by the same token, breaks that promise by instilling a vanishing point which organises everything around *itself*: all the lines converge there, in reverse, at that point of nothingness to which all the information is referred. The dyad of eye and world is broken by this cardinal of a system of vision where everything is visible, is viewable from the outside, is image. The viewer is cast out from the centre of the world, the Eden of dyadic vision; he exactly *becomes* an outside, object of another's sight. The surrealist metaphor of Merleau-Ponty could not be more succinct, in describing this continuous extraversion in vision (for it is not, in fact, a Fall, or archaic event, but a fate, a *perpetual* aspect of vision): the turning inside-out of a glove.[17]

The *Oath* already states the reversible or inside-out structure of vision in its *veduta*, but within the cubic or boxlike space now stands the frieze. By itself the frieze, like the *veduta*, might proffer the beholder a complete prospect, a master-plane that distils into itself the information of a cubic space it subsumes and overcomes; yet its insertion into the *pre-eminently* volumetric space of the *veduta* destroys that unique and privileged prospect by reaffirming the aspect of volume whose suppression gives to the frieze all of its coherence, intelligibility, and authority. That insertion raises all the possibilities of other and oblique views which relief negates, views which one would obtain if the figures in the *Oath* were free-standing sculpture, yet views from which the beholder (by this *irrational* placing of a planar design in a cubic space) is now excluded. 'Well, Monsieur. In the *Horatii* you have managed to get three figures on the same plane: something never before achieved in painting.' This sarcastic comment, from Pierre, the First Painter of France, goes to the heart of the matter: the compression of the male figures into a single plane is uncanny because this is at the same time an intensely volumetric painting. The plane of the frieze cuts across the Roman interior like a blade. Like a sword; it comes almost from another spatial universe. And its effect is to force on the viewer two competing systems for scanning or interpreting the painting's spaces: that of the *veduta* and that of the frieze.

Both systems promise to deliver to the viewer a coherent prospect, an image given in completeness, in presence; yet the *veduta* turns vision inside-out, while the frieze, because placed within the *veduta*, becomes subject to other views than that unitary, concentrated view which relief singles out and privileges. The frieze now comes under the power of the vanishing point: instead of surrendering itself to the line where the viewer *is*, it is made visible from where the viewer is not. *Veduta* and frieze function, in fact, as extreme versions of the device in painting that is known by the name of *anamorphosis*. In anamorphosis, an image is coherent around a place the viewer does not occupy – he has to change his position to discover the skull, the hidden portrait, the saint in prayer. For the *veduta*, and for the frieze within the *veduta*, the point of coherence switches from the place of viewing to the vanishing point; the image coheres not simply around a place the viewer can move to, but around the point which above all others stands for his *absence*, his exclusion from presence in the represented scene.

V

So far I have been speaking of only part of the *Oath*'s circuit of visuality. Both the figures in the painting and the viewer outside are exposed to a force of 'alterity' in vision, a force one might call the gaze, the Gaze of Otherness. But what of David? Where does he stand in this circle of sight?

In all of David's work up to the *Oath* one detects an aloofness in the handling of styles, a wary manipulation of styles – Pietro played against Poussin, Greuze played against the *tableau d'histoire* – in a game of connoisseurship, the effect of which is to introduce a 'hesitation' into the image: David throws inverted commas around his styles, he speaks in personae, across the delay or intermediary distance of the styles. The *Oath* marks the end of that playfulness of the early David, for now he paints as no one before him has painted and with a fury of commitment, in the style of Neo-classicism. The overview, the ironic interval, the inverted commas, all these gestures of fastidiousness vanish in a style without qualifications, a style coloured exactly by its refusal of complication, its banishment of 'neo-baroque' and 'neo-rococo' revivalism, a style of purgation that sheds these epicycles as indulgence, dalliance, waste (to David's pupils the war-cry will always be 'Van Loo, Pompadour, Rococo!'). David returns to the Source. Yet let us recall what was said earlier about the pain of belatedness inherent in the painter's task. To return to the Source is to repeat the questions, 'Which was the first word the child *read*?', and 'Which was the first image to be painted?' There *is* no first image: to be recognised, the image must be referred to prior images, earlier signs, and in the logic of inauguration here, what is first only becomes first retroactively. I paint; but to communicate to my viewer what it is I see, I must paint in the visual language that is already spoken; I must find signs that pre-date my vision, signs into which my vision must be inserted, in what is always already a state of belatedness

If the precursors are agents of anxiety in painting, it is not necessarily because the masters painted better, but because it is through their images that I must fashion my own. They take from me what might have been mine and what still must be made mine, for if I yield to what they have said then I will no longer speak, but be spoken; no longer see, but be seen. Tradition is what looks at me as I paint, and just as before the gaze of another the lines of force that placed me at the centre of my lived horizon reverse, making of me a spectacle, a visible object to the other's sight, so before tradition I as painter lose my uniqueness and my plenitude of vision, and am made a latecomer whose visions cannot be retained as my own. If I succumb fully to the images within which I am condemned to articulate my sight, I shall cease to be an artist, and become instead the blinded vessel of others' sight.

For the strong painter perhaps there is always this elective dream, which can never be realised: to paint the freshness of the world's colours. But for painting there can only be a dawning into belatedness. And for Neo-classical painting the exemplary expression of the sense of belatedness is its perception of the lost source of all of its activity, Antiquity: Antiquity is where the works of Zeuxis were made, then destroyed; the place of lost origins, it is the place *par excellence* of the origin *as* loss. For the painter who is weak because he wishes to make himself strong (for Mengs, for Gavin Hamilton) Antiquity seems a site of *possible* beginnings, as though by refusing belatedness the painter could steal back to the era of alleged inauguration, and, tricking time, could rediscover in the present all the lost primacy of the past. Yet for the painter who attempts to outwit his own modernity the result can only be a flood of repetitions, and deathly, stencilled echoes. Strength here is to be found only in what David discovers in the *Oath*, and again in *Socrates*, and in *Brutus*: the acceptance of latecoming, of tradition, and of tradition's gaze. In the place where the I might have been, there it, the tradition, stands, but in order that an eye might arise; an eye rid of its primal dream, yet not ridden, or derided by tradition.

The significance of the *Oath*'s 'stylistic revolution' is that it decontextualises the painting from its own immediate past, from the intricate, allusive connoisseurship practised at the Académie, and notably by David himself; while at the same time it recontextualises the painting in the field where the anxiety of influence is, for the art of academies, at its most intense: Antiquity. The antique here is felt as alien, as an alteration of normal vision – and we should remember here the extraordinary impact of the *Oath* on its first audiences, and on the subsequent evolution of French painting. It is a painting *radically* unlike those that surrounded it, at the Salon of 1785: its force is irruptive, invasive. The contrast here is with Antiquity as theorised, for example, by Reynolds, as that which, if only painters could return to it, would necessarily always seem familiar and natural, would seem *home*, because in the art of Antiquity the central and familiar forms both of nature and of tradition had been stored.[18] Or the contrast is with Antiquity viewed according to Vien, as a purifying influence on French art and as a means by which French painting might discard the excesses and false elaborations of the rococo age, and again become natural: the return to the antique is accompanied, in Vien's programme, by a return to the live model. With David in the *Oath*, the antique style is so purged, so stripped away, that when it arrives at the Salon it presents itself as an absolute break in the paradigm, as a trauma for French painting.

Seen against the pacific background of Vien, and the subtle diplomatic, bureaucratically adept painting of the Academicians, this is a truly violent work. Antiquity appears in a guise that could not be further from the homecoming it meant to Reynolds, for it is everything *but* the familiar, the normal, the centrally placed. It is the *unheimlich*. And by means of the historical disaster that left behind only Antiquity's sculpture and virtually none of its paintings, Antiquity features as an alien and alienating force *within* the painting. The presence of Antiquity in the *Oath* is that of *statuary*. The ambiguous properties of the *veduta* work once again in another key, for the *veduta* among other things supplies the clearest possible framework in which to see stone – arcades, walls, flagstones, cornices – and to see the body against stone, and to calibrate the volumes of the human body with an accuracy which is finally that of the sculptor or the stonemason. Antiquity gave us its sculpture, not its paintings; if we return to Antiquity (despite Reynolds' optimism) that return can be as though to a petrifying force, to a power which objectifies or reifies the visual field, and transcribes it in terms that are in essence those of another system than the visual. If the gaze of another reverses the lines of force which had centred in my singleness of witness, and makes of me an object, a volume in objectified space, it can be said that 'I am sculpted by the gaze'. David, so far from contending against sculpture in order to assert himself as a pure or original witness, presents his figures as though on a frieze, or compressed into the hard, carved space of stone relief; where sculpture becomes the densest of the painting's metaphors for vision, as that which represents the objectification of the world before the medusal gaze of the other, and as that which at the same time represents the priority of the precursors and of their visual systems over the painter working in belatedness.

David is a deep painter, and I would say also a painter frightened by the deeps his vision opens up (with Ingres it is different: he relaxes there; his gift is to take the energy David finds deadly and inhuman, and to tame, to personalise it). On the surface of David's greatest canvas we see the surfaces of things, but what is really being painted is the inwardness of vision, and what it means to be a sighted being who does not see angelically, in essence and beyond time, but mortally; along with others, in tradition. In a sense what he paints is *the mortality of sight*. It is a subject that addresses an issue neither Ingres nor Delacroix face so directly: death. And it leads him to insights which even now I doubt that we possess an adequate language to describe (the point is that David's paintings

36   David, *Marat assassiné*

À MARAT.
DAVID.

are that language): the *inscription* on flesh (and retina) of the signs that make us human; the social and ultimately the political nature of those signs – the words of the Horatian oath, but also the last words of Socrates, the death sentence passed by Brutus, the Oath of the Jeu de Paume, the torn ballot paper suspended over the torn body of Lepelletier, the *Roma* engraved on the shield in *The Intervention of the Sabine Women*, the 'Bonaparte: Hannibal: Karolus Magnus' graven on the rock in *Napoleon Crossing the Saint-Bernard*, the epitaph carved by the soldiers at Thermopylae. What interests him is the fatal character of those signs, and their deathly antagonism to living flesh, and here his inscriptions speak for painting itself, for in painting what we never find is the light, the air, the quick or lustral quality of living sight. As the social subjects of vision we are condemned also to see across systems that were there before us, and will remain when we ourselves are dust. In the signs of even the most vernal paintings we see *always across* our own death (illustration 36). A MARAT: DAVID: L'AN DEUX. We have not yet caught up with what is implied in that most eloquent of signatures.

Visionary delays: Ingres in the atelier of David

They were offered the choice between becoming kings or the couriers of kings.

Franz Kafka

I

DAVID'S RECANTATIONS in the period following the Revolution are notorious.

> The people's representative, the painter David, stood at the Tribune, where he stammered out a few incoherent words in which he sought, but in vain, to deflect the wrath of several of his colleagues, eager to have an official accusation charge laid against him. He was pale; the sweat from his brow dripped down from his clothing and fell to the floor, where it left broad stains.[1]

The polite interpretation of David's Revolutionary activities is faithfully stated by Delécluze:

> Everything seems to suggest that the pictures of the Tennis Court Oath, of Lepelletier, of Marat, and of Bara had been completed by David almost, as it were, without his knowing, during his bout of political fever. By the very nature of the subjects, and even in the way in which they were painted, they were quite different from all that the artist had produced before and what he was to do later. These productions could almost be compared to those of a sleep-walker who has been working without suspecting it. Therefore these four pictures mark an important but quite special stage in the development of David's talents.[2]

The visual expression of David's rehabilitation is *The Intervention of the Sabine Women* (illustration 40), and it is hard not to think of it as a 'normalised' painting. Its appeal is to a climate of normal assumptions and expectations concerning the viewer, the painter, and tradition; assumptions and expectations to which we ourselves might continue to subscribe. Its invocations to the past are complex, yet clearly it is a *new* painting, in a new and 'advanced' style – it is David's latest painting, and Neo-classicism is not irruptive or invasive as it had been in the *Oath*, but chic. The vision in the image *comes from* David, its unproblematic source, and owner of the painting now in a direct and legal sense: people pay to see the painting, and the proceeds amount to some twenty thousand francs.[3] The signature on the receipt for that sum would be on a par with David's signature on the canvas: David *owns* this painting as he could not be said to own, for example, the *Marat assassiné*. The word 'David' closes the painting by an act of legal possession which is the counterpart in law to the original possession by David of the image itself. It is true that David summons images from tradition into this painting; but those invocations are still containable under a law of ownership – so far from querying juridical and aesthetic ownership of the painting, they give it pedigree. And for the viewer a similar contract of ownership is at work when he buys the ticket at the door which gives him the right of viewing: he is paying for a unique experience, a single product (the 'unitary' work of art), made for his literally unique consumption (tickets are not transferable).

We are now firmly in the Directoire: the people and the people's vision are in abeyance (the infamous *Marat* disappears from view), and the star of property is rising. David's Revolutionary paintings had belonged to a dispensation in which vision had been overtly social in organisation. Through his orchestration of the Revolutionary pageants, to which his painting from 1789 to 1794 had been increasingly related,[4] David had made painting a collective experience, and the questions of 'origin' and 'originality' had been answered by a practice that located the vision of things in the Republic, the body politic. *Marat assassiné* showed the remains of Marat, his bath, his writing chest, his quill, in the same ensemble that David had publicly staged for Marat's funeral at the Church of the Cordeliers (illustration 37), and the painting owes its emptiness, its greenish light, even its atmosphere of reverential piety, as much to that image in the public domain, as the scene David had encountered when he visited Marat's private apartment immediately before the assassination. The image of Brutus, as Herbert has shown, had become as familiar as any public image

37 Anon., *The Funeral of Marat in the Church of the Cordeliers*

could, in this period before the technological dissemination of mass imagery.[5] Essentially the *Tennis Court Oath* (illustration 38) is a popular engraving enlarged to the scale of history painting (illustration 39), and it was from the economy of the engraving that the painting arose.[6] David's signature on the Revolutionary paintings is an incidental nomination, an inflection of public visuality, and it announces itself as a refusal to recede into private singularity: it is still 'A Marat, David'. David now claims to *own* the *Intervention of the Sabines*. Yet it is still *seen* by the public – in droves; and it invokes a series of precursors as multiple as any invocation in the early David. How does the concept of ownership work, here? And above all, in the genre of *public* painting – the *tableau d'histoire*?

38 David, *The Oath of the Tennis Court*

39 Flouest, engraving of *The Oath of the Tennis Court*

To answer this question we would have to look to institutions and to structures of law as these operate juridically to define ownership by the painter of his product, and ownership by the viewer of his right to view. Who owns the Cathedral? Who owns the *vision* of the Cathedral? Who at present owns the vision of the *Intervention*? The history of the boundaries of ownership in vision remains to be written; but no matter how such a history might describe the changing boundaries of 'original possession', what we would realise more and more from the empirical findings of the history is that two terms are in constant fluctuation: *origin* and *boundary*. From the arguments stated here it should be clear why the first of these must be considered as logically impossible. There is no original image anywhere: not in the world (the 'first' image); not in the painter's head (except by a concession, half theological, half lyrical, to the noumenon); nor will we find an original in the viewer's head (by the same logic of the 'perceptualist fallacy' that applies to the viewer). Painting as a system of signs knows only difference, succession, the intervals and movements from sign to sign, and no unitary or prior origin can be expressed or located anywhere in the circuits of painting-and-viewing. The image is an entity *without origin* (at the same time that, in the art of the West, it constantly witnesses – in the legal sense – its first or Zeuxian presence).

As to boundary, and to the lines drawn around 'agreed' origins of the image (the individual painter, the team in the atelier, the artisanate of the Cathedral; or the patron, the patron class, the people), all these are the historical fluctuations of imaginary boundaries that express real political, economic, and legal needs, and they have a right to their history, for only in history do they manifest and move. But in history the line that marks off 'origin', in so far as this refers to undemonstrable and transcendental origin, is *always* a fiction. It may be marked by an enclosure – the entrance to a public museum, or private collection; or it may be marked by a frame – the four sides of the frame are the boundary for *this* painting, the line that certifies everything within the frame as original, as having its origin here; it may be marked by a whole series of thresholds, like the approaches to the tabernacle in the Holy of Holies (*boundary* in a state of extraordinary purity and intensity); or it may be marked by the artist's signature (David). All those fictions of boundary are so many lines drawn around a zero, a nothing, a *vide*. Yet their persistence is an intrinsic feature of social visuality, and from the point of view of the painter the drawing of such boundaries has a greater urgency and necessity than for almost anyone in the circuits of vision, since it is only by drawing the line that he can become himself, this unique painter, this *creator*; and by the same token nothing expresses the difficulty, the impossibility of drawing that line more pressingly than tradition, for being in tradition is nothing if not the permanent realisation of non-originality. How does a painter such as David, who in the work of the 1780s, and particularly in the *Oath*, had realised and enacted the drama of non-presence in vision with a forcefulness few painters have ever achieved, how does this artist for whom tradition had been a power felt in all its potential to negate the self-enclosure of vision, how *does* this man recant?

Let us look at the painting (illustration 40). The 'boundary' is achieved by the simplest of tropes: indented quotation. Within this image we will find the echoes, clear or muted, of many images: a list can be promptly drawn up (and nowhere better than in classical source analysis). At once we will see:

(1) Flaxman (*The Trojans Seize the Slain*, for the 'grec pur' of outlined warriors, the flattened space, the Phrygian cap)

(2) Domenichino (*The Martyrdom of St Andrew*: for the background, the 'décor')

(3) Agostino Veneziano (the rearing horse, at the extreme right)

(4) Raphael (*The Massacre of the Innocents*, via Raimondi: for the woman whose hands meet over her forehead at the centre of the composition, and for the children in the foreground)

(5) Poussin (*The Rape of the Sabine Women*, for the stance of the warring males; *The Massacre of the Innocents*, for the woman running with her child)

(6) Guido Reni (perhaps: for the open mouth of the woman who runs, from Reni's handling of the same subject)

40 David, *The Intervention of the Sabine Women*

The inventory may certainly be extended, and the more it is, the more the painting will be seen to achieve its 'originality' precisely by declaring its power to *cite* (site, sight) the precursors' visions. Citation here is the figure whereby the master-image claims its arising out of tradition, so that however many precursive images are cited, and however disparate their provenance, that very profusion will establish the authority of the present image to act as the citations' matrix. The figure here works like a genealogy in reverse: exactly by declaring its secondariness and *declension* from tradition

> PRECURSORS
> PRESENT IMAGE

the image asserts its (fiction of) originality:

> PRESENT IMAGE
> PRECURSORS

The originality is only an effect of troping, a turning that *seems* at the same time to be a point of inauguration, and perhaps no character could be found better to indicate the duplicity of the trope than the letter alpha: seen as a loop around an enclosure, a lasso framing space, the alpha stores in itself the essential image of a first place; but seen also as a loop or turning in what is in fact seamless, the double loop of infinity whose coils have been arbitrarily cut, the alpha inscribes the face of difference as the true character of the character in the cleavage of the lateral v.

II

This is not to deny that in certain respects, the *Intervention of the Sabines* is a painting in the direct line of David's meditation on human vision, as this had appeared in the *Oath* and the *Brutus*. The aim of the work is, after all, exculpation: in obedience to political pressure, David must produce a work that will join the paintings of the 1780s, so that his reputation as the creator of the *Oath*, the *Brutus* and now the *Intervention* can slide over and conceal his aberrant Revolutionary production from 1789 to 1794. The *Intervention* opens on to the same pig-headed world of Roman valour and patriarchal vision as before, and once again David explores the emotional implications of the frieze. In placing their bodies as though on the surface of a frieze the males are shown as defining themselves, heroically, before a gaze that is not physically present *in* the scene. The posture of the warrior on the left makes more sense to the viewer than it possibly can to his adversary, for it is turned directly towards the viewing space and less advertently towards the enemy, as though the place to which the heroic image is aimed is not primarily the gaze of the opponent, but rather a non-specific gaze of otherness located in subjectivity, and then, at a subsidiary stage, ascribed to the actual enemy. Similarly in the case of the warrior on the right, the strange turn of his rear towards the spectator suggests that he conceives of his body, even (and particularly) the zones outside his own vision, as an image directed at an otherness surrounding him, looking at him on all sides, and only secondarily perceived in the gaze of actual hostility emanating from his opponent. These areas of the painting define the same kind of alienation in masculine self-imagery that had been portrayed in the Horatian brothers. And if we look carefully at the portrayal of the women we can see that at least here David's thinking has evolved beyond the point reached in the 1780s, though along lines laid down by the *Oath* and the *Brutus*.

There are four principal women (illustration 41): Hersilia, at the centre, the painting's heroine; behind her, a woman whose hands meet over her brow; a withered crone who is about to rend her tunic; and a bare-breasted mother, with arms extending down towards her children in anguished supplication. What is important

41 David, *The Intervention of the Sabine Women* (detail)

here is the twinning of the poses. The upper arms of the woman behind Hersilia are in close parallel to those of Hersilia herself, so that the change-over of the forearms from their closed position over the brow to the open and outstretched gesture of Hersilia, seems a single action, two stills in a single arching movement. Again, the arms of the ancient about to tear her garment twin with those of the younger woman in front of her whose tunic has been torn, as though despite the pronounced difference in their age and condition, these two figures evolve into one. The idea which emerges from such repetitions is that of the generic body of Woman, and it is to be noted that the women in this painting are not content with being marginalised as decorous images, like the women in the *Oath*, or prevented from entering into the pathways of male visuality by their immurement or coralling within the domestic zones of the house, like the women in *Brutus*: they *force* their image into the visuality of the males, and what they display there, collectively, is the fact of gendered difference.

The males are reflections of one another: Tatius' concave shield matches and complements the convex shield of Romulus, Tatius' angular or submissive pose matches and complements the taut and dominating pose of Romulus; as if the male universe were self-enclosed and self-contained, and its inhabitants were distributing among themselves (as in the far more overtly homoerotic *Leonidas at Thermopylae*, with its Spartan loves – Illustration 42) male and

42   David, *Leonidas at Thermopylae*

female roles, disavowing the actual fact of sexual difference, and deflecting their ideas of gender on to the fetishistic apparatus of sword, sheath and shield. The women are attempting, in unison, to break open the mirrored world of masculinities: they are not engaged in displaying the pathos of victims, like the swooning girl in *Brutus*, or in hiding themselves from the males, like the hooded figure in *Brutus*, and the downcast, enervated women of the *Oath*. They are driving a wedge into the dyadic vision of the men; they introduce true difference, differently gendered bodies, and their task is larger than the individual – it requires a group momentum. The woman behind Hersilia seems to come up to and press her arms against a wall of invisibility, a barrier of patriarchy that keeps the women, as though by a law of purdah, out of view. But Hersilia, partly propelled by her companion's efforts, succeeds in breaking through that barrier and in penetrating into the vision of the men, her arms dividing the dyad and interposing the collective force of the female body. Everything happens as if Hersilia were trying to reorient the masculine vision, align it round another term than a gaze of aggression located in mirrors; around a body which, by insisting on its different nature, breaks open the dangerous visual lock of Narcissus.

David's dramatic understanding of his figures, and of their appearance before each other and to themselves, is certainly as subtle and as deep as it had been in the *Oath* and *Brutus*, yet the idea of alterity in vision – the 'othering' of sight – is confined *to the figures*: it does not extend to the place of the viewer, or to the painter. Spatially, the *Intervention* altogether lacks the complexity of the *Oath*'s play of frieze and *veduta*, though the residue of both forms can be found. The image takes its principal design from Flaxman (illustration 43), where depth is eliminated in the wiry line of surface. We can say of Flaxman's drawing that it contains no illusion of space, only an idea of space: devoid of shadow, depth and interior modelling, it offers its figures to only one point of observation, the eye placed above the page. David is keen that the

43 John Flaxman, *The Trojans Seize the Slain*

Intervention have the appearance of sleekest modernity: it must be executed in a pure Directoire style, and carry no overtones either of the Revolution or the *ancien régime*. To this end his reliance on Flaxman is advertised as the most visible agent of influence in his painting, and here David shows, as usual, a preternatural sensitivity to shifts in contemporary taste. In 1795, when the first ideas of the *Intervention* were beginning to form, Flaxman had only recently become known in France: in England the Flaxman *Homer* had appeared only two years earlier, the Aeschylus drawings of 1795 could only just have arrived in France, and Flaxman's European reputation peaks in fact ten years later – around 1805, when editions of his work are published simultaneously in Rome, London, Paris, Hamburg and Leipzig.[7]

As Flaxman's reputation rises, so the popularity of the *Intervention* increases: David's choice of influence was strategically brilliant. Yet Flaxman is also the most negative kind of influence David could have absorbed at this time, since the planarity of Flaxman's work rules out all the spatial intricacy, the play of anamorphoses, which had characterised David's history painting of the 1780s, and particularly the *Oath*. By rendering the image as design, as linear configuration, and by placing the frieze of Tatius, Hersilia and Romulus somewhere 'in front' of a *scaena* or backdrop (the theatrical citadel, the wretched matchstick spears) David takes the viewer *out* of the problematic visuality inhabited by the painting's figures. The viewer simply looks at the scene: nothing more is demanded. He is not *implicated* in visual disturbance, as he must be when he scans and construes the spaces of the *Oath*. The 'frieze' is a plane designed to be consumed completely from the spectator's viewpoint. Within the painting, the frieze is semantically charged with ideas of the gaze: the males' sense of their visibility from all sides, and the need to project self-imagery which nonetheless can never satisfy the demand which the gaze contains; the females' sense of male vision as a barrier that must be penetrated, a wall to be torn down. For the figures in the drama, the frieze sums up a whole sequence of problems and complexities in sight: but for the viewer it is simply there, spectacle. Though ultra-modern in look, the painting proffers itself completely to the viewing space, and this explicit surrender of the image to an audience is in fact the most *retardataire* element in the *Intervention*, and signals a regression to such outward-turning, theatrical pictures as *The Death of Seneca*. By incorporating this ascendant fashion David in fact runs counter to the direction of his development from *Antiochus* to *Brutus*: the viewer is taken out of the battleground of visuality, away from the hostilities. The drama does not personally concern him: across an Ionian distance he sees a representation of disordered visuality, but sees it *as* representation. The *Oath* had found its own exit from the circuits of visuality impossible to find: the image, as part of vision, belonged *with* the disorder it represented. Here, the painting sidesteps and extricates itself; its complaisance and complacency lies in its satisfaction that it is representation, *tout court.*

Nor does the *Intervention* include that other drama of embattled vision, whose protagonist is the painter. Tradition is not a problem here: on the contrary, David sets himself up as its master, master-painter in the worst sense – one who contains 'influences'. When classical source analysis uses this word it enormously under-estimates (if it doesn't simply bracket out) the problems tradition presents to the painter (as opposed to the viewer); but that for once is exactly how David tropes tradition – as influence, allusion, safely contained quotation. What he seeks, at the most perverse level of his recantation, is self-effacement. He is not the David of the Revolution. He publicly disowns the *Oath*: 'The *Horatii* expressed the taste for Roman monuments, which were the only ones I could study during my stay in Italy. Ah! if only I could recommence my studies in the present age, when Antiquity is better known and understood: I would go straight to my goal, without losing the time I spent laying the road I had to travel.'[8] He is now a painter who quotes directly from tradition; a doxologist. His quotations are without irony or inflection: he has ceased to orient himself or navigate among the images of the past, or to even suggest that tradition can threaten its sons. Least of all is tradition an alien or irruptive force, as it had been in the *Oath*, a drama in which everyone was caught in the network (the *rets*, the *rais*) of sight. David mixes, concocts, *decants* his image with the palette of a connoisseur; and the tragic aspect of the *Intervention* is that David is now *that*, the being the artist must always seek to overcome if he is to survive as artist: a mere viewer. In real terms he is now barely distinguishable from Hamilton or Mengs. Painting *for the audience* and from its point of view, he caters to the ideas of chic it has and will have; he is not emergent from tradition, but tradition's derided eye. This is a painting of assemblage, collage: David cannot seize an image from the past, since he wishes to *become* the past, to regress to the beginning of a career, to immerse his being in tradition and so to cleanse it, and in public view.

III

It is in this context that we must understand the developing talent of Ingres, David's greatest pupil, and active in David's studio for an exceptionally long period of apprenticeship, from 1797 to 1806. The production of *The Intervention of the Sabine Women* dominated the work in David's studio during the crucial first years of Ingres' tutelage, from 1796 to 1799. The actual painting was assisted by favoured students, work in progress was constantly evaluated by the student body, and David's pronouncements on this painting indicate an anxious willingness on his part to yield to student (now we might say to graduate) opinion.[9] Yet so far from satisfying his school, the *Intervention* provoked a minor war. Debate centred precisely on the problem of how to control 'influence', and to grasp the disappointment, the confusion, and the drastic resolutions passed by David's students, we must reconstruct a post-Revolutionary artistic scene in which 'influence' had become an almost unmanageable problem.

During the Revolution things had been otherwise: painting had been guided by events. In the case of David himself tradition had ceased to be an obvious preoccupation. The *Tennis Court Oath*, *Lepelletier*, *Bara* and the *Marat assassiné* had taken populist vision as their context, through alliance with the print and the Revolutionary pageant. We know from the historians, and from the documents themselves, that the period from *Lepelletier* (spring 1793) to *Marat* (summer 1794) had been one of a generalised visual paranoia in Paris; material life is saturated with dangerous significance.

The Terror was such that in certain districts of the city, when the night patrols walked the streets, no one dared open his window to see what was happening outside. Seated round the table, pale with fright, each made his guess as to the number of the house the hand would choose to knock at. . . . A single dish, modest, even crude, sufficed for dinner; for everything was capable of being seen as a crime ('tout pouvait être transformé en crime').[10]

It was a period when one could be denounced by one's servant for wearing clean linen; when debates could take place in the National Assembly concerning right sumptuary conduct: is it counter-Revolutionary or is it patriotic for women to wear oak-leaves in their hair? is it an insult to the General Will for a Quaker not to remove his hat before the Bar? is the red cap a true sign of Liberty, or the mask of intrigue? During the Jacobin supremacy, life and death turned on the interpretation of signs: to uproot a tree of Liberty, to sing 'O Richard! o mon roi!', to deface the image of Marat, these were crimes of the utmost seriousness.

It is from the Terror that the *Marat* ultimately takes its edge and its urgency, for like *Lepelletier* it was destined to be placed in the assembly of the Convention, at the centre of the network of visual and rhetorical signs whose correct manipulation, through speech, costume, and behaviour, was essential to personal survival. Painting was part of a nexus of fatal signs extending from the Convention into the Clubs, to the streets and into the private hearth whose privacy is no longer sacred. To recapture some of the implications of this general terror of signs one need only look at Regnault's *Liberty or Death* (illustration 44), a work designed to hang in the headquarters of the Jacobin Club, and directly cognate with David's *Lepelletier* and *Marat*. Although executed by a painter with a fully evolved personal style, a painter well able to command the resources of 'high' art, it bases itself on the iconography of the popular print, blown up, as in the *Tennis Court Oath*, to Salon proportions; while its style – the large voids, the squared central face, the mixture of rapid brushstrokes for background and hard, enamel finish for the flesh – anxiously copies David, and not only from a desire to emulate, but from trepidation at departure from David's Jacobin orthodoxy.

Grim though the period from 1792 to 1794 must have been for the Parisian population, at least the painters knew what style to follow. Even Prud'hon, the most subtle and idiosyncratic of painters, is found turning out the Jacobin emblems as well as the best (illustration 45), while David mutates into maker of direct propaganda, inventor of such images as *The Army of Jugs* (illustration 46) and the alarming, incoherent *Triumph of the French People* (illustration 47). After Thermidor, in the Paris of the *muscadins* and the *merveilleuses*, material life sheds its frightened and frugal character, and becomes aggressively, vulgarly opulent. The shift from public to private visuality can be traced in the work of David's imprisonment in the Luxembourg, and especially in the

44 Jean-Baptiste Regnault, *Liberty or Death*

View from the Luxembourg (illustration 48): abandoning the ruined Jacobin city he paints an image that is less an exercise in landscape, than in erasure. He withdraws into and almost *behind* private vision, to contemplate what the basic elements of sight are like – air, light, space, distance, colour – once the gridwork of signs has been lifted: or some at least of its screens removed. The painting breathes recovery after a long delirium, and in fact is the true recantation of which the *Intervention* is the public and trumped-up version. David's only depopulated painting, its inner resemblance is to the withdrawn, ascetic analysis of vision conducted in the *Oath*, the *Socrates* and the *Brutus*, for this is a totally introverted work, a painting about the wish to see vernally, without the

45 Pierre-Paul Prud'hon, *L'Égalité*; engraving by Copia

46 David, *The Army of Jugs*

47   David, *The Triumph of the French People*

48   David, *View from the Luxembourg*

overlay of signs, and about the relaxation and convalescence of a vision that had learnt too much about the connection between signs and death.

One wishes that such convalescence could have lasted for David, and one notices again how secluded, how inturned, his vision in the 1780s had been. But, for the painters after Thermidor, Paris is a whirl of fashions, distractions, and eclecticism. The controls of ideology that had operated on public vision, in the atelier and elsewhere, are lifted. The conservatives return. Seroux d'Agincourt had spent the Revolutionary years in Italy, studying medieval art: in 1796 his disciple Paillot de Montabert enters David's studio, bringing with him the fruits of d'Agincourt's scholarship. Certain of David's students begin to study the techniques of fresco and encaustic, and to look seriously at Giotto, Fra Angelico, Perugino. At the same time, there is a marked increase in artistic publication. In the library of Girodet, for example, David's most celebrated pupil of the post-Revolutionary years, we find Herculanean prints, the Hamilton 'Etruscan' vases, six editions of Flaxman, Winckelmann, Sofia Giacomelli's *Paradise Lost*, Stuart, Montfaucon, Bartoli, even monographs on medieval tapestry.[11] In 1798 the victorious army brings to Paris the booty of the Italian campaign: carried round the Champ de Mars on triumphal chariots, and subsequently placed on public exhibition, are the *Apollo Belvedere*, the *Antinous*, the *Laocoön*, the *Gladiator*, the Raphael *Transfiguration*.[12]

David's studio, like every other, was awash with influence. This in itself might have posed no threat if the school of David had possessed strong direction. In his prime David could be an overwhelming influence: Drouais' *Marius at Minturnae* (illustration 49) looks as though it has been cloned from *The Oath of the Horatii*. But the *Intervention*, the focal work in David's atelier, was clearly and deliberately abject before influence; and however satisfying the deliberate self-opening to tradition may have been personally to David, to his students the rising tide of influence was far more disquieting. In the discourses of the spokesman for the mutinous *penseurs*, Maurice Quai, the tone is almost one of panic; the school is leaderless.

David began the great work of reform in art, it is true; but the instability of his character and the limitation of his ideas lost him to politics. He lacks the energy needed to complete the revolution that must be achieved. . . . So many examples of bad taste, such as those supplied by Italian art, by Roman art, and even by Greek art . . . are tolerated in the schools that there are no grounds for hope that any improvement can derive from our studies.[13]

The public may have been convinced or beguiled by the 'originality' of the *Intervention*, but David's graduates see it, and its creator, in a different light. The worry that persists in David's studio is that the force of tradition has become insuperable. For

Quai and the *penseurs* the only solution is a return to first principles – everything after Phidias, and Aeschylus, is corrupt. The desire is for origins, and that desire is a function of anxiety that unless the visions of the precursors are screened out by wilful and systematic iconoclasm, nothing further can be painted. The younger artists fear their inheritance as they might fear a flood. They are not afraid of David – there are no signs of protest against dogmatic teaching: they resent the failing of his strength.

IV

It is therefore appropriate that Ingres, embarking on his career as a painter, should begin with images of sheer power and command: the portrait of *Bonaparte as First Consul* (1804; illustration 50) and the *Imperial Portrait of Napoleon* (1806; illustration 53). And given the tides of contradictory influence in David's studio, it is also understandable that in the first of these works Ingres should turn to the most powerful delimiter of influence, the trope of aegis. *Bonaparte as First Consul* is an erudite, even an antiquarian work, and the stylistic model it selects is the product of the research encouraged by David after 1800 (though apparently not carried over into his own work) in the techniques of 'archaic' painting.

49   Jean-Germain Drouais, *Marius at Minturnae*

The painting makes constant references to the pre-perspectival
painting of Northern Europe. The floor is raked at an unnaturally
steep angle which destabilises the placement of all the objects in the
scene – the Consular chair, which rather hovers over than rests
upon the carpet beneath; the feet and pumps of the First Consul
which point downward at an obtuse angle to the calf; the draped
table, whose legs occupy positions that can hardly be inferred from
the confusing information supplied by the ledge of its shrouded
surface. This deliberate confusion of perspective is intensified in the

50 Ingres, *Bonaparte as First Consul*

view of Liège Cathedral, where the turrets and gables project towards a variety of incompatible vanishing points, and where all the architectural edges have been flattened out, each right angle fanning into an oblique by a distortive supplement of perhaps ten degrees. Registration of texture and of reflection is unusually intense: the velvets of the Consular costume, chair and table drape; the sparkle of gold adornment and embroidery; the creased silk of the stockings, the hard glitter of the jewels on the sword – these faithful details invoke a primitive and microscopic realism associated at this date with the name of 'Jean de Bruges'. The painting places itself under the protection of Van Eyck. In this surrender to a specific master, Ingres re-enacts the same duplicity of homage performed by David before Pietro da Cortona in the *Antiochus* and before Poussin in *St Roch*: the latecomer genuflects before the precursor, but the seeming passivity before influence conceals the active and combative use of that influence, as an instrument for screening out the compelling and potentially crushing weight of tradition. We cannot *see* Ingres in this work – he has vanished behind the style of 'Van Eyck' – but the apparent self-effacement is deceptive. It is a work of extraordinary daring – to contemporary viewers it was barely comprehensible, and critical discussion of Ingres' painting in the years after 1804 habitually employs the vocabulary of bewilderment. Such invocation of Van Eyck is itself exceptional, the intrusion of a deeply alien influence into the normally conservative domain of official portraiture. But it is not just that the source is alien: the *use* of the source is almost without precedent.

To gauge the extent of Ingres' innovation in the deployment of sources, let us refer back to that paradigm of 'normal' invocation: David's *Intervention*. The quotations are numerous, but each quotation is held within a stable matrix or frame (and 'frame' here should include the idea of 'signature'). The *Intervention* acts as a master-image within which a number of lesser images are contained at a 'lower' level, of sub-set; in much the same way that in fiction a text may contain within itself lesser enquoted texts, such as the words of dialogue. As in classical fiction, the *Intervention*'s sub-sets are clearly subordinate to the 'main' set: they occupy minor and restricted portions of the final image – Domenichino in the décor, Flaxman in the male protagonists, Raphael in the female group, Agostino Veneziano in the rearing horse. None of these quotations is allowed to expand beyond its allotted zone – there is no question that any of these sub-sets might take *control* of the image: they are held firmly, so to speak, within their inverted commas. While those sub-sections in the final painting which are placed within the confines of quotation may offer quite separate solutions to representational problems, solutions not only distinct but even opposed – the rearing horse is a three-quarter view that implies diagonal and baroque recession in space, while the Flaxmanesque warriors are planar, and imply minimal recession in space – nevertheless the various sub-sections are not allowed to become *alternatives* to the form of representation used by the painting as a whole. Digressive in nature, their manipulation by David divides the image into two levels: a controlling image, and a secondary level at which quotation is allowed to occur without disturbance to the dominant set.

In *The Intervention of the Sabine Women* the two levels are arranged in strict hierarchy, and between them exists an interval which we might call the alpha point or authority of the image. The master-image owes its status of dominance precisely to the distance installed between 'itself' and the lesser images to which it alludes: it is in this space that the word 'originality' may be inscribed. To put this another way, the viewer can accept the image before him as an autonomous and self-authorising entity if he can clearly see that between the master-image and the lesser images inserted within it, a factor of *dissociation* is visibly at work. Without that distance and that relation of dominant to sub-dominant levels, uniqueness of painting and uniqueness of viewing are engulfed by the past. For the painter, interval and stratification are crucial means of self-protection from the blare of influence: lose that ground, and the painting becomes a babel of sight.

V

Hence the shock, the bizarre or subversive quality, of Ingres' *Bonaparte as First Consul* (illustration 50; 'This painting looks strange'). The *entire* surface of the painting, and not simply local and restricted areas, has been handled in a consistent idiom of 'gothic' quotation. If we look for features that might correspond to the familiar alpha point or separation of 'main' from 'quoted' texts, what we find is almost an inversion of the normal order, as though quotation formed the main text, and the real world were 'indented'. Temporal dislocation is so pronounced that items of modernity – and nothing can have looked so freshly modern as the improvised costumes of the Consulate – seem intrusions from the future. The protracted, exhaustive quotation from a remote artistic past, a past contemporary with the gothic of the Cathedral and precincts seen from the window, raises the lower or quoted register to the status of control while the real objects of the modern world (normally associated with the higher or master level) are made to appear as quotation or digressions away from the gothic present. The décor of the Consulate is given the appearance it *might have had* (the *tense* of the painting is strange) if it had been glimpsed during the gothic age. Where there is still an element of separation between controlling and subordinate levels, the levels are turned around. But essentially no such separation is to be found (this is a painting that sacrifices its 'alpha').

The ontology of the representation is altogether uncertain. Obviously the portrait is not realistic in the manner, let us say, of David's portrait of the First Consul (illustration 51). And yet the meticulous registration of textured and reflective surfaces – the gloss and nap of the velvets, the lustre and fraying of the quills – insists that the portrait is still and painstakingly devoted to realism.

51   David, *Napoleon in his Study*

The painting institutes a gap between a modern world the viewer intimately knows, and this, its stylisation. It is a kind of puzzle: to convert the stylised image back into the familiar world, we as viewers must decode all its information: tilt back the floor, rearrange the architectural view, redefine all the angles. And as with certain puzzles, we are given clues to assist us in the work of decoding. The particular key offered here is the right angle: all the right angles in the image have been distorted by around ten degrees; adjust the image by that angle and its space will return to 'normal'.

The basic action of the image is to hint across its deformation towards a possible re-formation or solution, to be accomplished in the viewer's mind. It is not at all a chaotic painting: its deflections and reshapings have been plotted with clear inner consistency. The central idea is one of imminent or withheld completeness; and here Ingres shows himself as a true successor to David. Just as David's history paintings of the 1780s supply viewpoints which the spectator cannot occupy, so here the spectator is intimated a viewpoint which, if he were to decode all the spatial information correctly, he might be able to occupy, but which he cannot occupy *now*, as he actually looks at the work's surface. And to make the accession to coherence still more difficult, several viewpoints are in fact proposed. To perceive the angle between the First Consul's legs and feet as oblique, the viewer must presumably be close to the figure, somewhere near arm's length (he could put his hand on Bonaparte's shoulder): yet to perceive the whole figure, from head to toe, he must be further back. But if the viewer works out how far back he must mentally place himself, because of the tilt of the floor the final choice of position becomes strange, since the idea of a raked stage means that with each pace back the viewer goes *lower* – yet the figure is not seen from below; the feet, in particular, are seen from above. As we probe deeper into the spatial conundrum of the painting, the possibility emerges that the bodily scale of the First Consul has been reduced by a factor of two – that the figure appears to us as it would appear to itself in a mirror; and indeed, it is in the experience of mirrored reflection that a full pace backward appears as a half, and that the viewer has the combined sensation of being both close (so that the angle of foot to calf seems oblique) and distant. Despite its painstaking detail (though also because of it: the mirror is the place of detail), the portrait of *Bonaparte as First Consul* is a repetition less of a real than of a *reflected* world, familiar yet distorted, once by the mirror, and once again by the Van Eyckian disruption of perspective. The painting is conducting, in fact, under the guise of homage to tradition, an obvious assault on the classical or Zeuxian premise that painting repeats or resurrects the original presence of the world. Ingres' portrait supplies all the markers of attentive realism. But the completeness of representation contained in the realist promise is then held back. Instead, the image gives the world under subtraction: minus its spatial coherence, which must be reconstructed; and minus its truth, since its origin lies less in the immediacy of vision, than in the mediations of the mirror, and of tradition.

Visually, the portrait is the most sophisticated kind of pun or play of substitution between the images of 'Jean de Bruges' and the images in mirrors: the distortions of 'archaic' painting are reinterpreted in terms of the familiar experience of the mirror; the distortions of the mirror are reinterpreted in terms of Van Eyck. Now we must ask the question *why*: why this strange and complicated pun? why these refusals to present the painting in the expected vernacular idiom of French portraiture, an idiom which David uses to great effect with the same subject? what is in common between painterly archaism and mirroring, and what kind of link does *Ingres* propose between them?

Let us take the question of mirror reflection first. From one point of view, the mirror can be said to carry out with complete success that reduplication of the world which, in the classical account of the 'realist' tendency of Western art (Pliny, Vasari, Gombrich), is the constant aim of the tradition. The perfect replication of the real in its mirrored reflection is thus a kind of utopian fulfilment of painting's realist project, and between the mirror and painting there exists a bond of similarity which European painters have not hesitated to stress: one need think only of obvious cases where the similarity is stated – the convex 'witness' mirror in Van Eyck's *Arnolfini Marriage*, the self-portraits of Dürer, the mirror that gives us the odalisque's unseen face in the *Rokeby Venus*, or the explicit play between mirror and canvas in *Las Meniñas* (though in each of these cases there is also play *against* the equation of mirror and painting; the painting is always that which exceeds or goes beyond the mirror). In the immediate context of early Ingres, one should think also of the actual use of the mirror as a painting aid: of David's mirror self-portrait, painted during his imprisonment in the Luxembourg, and of Ingres' own self-portrait of 1804 (illustration 52). The mirror is not only an emblem for painting's replicative goal (or of the higher nature of painting's replications); it is used by both David and Ingres as a direct instrument in realising that goal.

Yet, although the mirror is an instrument that gives us the world in all its original presence, the status of the mirror is also ambiguous. It has another, less plenary aspect, an aspect doubtless crucial in the case of the child, though that first encounter with the mirror can hardly be regarded as a special case, or confined only to childhood development. We know from clinical psychology that the child realises from the behaviour of others that it exists somewhere in space and that it is in constant transaction with the vision of others: it soon learns to retrace with its own eyes the path of an adult glance. We know also that at some point the child apprehends its existence as an image *for* others, and that this image is not simply a spectacle, but an identification, an image to be assumed by the self. What clinical psychology cannot be said to have determined is whether in this mirror phase of development encounter with an actual mirror is necessary to precipitate the identification; but whether or not a causal and precipitating function is ascribed to an actual reflection, it remains that it is only in the transactions with a mirrored reflection that the child apprehends its full existence as an image for others. Henceforth the child cannot place itself at the single centre of its universe, but by a Copernican shift, must think of itself as a decentred image seen from a place the child cannot occupy, an image which nevertheless is to be assumed by the child as its visual identification. For the child the mirror is accordingly a place of spatial *disruption*: the laws of the mirror are not the same as those of ordinary space, as Alice discovers; in particular the mirror installs a principle of discrepancy between the mirror image and its original, and learning how the mirror works involves checking, point by point, the original

52 Ingres, *Self-portrait at the Age of Twenty-four*

against the double. The uncanniness of the mirror is not confined, however, only to childhood. In adult life it is still by checking the appearance disclosed by the mirror against the complex social codes of self-presentation that the individual adjusts his or her persona in everyday existence. Here also the mirror is a place of the gap and the discrepancy, between the actual reflection and the social codes of presentation, and in both childhood and adult experience the mirror repeats its action of alterity: the mirror does not simply reflect things as they are, in plenitude and presence; it opens an interval between the place the self feels as its actual residence or location, 'behind the nose', and the unknowable place at which the self will appear as image.[14]

It is in this experience epitomised by the mirror, yet occurring constantly in the socialised existence of adult life (and here one must point to an anxiety which not even psychoanalysis has fully named, yet which seems rooted in the human condition: fear of being observed), that the individual passes from vision – simply seeing the world and opening, like a camera, on to its light – into visuality, the subjective experience of seeing-and-being-seen. In vision, the world is a continuum without division, but in visuality the continuum is split – on this side ('behind the eyes'), consciousness without image; on the far side ('in the eyes of others'), image without consciousness; the self must articulate itself across this divide. And even if we discount the whole psychoanalytic tale of the 'mirror phase', nevertheless this remains as the disconcerting truth of the mirror: it gives back ourselves to ourselves; but in a form which is not quite our self. Those eyes are our eyes, but they look *at* us; and in those eyes that are both our own and not our own, what we experience is a 'being looked at' which surrounds our consciousness on all sides ('self-consciousness'), but is here mysteriously collected by the mirror into a line of vision: the gaze.

The device of the mirrored reflection in *Bonaparte as First Consul* is far more concerned with the negative than with the plenary aspect of the mirror – with alterity rather than identity. Ingres' self-portrait of 1804 (illustration 52) gives us the mirror's positive and unproblematic face – the viewer can identify himself exactly with Ingres' own vision: what he sees, we see. But *Bonaparte as First Consul* is not a self-portrait: it repeats the spatial emphases of the mirror (the uptilting of floor surfaces, the obtuse angle of foot to leg, the frontal gaze) but we cannot accept the eyes of the figure as a relay of vision out to the viewer. We are given the *sense* of a mirrored reflection, but we are as much excluded from the figure's viewpoint as, in the self-portrait, we are invited to share and identify with it.

The withholding of presence in the device of mirrored spaces is restated in the register of style. In the *Intervention* David had held all his stylistic quotations or subsidiary images within a higher or containing image. Yet in the portrait of *Bonaparte as First Consul* there is *no* higher or meta-image: no ruling idiom in which the archaism of the image can feature as indented quotation. As a result the image appears not as a 'natural' or uncoded statement within which artificial and coded quotations feature as subsidiaries, as they do in the *Intervention*, but rather as a through-coded statement which the viewer must somehow decipher. The disappearance of the 'higher' level entails that the painting may be understood only if the *viewer* supplies the missing meta-language. This he can perform by regarding the image before him as a sub-set or object language within the master set or meta-language of archaic, Northern, pre-perspectival painting. The point is that the image does not decode or explain *itself*: it must be referred, in the viewer's mind, to information which the image does not of itself provide. To view the portrait is to experience at the level of style a gap between the image and tradition which repeats in the key of styles the interval that cuts across being in the mirror. The present image is senseless until referred to an absent aggregate of images ('Jean de Bruges'). That referral is an event occurring, of course, throughout visual recognition. But this particular image intensifies the discrepancy, cultivates the gap, widens the interval, and to such a degree that no viewer can simply pass over it automatically or half-consciously. Looking at David's *St Roch*, for example, the viewer is aware of Poussin as a nearby and canonically familiar source: referral of *St Roch* to 'Poussin' requires no particular effort. But the strange and archaic source to which *Bonaparte as First Consul* must oe referred ('Jean de Bruges') is eminently un-canonical. The referral has to traverse immense and unfamiliar distances; it cannot be carried out simply, or at once. Ingres 'hesitates' his image, once across the mirror, and once again across style. Recognition of the painting does not unfold through presence, in the now of viewing, like the mirror in its benign or plenary aspect; but in transit, across the gap of centuries that separates medieval Flanders from Napoleonic France. In this gap, which one might call the *delay* of style, the negative or subtractive act of the mirror finds its counterpart, in tradition's gaze.

VI

Early Ingres is a master of tradition and its tropes, and nowhere is his mastery more confident or more playful than in the *Imperial Portrait of Napoleon* (1806; illustration 53).[15] If *Bonaparte as First Consul* had organised tradition by narrowing influence to a single term – 'Jean de Bruges' – through the trope of aegis, here Ingres goes the other way and opens the aperture of influence as wide as possible, through the trope of synecdoche or totality. *All* the precursors are there, from first to last.

Ingres begins with Phidias. This is as much a contemporary reference as a classical allusion. Among the trophies of the Italian campaign, there had arrived in Paris a *Castor and Pollux* attributed to Phidias and mentioned by David in the *livret* on the *Intervention*. The *primitifs* in David's atelier maintained that a return to antique sculpture would assist in purging painting of its modern deformities, but even within Antiquity they found corruption: only the style of Phidias was perfect, and all subsequent sculpture was to

53 Ingres, *Imperial Portrait of Napoleon*

be viewed with suspicion. Ingres' invocation to Phidias thus signals the debates and ideas of Maurice Quai, and should perhaps be seen as a trope of masking, in the way that early David masks Peyron under the features of Peyron's avowed hero Poussin. Phidias is first invoked across his statue of Zeus, which Ingres would put to more explicit use in the figure of Jupiter in the *Jupiter and Thetis* of 1811 (illustration 67); here, the quotation seems confined to the idea of the enthronement of a supernaturally powerful male deity. To the *Zeus* Ingres has added the reputation of Phidias' second master-work, the statue of Athene in the Parthenon, a work of colossal scale that had been fashioned in ivory and gold – the principal materials and colours of the *Imperial Portrait*. Moving forward in time, Ingres next invokes the age of the Caesars (the wreath, and the notion of the Emperor as numinous); then of Byzantium. By flattening the spaces in the painting and by stressing the low, chiselled design of the throne and the Imperial costume, he recalls the incised planarity of a consular diptych or ivory plaque of perhaps the fifth or sixth century; the arc around the throne is made to seem like an *aediculum*, signature of deepest archaism. The Dark and Middle Ages Ingres can safely leave to the costume and apparatus of the Sacre, for Napoleon was eager to appear as heir not only to the Caesars, signalled by the Imperial wreath, but of the French kings; the sceptre indicates that this is the legacy also of Charlemagne. Carolingian style is perhaps the least represented in the painting, but it is undoubtedly there, partly in the device of the foot protruding from the Imperial tunic and hovering over the indented cushion, which takes us back to illuminations of Old Testament kings and patriarchs, and partly in the painting's scale, which though large is constructed as though in cameo space, smaller than the hand, like an Ottonian miniature. The styles of the Renaissance and of Italian painting are conspicuous by their omission: gothic and the North have screened them out, and there is a fairly straightforward appeal to Van Eyck's God the Father in the *Adoration of the Lamb*. But the Renaissance is at least remarked upon in the curiously marginalised reference to Raphael's *Madonna of the Chair* in the Zodiac's Virgo.

We are now in a position to see how astutely Ingres deploys the trope of synecdoche or totality – *everything* is included: Antiquity, Byzantium, the Dark Ages, the Carolingian Empire, the Northern Middle Ages, the High Renaissance or Age of Raphael; the painting is like a speeded up film of Western art from Phidias to Raphael, in ten seconds. Sheer velocity of reference makes the tradition weightless; or at least allows Ingres to escape its gravity. No single provenance is allowed to detain our or Ingres' attention for long enough to acquire a field or density of its own: the pull of one influence is so rapidly followed by the pull of the next that Ingres, though continuously quoting from styles, succeeds in travelling *round* them all. Ingres' deployment of tradition is similar to David's in *Mars and Minerva*: the earlier style is not allowed to stand alone; immediately adjacent the image places the style of the later period which completed it and rendered it obsolete. By the same token, later styles are not shown as autochthonous or self-empowered, since juxtaposed against them we see the origins from which they in turn struggled to escape. The effect is one of cancellation or deletion: Rome and Greece counter each other's respectively completing and originating power; Charlemagne counters Justinian; Raphael counters Van Eyck. What might have been a crushing and debilitating sense of belatedness is resolved by showing that not even the illustrious ancestors were exempt from their own latecoming in time. By cultivating the panoptic vision to which none of the ancestors had access, Ingres converts the weakness of modernity – its position at the *end* of centuries of endeavour – into elevation and elation: Ingres sees more than Byzantium, since Byzantium had lost sight of Athens and Rome; Ingres knows more than Raphael, since Raphael did not know Van Eyck. To Ingres the panoptic view is spacey and dazzling: he places himself as *outside* tradition, not at its close, and the temporal dislocation of his modernity is worn proudly, like a badge. Literally: the Raphaelesque Virgo, Ingres' personal imprimatur, and placed within inches of his actual signature, dislocates the entire circle of the Zodiac (illustration 54). There is no conceivable way of getting Virgo to stand opposite Pisces, as Ingres, in the subtlest and lightest of the painting's many touches of humour, pretends it can. By making Raphael his signature, Ingres renounces the burden of having to authorise his image from an alpha point of personal origin: given the choice between being a king or the messenger of kings, he chooses to become a messenger. And by projecting Raphael into his personal birth sign, Ingres implies that all the styles (and not only the fallen styles of modernity) have their eras, with each artist locked in successive place after his precursors, as Virgo succeeds Leo. All this shows an instinctual wisdom of approach to the problem of tradition. But at least in this work Leo is emphatically *not* Virgo's precursor, and in that wry, barely noticeable twist of the zodiacal series Ingres declares openly what the painting as a whole is determined to achieve: his personal immunity from the hazards of influence, that astral disease.

VII

The extent to which the problem of inheritance affects the work of Ingres, and from the beginning, can be gauged from the three Rivière portraits of 1805–6 (illustrations 56, 59, 61). For David, portraiture was the one area where no overt engagement with the precursors need take place and no conflict over the ultimate possession of the image need arise. After the Jacobin portraits of

Lepelletier and Marat, in which portraiture and history painting fuse in the heat of the Revolution, David's artistic production separates back into two streams: the *tableau d'histoire*, which David approaches with increasing loss of nerve; and portraiture, which curiously David does not seem to perceive as existing in the same stressed terrain of influence as his official, guarded statements, the *Intervention* and the *Leonidas*. We can measure the relative ease of portraiture and the increasing difficulty of history painting simply by measuring the time it takes David to work in these now very different spheres of art: the head of Bonaparte, according to Delécluze, was finished at a single sitting; *Leonidas at Thermopylae* took twelve years. The fracture of David's pictorial thinking is

54 Ingres, *Imperial Portrait of Napoleon* (detail)

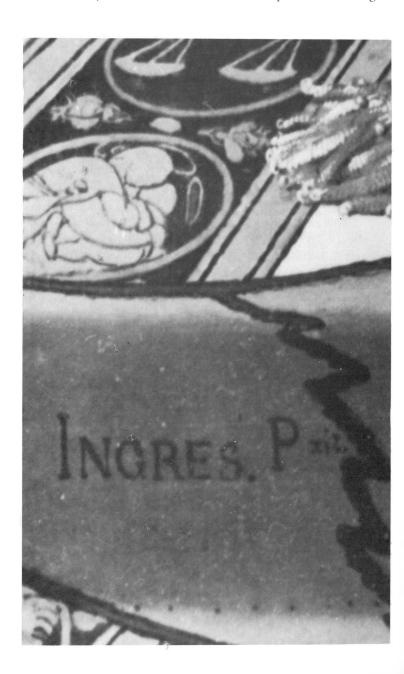

certainly understandable. To make a portrait, the painter must have mastered a repertoire of variable schemata for each component of the costume, hands, and face; formulae which, when gathered together and concentrated on what is always a small area of the canvas, ensure that in proportion as the markers of facial uniqueness create a unique representation of the sitter, the image itself becomes the painter's unique creation, one which no predecessor can claim. Portraiture supplies David with the means of guaranteeing possession and ownership of his images, and this consolation becomes more and more important to David as his capacity to innovate within tradition (located, for him, in history painting) declines and finally disappears. In the same late period of exile when David is turning out such dismal mythologies as *Cupid and Psyche* and *Mars Disarmed by Venus* (illustration 77), he is also producing such portraits as *Three Ladies of Ghent* (illustration 55), a work which proves that at least in the genre of portraiture David was capable of endless personal self-renewal.

55   David, *Three Ladies of Ghent*

The image of these three women implies an entire society, closed, provincial, where the atmosphere of suffocating domesticity is made even more unbearable by the need to maintain strict standards of public appearance. To this narrowly prudent world David responds with the utmost sensitivity. He is fascinated by the scars such as milieu inflicts on the individual – the pinched mouths, the crabbed expressions, the misplaced opulence of ugly lace and dowdy fur – scars which his urbanity might easily have mocked, but which he manages to invest with sympathy, perhaps because the scars look so deep. To the last, David's portraits issue from the humane side of his personality and from the most technical side of his craft. He uses the schemata of facial representation with unique facility – and by the same token he does not ask himself questions about his instruments: it does not occur to him that these too come to him from tradition, or that it might be possible for the portrait to induce the same kind of anguished self-examination and defensiveness about tradition and innovation which had enfeebled the *Intervention*, virtually paralysed the *Leonidas*, and which at last turns his work to leaden whimsy, in the sad boudoir mythologies of his final years.

For Ingres, not even portraiture is exempt from the problematic of being-in-tradition. Where for David there had been two routes for painting, one crushed by the gravity of the past and the other a route of escape, for Ingres there is only one activity, painting; and with portraits also, the difficulty is not how to paint them but how to clear a space within tradition where their vision can be enclosed and protected. To this end, the portrait of Philibert Rivière activates the powerful trope of aegis (illustration 56): it seeks refuge under the protection of Raphael. No viewer can fail to notice the folio print of the *Madonna of the Chair* (illustration 57). The difficulty lies in how we are to interpret the quotation; and the easy answer – that it is there to establish M. Rivière as an enlightened connoisseur – will not do.

Let us look at the Raphael (illustration 58). What is distinctive, in this context, is its reconciliation of the demands of three-dimensional space and the demands of the circular frame, though to achieve the reconciliation the painting performs some rather curious distortions. The shape of the chair, for example, which both in its squareness and its spatial recession might conflict with the circularity and the flatness of the tondo, is reduced by ellipsis to a single cylinder. The cylinder's verticality, alien in the circular space, is neutralised by at least seven bands or rings which counter the vertical thrust with a stronger lateral momentum. These release a sideways curve that comes forward to the painting's centre, at the Madonna's right arm, then turns back into the painting with the hands and forearm of John, and the space becomes a gentle curve moving from left to right and making the tondo seem slightly convex: its two dimensions are inflected, very slightly, into three.

56   Ingres, *Portrait of Philibert
Rivière*; Paris, Louvre

57   Ingres, *Portrait of Philibert
Rivière* (detail)

To preserve the logic of its circular design, the painting proceeds to obscure its anatomical arrangement. The legs of the Madonna, which if rendered visible might carry the image into an implied space below the edge of the frame, are so copiously draped that the viewer is unable to locate the limbs beneath. Articulation of leg to torso is simply omitted (let the viewer try to imagine where to place the figure's waist). The function of disposition in three-dimensional or anatomical space is in fact transferred to the two dimensions of the panel's surface, and, to ensure that the resultant design dominates the entire surface, a series of minor distortions follows. The prominent left thigh of the Child is amplified; the Madonna's upper arm is shortened; the calves of the Child are broadened towards the edges of the frame; the lower back of the Madonna is obscured by emphasis in gold, which lead the eye inward to the centre of the painting, so that the figure can seem without a spine, simply shoulders and arms suspended in space. The list of exaggerations and displacements could be considerably

58   Raphael, *Madonna of the Chair*

extended: but the underlying principle is the production of *rhythm* between dimensions: the law of two dimensions modulates with the law of three.[16]

At this point the reader might well expect an account of the portrait of M. Rivière in terms of the *Madonna of the Chair*. There are, after all, many points in common between the two paintings. Both employ poses where a chair touches the left of the frame. Both give prominence to the knee, and swell the calf. Both submit the physical facts to a commanding 'will to form'. And Ingres' portrait of M. Rivière continues to make subtle, almost subliminal reference to Raphael's portraits of male sitters: to Angelo Doni, to Cardinal Bibbiena (the rings, the clasp of the chair), to Julius II (the angle and disposition of the chair, the placing of Rivière's right arm), to Leo X (the picture within a picture, the books placed on a table draped in velvet, the bright metal rim). In a painting made for and about a connoisseur of Raphael the subtlety of allusion has obvious, and courteous, import.

But what is strange here is that the motif of two dimensions against three which dominates the *Madonna of the Chair* applies far more cogently to the *other* two portraits in the *Rivière* group, both of which have *curving* frames. M. Rivière is seated in a clearly *rectilinear* frame and space, where straight edges, squares, and rectangular forms abound. The invocation to Raphael is far more appropriate to the portrait of Mlle Rivière (illustration 59), whose left arm, boa, landscape with mist and turret, and placing against a clouded sky cut by a curving frame, repeat the familiar forms of *La Belle Jardinière* (illustration 60). Even more exactly the allusion to Raphael applies to *Mme Rivière* (illustration 61), a painting directly modelled on the 'Tao' design of the *Madonna of the Chair*. The quotation hidden in the portrait of M. Rivière, the father, precisely does *not* 'explain' his painting: key to the portrait of his wife, but not to his own, it sets up a play between historical source and modern reverberation that is more complex than even the *Bonaparte as First Consul*.

The insertion of the *Madonna of the Chair* into M. *Rivière* is on rather a different plane from the allusions to Raphael's male sitters, which traditional source methods can describe without difficulty. The special nature of the quotation is as elusive to that traditional analysis as it is clear from the perspective of linguistics, from which once more I shall borrow the concept of meta-language. The inclusion of the *Madonna of the Chair* presents the work of Raphael as a meta-language within which all three *Rivière* portraits may be securely set. That meta-language places the portrait of Mme Rivière directly within itself, since its play of two dimensions against three, its distortions of anatomy (visible particularly in the dislocation of the legs from the torso), its intricate linear echoes of surface to frame, its submission of all forms to the wilful logic of the 'Tao' shape – all these are expansions of formal ideas contained in the *Madonna of the Chair*. By substitution of *La Belle Jardinière* for the *Madonna of the Chair*, a similar meta-language embraces and absorbs the portrait of Rivière *fille*. Looking at least at the female portraits, the viewer *knows* that these images have to be seen against the 'higher' language of Raphael from which they descend. But the relationship between these images and their sources is very different from the 'normal' relationship of image to source evident, for example, in David's *Intervention of the Sabine Women*. There, quotation had formed a sub-set of the given image: here, the given image is a sub-set of a generalised meta-language of 'Raphael'; much as *Bonaparte as First Consul* is a sub-set of a

59   Ingres, *Portrait of Mlle Rivière*

generalised 'Jean de Bruges'. But the point is again the *distance* between 'meta-language' and 'object language'. When the viewer looks at *Mme Rivière* through the grid of the *Madonna of the Chair*, what he notices are the *differences* between them: there circular, here oval; there sacred, here profane; there primal, original, classical, here secondary, derivative, modern. Let us imagine that during some historical disaster the portrait of M. Rivière had been destroyed; or that the quotation from the *Madonna of the Chair* had not been included. We would still be able to detect the *Madonna of the Chair* as a muted harmonic within *Mme Rivière*, faintly audible in the register of connoisseurship, as the echoes of Leo X, Julius II,

60   Raphael, *La Belle Jardinière*

Angelo Doni and Bibbiena are in the case of *M. Rivière*. But by supplying the *exact* source – the *Madonna of the Chair* – Ingres ensures that vision will attend consciously and conscientiously to the *interval* between the two paintings.

The meaning of a sign cannot be disclosed by that sign out of its own being: meaning exists in the *movement* from one sign to another sign. In Ingres the meaning of a painting is always, and explicitly, *another painting*. If *Bonaparte as First Consul* had commenced Ingres' assault on the Zeuxian doctrine of presence, now the assault is enormously intensified. It is the *principal* statement of the *Rivière* group. The *Madonna of the Chair* may claim *Mme Rivière*, but only across a gap – the interval or interstice that exists between the folio on M. Rivière's desk and the portrait of Rivière's wife. Raphael may claim *Mlle Rivière*, but only across another relay (or delay): *La Belle Jardinière*. What the female group activates is a series of *displacements* in which no sign stands alone: the work of painting and of viewing consists in the conscious and

61   Ingres, *Portrait of Mme Rivière*

heightened experience of a signifying *chain*. And in the case of M. Rivière, the action of the higher or explanatory language of 'Raphael' exactly fails to absorb or recuperate his portrait. We know that there must be a connection between the *Madonna of the Chair* and this painting, but the links are difficult, if not impossible, to state. Perhaps the theme of two dimensions against three has been taken up in the cameo surface of his ring? Perhaps the idea of a representation within a representation lies behind the curious visibility of the cameo face and the lion heads? But essentially the viewer is left with an enigma. The enigma *is* the distance between the posited meta-language and this painting. With the female portraits, links in the chain are supplied, but in the case of M. Rivière they are absent. Between the *Madonna of the Chair* and this picture, there is *only* interval. The meaning of the quoted painting is not to be found here, but in the *next* painting, of Rivière's wife, and the one after that, of his daughter: and in the interval between *M. Rivière* and its quotation. The invocation to Raphael sets in motion a chain of images-in-displacement: the *Rivière* portraits are not free-standing or self-contained, but mobile; their forms unfold under postponement or deferral, in a vision where nothing is arrested about an alpha point or origin (even Raphael, the possible primogenitor, features as a secondary presence, a copy).

What is lost here is a certain male dominion: it is less the case that the image of Rivière *père* acts as key to the portraits of his wife and daughter, than that his own portrait is caught in a chain of images moving by displacement across the image of woman, Madonna; just as Raphael, distant primogenitor to the portrait sequence, acts less as its anchor than as a principle of allusive and elusive motion across its surfaces. In Ingres there are no kings, only couriers of kings. What the citation of Raphael signals is not origin, but the opposite: the separation of signs from origin, their sliding free from base, in a movement where authority over vision gives way to vision under desire. Representation less of Raphael than of desire within the image, citation anticipates here the great phase of Ingres' development, when desire and the name of Raphael will become almost interchangeable terms.

5 Tradition and Desire

in me tota ruens Venus
Cyprum deseruit   Horace

I

WHEN A PAINTER feels to the full the pressure of the past, when
his facility enables him, as it did the young Ingres, to impersonate a
variety of precursors, and through his impersonations to experience the past as a multiplicity of styles, then the personal
struggle with tradition is bound to be intense. Let us take once
more the portrait of Mlle Rivière (illustration 59). Ingres is paying
an obvious tribute to Raphael, but equally obvious is his refusal to
let Raphael capture and reincorporate the image into the past and
its repetitions. In one direction, he reinforces the contemporary
character of the image, by stressing the theme of ephemerality.
Mlle Rivière is evoked through metaphors of spring: in the phrase
of Kenneth Clark, she is 'the snake, the snowdrop, the tulip and its
sheath, the young bird'.[1] The portraits of her parents are
representations of marriage and both are seated in a rich domestic
interior that marks the stability of their union; they are adorned
with all the accoutrements of bourgeois security. But their
daughter is outside this social and sexual fixity: she retains their
wealth, but she has no space of her own, only the open and
generalised space of the landscape. She is not dressed for the
countryside where she stands but rather for the salon and for
domestic space, for the interior of another house, but in this
landscape through which she walks so incongruously dressed the
houses are almost invisible: what predominates is the church. Her
situation is clear: she is in transit between the roles of daughter and
of wife. The richness of her costume indicates the paternal wealth
from which she is destined to be separated; it serves to define the
wealth of her future husband; and it emerges therefore as a
temporary display whose beauty consists in its temporary nature,
just as her own beauty is liminal and transient. Ingres, with his
couturier's instincts, highlights exactly those features of her
costume that distil the fashions of 1805: the looseness of her long
gloves above the elbow, their sharply truncated fingers, their
careful stitching, their bitter tan. None of this beauty can last, and
here transience protects the image from absorption by the past.

From its secure anchorage in present time the painting can afford
to invoke Raphael. Yet the severity of outline, the hardness of the
lighting and the high-fidelity realism of such passages as the folds
of the gloves move back to an age older than Raphael, and from

this archaic idiom the work of Raphael can be seen as itself belated: Ingres projects on to Raphael Ingres' own temporality, and while invoking Raphael as source at the same time Ingres denies him his priority. Having, so to speak, surrounded Raphael on two sides, from the future and from the past, Ingres has in fact positioned the alleged source in a temporal series which substitutes for the idea of origin the idea of *displacement*: the image moves through three zones of time – 'archaic', Raphaelesque, and modern – none of which can lay a definitive claim to the image. Instead, it shuttles across them, in transit and between thresholds (like Mlle Rivière herself). Ingres has done much more than simply 'distort' Raphael into an image Ingres may claim as his own. What interests him is this motion of displacement; the image is prevented from 'fixing'; it slides between eras and across styles – its temporal mobility or oscillation is such that no single style can arrest it into presence.

This temporal elusiveness or sliding is repeated in Ingres' spatial handling, especially in the focal zone of the painting, Mlle Rivière's face (illustration 64). Its uneasiness can be traced to opposed conceptions and even to opposed technical approaches to the problem of the portrait head. Ingres constructs his heads in two distinct stages. First, as a *volume* bounded by precise outline; second, as a *surface* on to which the facial features – eyes and eyebrows, nose and mouth – are *separately* superimposed. The distinctness of the stages is all too clear if we look at examples, quite frequent in Ingres' output, where the superimposition has come unstuck.[2] The fissure or geological flaw between the two stages – earlier and featureless oval, then later and 'disembodied' facial characteristics – can be detected quite clearly in such works as *Mme Devauçay* (illustration 62), or *Mme de Senonnes* (illustration 63). In *Mme de Senonnes* the fault can be sensed as the discrepancy between the first axis running from the parted hair to the chin, and the second axis formed at the juncture of eyebrow to nose in the 'overlaid' features. It is as if a slide were thrown on to a screen from a projector whose base has been tilted out of true.

The balance between the stages is more resolved in *Mlle Rivière* than in these later works, but if we look carefully at the head we will find the same lantern-slide effect (illustration 64). If we isolate the facial features in our mind, the blank ovoid behind them shows through, as though her features could be peeled away, like a lamina. Mentally putting the lamina back into place, we can see at once the areas which remain problematic: the interval between mouth and chin is unnaturally abbreviated; the eyes are too broad for the oval that encloses them, and though this is countered by an ambiguous placing of the cheekbones it leaves the expanse of the brow over-extended and over-exposed. I point to these details not to accuse Ingres of faulty anatomy, but rather to demonstrate that for Ingres anatomy is a way of introducing a marked spatial fault between two dimensions (the planimetric facial features) and three (their volumetric support). When the laws of perspective are behaving themselves and when perspective is in full resolution, design coheres equally well when scanned by the viewer as a planar enclosure bounded by surfaces (the frame, and the repercussions of the frame occurring within the image as composition) and as volume in virtual depth or recession. Yet under normal circumstances the viewer does *not* scan the image twice in this way, in two phases of interpretation, since they are exactly welded into one: that unity *is* the perspectival coherence. In this painting, however, the viewer is compelled to scan twice, and the plurality of interpretative grids corresponds to the plurality of stylistic languages, none of which can interpret the image as a whole. In this respect *Mlle Rivière* is the inverse of the *Madonna of the Chair* (illustration 58), where two dimensions and three are harmoniously fused (it is a problem to convince people that a play of two against three is involved at all): here the image is mobile *between* the

62   Ingres, *Portrait of Mme Devauçay*

two and the three (the problem is to demonstrate that this is not simply incompetence). As a result, actually to view this portrait is a strange experience: accustomed to the notion that painting in general and portraiture in particular resurrects an original presence, the viewer is troubled; troubled, when obliged, by the logic of the painting group to which the portrait belongs, to cross-refer it against painting before Raphael, against Raphael Madonnas in landscape settings such as *La Belle Jardinière*, against the *Madonna of the Chair*, and against the fashions of 1806; and troubled when the unity of perspective with which the viewer is familiar is divided in such a way that the painting must be scanned in two successive viewing acts, neither of which is privileged over the other, and neither of which definitively claims the image's space.

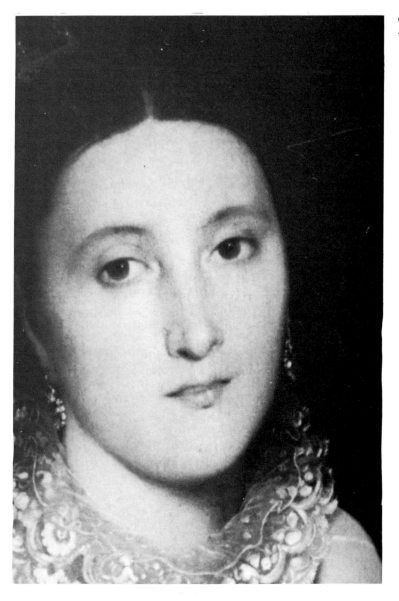

63 Ingres, *Portrait of Mme de Senonnes* (detail)

What these sensations of stylistic and spatial unease have in common may be called counter-presence, a trope that enables the force of tradition to be defeated by absence, or desire. The process is clearly described by Kojève:

Now the analysis of 'thought', 'reason', 'understanding', and so on – in general, of the cognitive, contemplative, passive behaviour of a being or a 'knowing subject' – never reveals the why or the how of the birth of the word 'I', and consequently of self-consciousness – that is, of the human reality. The man who contemplates is 'absorbed' by what he contemplates; the 'knowing subject' 'loses' himself in the object that is known. Contemplation reveals the object, not the subject. The object, and not the subject, is what shows itself to him in and by – or better, as – the act of knowing. The man who is 'absorbed' by the object that he is

64   Ingres, *Portrait of Mlle Rivière* (detail)

contemplating can be 'brought back to himself' only by a Desire; by the desire to eat, for example. *The conscious Desire of a being is what constitutes that being as 'I' and reveals it as such by moving it to say 'I'.*[3]

Transposing the terms of Kojève's description to painting, we can define the counter-presence or desire that is infused into an image as the force that separates itself from a tradition into which, if no such principle had been installed, the image would otherwise merge and dissolve. When consciousness contemplates the world as presence, simply as a field of objects, it cannot describe a boundary within which it can itself be located: it is the sense of lack, of something being absent, that draws the line. Desire divides the continuum into two areas: on the far side, the external world which may contain the object (the nourishment, the love, the image) that will assuage desire; on this side, the internal world that experiences itself as incomplete. By desire, the I is separated from and opposed to what is not-I; desire crystallises identity as this being, experiencing this lack; the human I is the I of a desire or of Desire.

In terms of painting and its tradition, the artist possesses no identity unless he can achieve distance from the work of the past. Until such distance is reached, he is absorbed by what he contemplates; tradition floods him and reveals only itself, not the subject that views. Separation from tradition occurs only when the painter is brought back to himself or revealed to himself by his desire, since the lack at work in desire draws a line around himself, while at the same time establishing tradition as the background against which his identity emerges. Only when the painter experiences the void within him which is his desire to produce an image, can he innovate against tradition: this moment, when the potential image is experienced as a lack within tradition, can be seen as the elective moment of his vocation and inspiration as a painter. The problem for him then, is that the void will at once refill with the imagery of the past, and annul his identity forged in desire, unless desire itself is maintained: it is a 'dissipative' structure, requiring energy for its maintenance, like a standing wave: the painter's effort is to resist the onrush of images in whose flood his imminent identity will drown. The preservation of desire is achieved by introducing breaks into tradition, nodal points that can interrupt the continuum of tradition by turning the force of tradition on itself: points and turnings which the present discussion has named as tropes.

All the tropes work to demarcate a boundary between tradition and the newly created image, or rather to create the new images by drawing, in different ways, a boundary against tradition. Ingres' trope of displacement or desire mobilises tradition as a series of references so organised that each pushes out the next and none lays successful claim to the painting as a whole. It is a trope particularly characterised by its dynamism – it seeks mobility of reference, a quasi-perpetual movement from one interpretative frame to the next; and to ensure that the movement goes on, it therefore distributes its references as equal privileges – no one interpretative frame is allowed favour over the rest, for what the trope looks for is expanded distance *between* referential frames. In those intervals forced between them, it establishes the image as an absence of other images, an image under lack or desire; and the intensity of that desire gives it strength to combat the works and the visual systems of the past that would otherwise claim it.

II

Displacement is the most crucial of the tropes in Ingres because of its direct connection with sexual desire. For Ingres, eroticism is never conceived as an excess or superflux of energy, or a plenitude of being. It is certainly possible to conceive of the sexual impulse in this way, and to place it under the sign of Abundance. But in Ingres, sexual desire is less a fulfilment than a postponement of satisfaction, and, though explicit depictions by Ingres of the sexual act do indeed exist at the Musée Ingres at Montauban, in his painting the consummation of desire is never represented. The *Valpinçon baigneuse* (illustration 65) is less an erotic presence than an intimation of its possibility. The figure is placed in a hushed interior whose silence is interrupted only by a splashing font; she turns from the spectator and covers her body with a sheet: we cannot see her face. Our attention is directed instead to a different personal feature: the bather's ear, as it experiences the liquid acoustic of her private world. The sensuality of the image is unquestionable, but the Valpinçon bather cannot be appropriated by the viewer's desirous gaze: the bather's senses, perfectly attuned to her environment, attend to silences and sounds our senses cannot share. Certain aspects of the bather are obviously intended for the spectator alone: the soft, yielding underside of the foot, the nape of the neck, and the gently modelled back are zones the bather cannot herself see; but while these details increase sensual enjoyment of the figure, they also isolate the viewer in voyeurism and erotic deflection, pushing viewing out still further from the image. Instead of satisfaction, the viewer experiences the interval between the viewer's and the figure's existence, the lack, not the presence, in desire. And this erotic absence is linked, in the most inventive passage of the painting, to the trope of displacement *in tradition*. The bather's turban repeats the stripes and folds of the scarfs worn in two directly invoked paintings by Raphael: the *Madonna of the Chair* (illustration 58), from which the turban takes its fabric, and *La Fornarina*, from which it takes its construction (illustration 66).

It is as though *La Fornarina* had been turned round and viewed from behind: even the tight-drawn hair and curve of the ear are the same. What the turban does is to complete the series of absences registered in the bather's absorption in her sonic world and in her rotation out of view, to link the painting as a whole to precursive images that claim possession of the new one, and by so doing to make tradition itself an absence that intensifies the lack or absence to which the painting is dedicated.

I would like to stay for a moment with this detail, the bather's turban, because it introduces a concept of much importance to our understanding of Ingres: the Muse. The artist who senses his own latecoming in time is surrounded by the monuments of history and culture across whose landscapes he moves as exile and wanderer: in

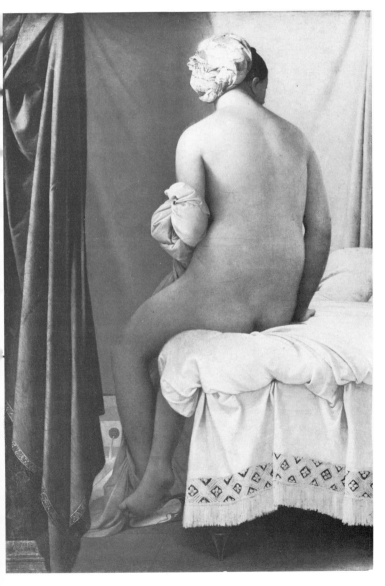

65 Ingres, *Valpinçon Baigneuse*

the phrase of Théophile Silvestre, Ingres is a painter from China astray in the ruins of Athens.[4] The relics of the past are permanent reminders of his dispossession and his belatedness. Yet in at least one place he can experience both space and time under the same conditions of immediacy that had belonged to the precursors in their own age: the body. To the latecoming artist, the body assumes an enhanced importance because it is an instrument, perhaps the only instrument available, which can break the spell of belatedness through the prime and freshness of the senses. By entering into his own body, the latecoming artist overcomes the weight of tradition and makes all the precursors his contemporaries in the spring of somatic time: the body can be a place where tradition and the individual talent are mediated and united.

66 Raphael, *La Fornarina*

ROMA - RAFFAELLO - LA FORNARINA
(GALLERIA NAZIONALE D'ARTE ANTICA)

In part, this merging follows in Ingres the course of simple antagonism against the past: the *Valpinçon baigneuse* is *La Fornarina*, but in another guise; she has been seized from Raphael, has been subjected to the strange and personal distortion Ingres characteristically inflicts on the object of his delight, and has been turned away from the picture plane where Raphael had captured her: her rotation marks her passage from tradition into the private ownership of Ingres. But more forcefully, Ingres' trope of displacement denies that anyone, not Raphael, not the viewer, not Ingres himself, can possess the image in presence. Ingres' copula between personal eros on the one hand and tradition on the other unites them in the lack that is common to both. By linking the bather to two very different works of Raphael, given equal privilege, Ingres ensures that neither can stake a definitive claim: the quotations neutralise each other and instead open on to the spaces between them. The intervals between images-in-displacement, the gaps in the series that runs from *La Fornarina* to the *Madonna of the Chair* to the *Valpinçon baigneuse*, are modulated into the central absence that constitutes his own bodily desire, tradition and desire joining in a single term, the Muse.

The Muse is technically female and in Ingres' work the juncture between tradition and bodily desire is almost always represented by women. Before passing on to some of her many incarnations, however, let us look at the *Jupiter and Thetis* of 1811 (illustration 67). Neither the male nor the female can be understood as bodily presences in any normal sense. Although Ingres could not have seen the murals unearthed at the Villa of the Mysteries at Pompeii, the comparison between the two is useful because it makes so plain the nature of the transaction between Thetis and Jupiter (illustration 68). Thetis is supplicant less before an individual deity than a generalised erotic image of the male, which has the exaggerated character of sexual fantasy: this is indeed reverence towards the phallus, and Jupiter's whole body is conceived in terms of tumescence and inflation. It is similar with Thetis, less a body than the glyph of one, boneless, invertebrate, deformed by the requirements of Ingres' highly specialised sexual needs, for with Ingres the female must assume a *reverberant* form, her neck recalling the loves of the swan, her hand (in Clark's phrase) half octopus, half tropical flower.[5] Ingres said that he wanted his painting to 'breathe Ambrosia' and it does: it is hard to think of any painting that represents so excitingly the process of physical arousal. Boucher is drab in comparison, because he still thinks of sexuality in the manner of Giulio Romano, or the *Kama Sutra*, as a matter of posture. *Jupiter and Thetis* goes deeper into the interior of sexual vision, to examine behind the contents of the sexual fantasy the underlying structure of unreality.

It is not in bodies that Ingres discovers the sexual, but in the deformation of the body out of presence and into the signs of sexuality;[6] he is concerned to gauge the *non*-correspondence between the actual and the sign in sex, to measure the intervals of desire. In the painting itself, he activates the trope of displacement so that the allusions to Phidias, to Pompeian painting, to Girodet and to Flaxman flash past as a series in constant movement. Even the inset frieze, showing the struggle of Jupiter against the Giants, shares this mobility. Invoking one of the most celebrated cameos of Antiquity, it joins the series of displacements and quotations that claims the main figures (Girodet, Flaxman, Pompeii, Phidias, and now this). But it also offers to interpret the figure of Jupiter: the eye is forced to compare the god and this second representation, and discover in the comparison the key to the cameo-like nature of Jupiter's torso. One part of the canvas displaces another, in the same way that in the *Oedipus and the Sphinx* (illustration 69) the left hand twins with and displaces the right. And as in *Mlle Rivière* (illustration 59), two equally likely candidates compete for spatial

67   Ingres, *Jupiter and Thetis*

68 Wall-painting from the Villa of the Mysteries, Pompeii

69 Ingres. *Oedipus and the Sphinx* (detail)

explanation of the painting: the bi-dimensional interpretation, which works with the linear, Flaxman-like design; and the interpretation in three dimensions, required by the (limited) recession of the podium, the tilt of Jupiter's left foot, and the inward move from foreground (cloud) to middle distance (the figures) to background (Juno). Yet neither can adequately account for the painting's space, from which both interpretations fall away; its space belongs neither to two dimensions nor to three, but 'something in between'.

The phenomenon we are describing is one in which a series of *erotic* displacements and a series of *painterly* displacements are conjoined, so that the lack or absence in human sexuality (as Ingres conceives of it), and the lack or absence with which Ingres carves out his images from tradition, come to reinforce and to express each other. It is a complex phenomenon, and one that is easily misunderstood. The misconception to be resisted is that Ingres deploys libidinal force simply *against* his inheritance, like an angered son. This is to miss what is important about sexuality in Ingres: that it is not a positive or *plenary* force, but a force of *vacuum*. For this reason, one line of classic feminist objection to Ingres' odalisques can, I think, be off target. In *Ways of Seeing* John Berger juxtaposes the head of the *Grande Odalisque* and a pin-up photograph.

Compare the expressions of these two women. One the model for a famous painting by Ingres and the other a model for a photograph in a girlie magazine. Is not the expression remarkably similar in each case? It is the expression of a woman responding with calculating charm to the man she imagines looking at her – although she doesn't know him. She is offering up her femininity as the surveyed.[7]

While this may be true for the pin-up, things are far less simple in the case of the *Grande Odalisque* (illustration 70). For unmasking of the truth of exploitation behind the odalisque tradition we must wait until Manet's *Olympia*.[8] Here, woman cannot offer herself with calculated charm; she is not offering herself at all. The *Grande Odalisque* is presented in terms of highest unreality. It is a radically dehiscent image whose construction further disintegrates the longer one examines it. Let the viewer try the following mental experiments. Measure the *length* of the vertebral column running from the neck to the coccyx, or the *width* (and location) of the pelvic girdle. Looking at the figure's left knee, try to imagine where (and how) the left leg joins the body. For those who enjoy the vertigo of lateral puzzles, let the left foot be imagined travelling down the calf towards the right foot, and try to calculate the ensuing positions of the left leg. None of this *can* be imagined, for the woman is not a three-dimensional being at all, but a bi-dimensional design whose plausibility evaporates when elaborated into the 'three-dimensional' flesh of this, Ingres' most impossible creation. Above all, she is not a stereotype (as the 'girlie magazine' figure most certainly is). Stereotypes can be said to be linked to cultural identity and enjoyment, in a standardising and homogenising process of building 'the civil subject'; but the *Grande Odalisque* is the opposite of this: a radical disruption of the standard and homogeneous image of woman, in a self-dissolving and self-unravelling movement of what Barthes used to call *jouissance*.[9]

The undermining of a coherent image of woman is all the more striking because the painting comes so close, comes to within a hair's breath, of persuasiveness. The *Grande Odalisque* promises a union of all the senses: touch, in the fan; scent, in the smoking censer; taste, in the hookah; sight, in the jewels; hearing, in the version of the *Grande Odalisque* where, as in the *Valpinçon baigneuse*, a spout gushes below the odalisque's right foot into a pool of water (illustration 71). The figure also promises a perfection of unity and self-containment in the finality of her contour. But all such promises are broken by the painting itself, which denies – *undoes* – its reality as authentic presence. And as in the *Valpinçon baigneuse*, the stripes of the turban take us once again towards Raphael and displacement, the *Madonna of the Chair* and *La Fornarina* claiming the odalisque as echo of their own initial sound.

The *Odalisque à l'esclave* follows the same construction (perhaps one might say de-construction). The rhythm of the breasts and hips seems closer to India than to Europe, and such details as the helmet, and the tile and fabric patterns (Fogg version, illustration

70 Ingres, *La Grande Odalisque*

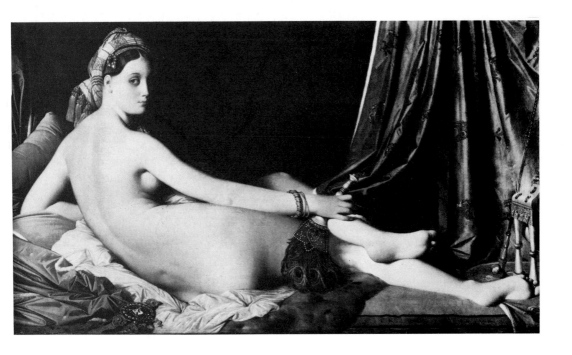

71 Achille Réveil, engraving of *La Grande Odalisque* (1851)

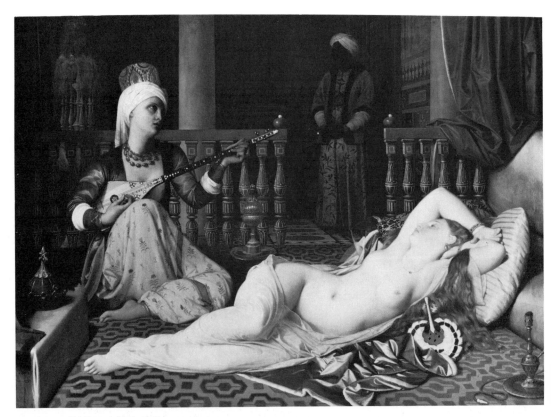

72 Ingres, *Odalisque à l'esclave*, Fogg version

72 and Baltimore version, illustration 73) are clearly taken from
Islamic, probably Persian sources. But the orientalism of the
painting should not blind us to more local and specifically Parisian
deviations. The *Grande Odalisque* and the *Odalisque à l'esclave* are
both closely related to the work of David's atelier in the crucial
phase of its stylistic disintegration, whose ensign is *The Intervention
of the Sabine Women*. Ingres' experience in the atelier from 1797 to
1806 was to mark him for life. Even at the end of his, so to speak,
graduate career, in *Romulus Victorious over Acron* (1812; illustration
74) we find him carefully transcribing into his work the
Intervention's fallen warrior (illustration 75). It is impossible not to
trace the *Grande Odalisque* back to David's *Mme Récamier* (illustration 76), on which Ingres had worked as David's assistant. The
swerve away from *Mme Récamier* is, of course, considerable,
though to David at least the connection between the works seems
to have been clearly recognised, and David goes on to claim his
figure back from Ingres in his late history painting *Mars Disarmed
by Venus* (illustration 77), a final expression of the tension of
influence David felt existing between himself and his pupils in the
decade of stylistic fragmentation 1796–1806. The first sketches for
what would become the *Odalisque à l'esclave* date from 1808, the
year of Ingres' lost *Sleeper of Naples*, owned by Murat and
destroyed at Murat's downfall in 1815; and there can be little doubt

73   Ingres, *Odalisque à l'esclave*,
Baltimore version

that the link between them is that of Girodet's *Endymion* of 1803 (illustration 78). Endymion has changed gender, but then his gender was always in doubt. What remains are all the most salient aspects of Girodet's painting: Endymion's raised and enervated right arm, crooked behind the head – a detail we see in all the versions of the *Odalisque à l'esclave*; the foreshortened profile; the cascade of drapery beneath; the elongation of the legs; the placing of an attendant figure to the left. In his re-envisioning of the Girodet, Ingres passes behind him to Girodet's Flaxman, lying flat on the picture plane: intensifying the linearism, Ingres banishes the misty radiance which Girodet had used to blur his design, and produces a figure completely contained within a single and sharply defined contour. The most perplexing problem becomes the placing of the figure's arms, and through Ingres' enormous number of variations on this theme, from the *Sleeper of Naples* through the *Odalisque à l'esclave* to *Zeus and Antiope*, while the lower body remains fairly constant, the arms constantly permutate. Probably the most perfect resolution is the drawing which exists today in a private collection in England (illustration 79). It is a

74 Ingres, *Romulus Victorious over Acron* (detail)

75 David, *Intervention of the Sabine Women* (detail)

breathtaking work, but precisely in its perfection and its authority it highlights what could never be resolved in any of the painted versions of the *Odalisque à l'esclave*: the relation of the figure to its décor.

Décor is the operative word. The figure is already complete *as* a drawing; she does not require a setting (illustration 79). But here we encounter once more Ingres' very personal conception of Eros. Certainly Girodet is a persistent echo through all the variants on the *Odalisque à l'esclave*, but Ingres is not invoking Girodet in the same way that in the *Grande Odalisque* he invokes Raphael. Once one has noticed the 'Girodet connection' it is hard to forget it, but the displacement at work in the *Odalisque à l'esclave* occurs less, in fact, in the 'exterior' references the image makes than those it makes internally (within the four sides of the frame). Again the odalisque is anatomically implausible: but what is absolutely implausible is the 'seraglio'. This is perhaps clearest in the painting's painted balustrade, where despite the rotundity of the supports, the volumetric curve of their inset design, and the device of reflections, the dominant impression is that of a cut-out with no depth at all. The spatial corrosions of the balustrade spread all round the painting, infecting everything except the reclining figure: the helmet on the table and the cylindrical head-dress of

76 David, *Mme Récamier*

the handmaid, both cut-outs; the landscape in the Baltimore version, a backdrop; the fountain in the Fogg version, with its candle-wax jets and dry-ice spray.

To understand this 'failure' to portray convincingly the interior of the harem, we have to recall a nineteenth-century orientalism in which the East is conceived as the fantasmatic Other of the West, and attend closely to the fact that the reclining female is white-skinned and auburn-haired – by way of the euphemism of 'Circassian', quite clearly a European. The *Odalisque à l'esclave* gives visual expression to a rich speculative and fantasmatic tradition which extends in France from the *Bajazet* of Racine and the *Lettres persanes* and *Esprit des lois* of Montesquieu, through Galland's translation of the *Mille et une nuits*, to Flaubert's *Salammbô*.[10] Throughout this tradition much interest is expressed in the secret world of the seraglio, thought of as a place of 'derangement' of 'normal' (occidental) sexuality where the relation of male to female is one either of omnipotence (the sultan) or of impotence (the eunuch), and where (this is of crucial interest) the women are fascinatingly *interchangeable*. This orientalist theme

77 David, *Mars Disarmed by Venus*

78 Anne-Louis Girodet de Roucy-Trioson, *The Sleep of Endymion*

79 Ingres, Study for *L'Odalisque à l'esclave*

of sexual derangement is engaging to Ingres because of its congruence with his own understanding of the *normally* functioning sexual imagination; here, too (in erotic fantasy) the imagery of desire represents desire in the form of restlessness, of interchangeable images, none of which actually *contains* desire. The interchangeability of the women in the seraglio matches the seriality of Ingres' own attempts to capture the elusive *Odalisque à l'esclave*, and through an orientalist fantasy *avowedly* presented as such (and in this openness of avowal Ingres is working against many tendencies in the orientalist tradition) Ingres succeeds in dramatising the movement of displacement that for him is the essence of desire-in-the-image.

The displacement here is of two kinds. There is first the seriality that comes from other, competing versions of the subject; the (informed) viewer does not simply experience *this* painting in the here and now of viewing, but rather the differences and intervals which separate and distinguish each version. Where, before, the competing images had come from tradition, now they come from Ingres' own production, and one way to understand Ingres' compulsion to repeat his designs is as the forging of a private or personal tradition to which the same displacing function can be ascribed, which had formerly been ascribed to the precursors. Repetition creates a body of provisional images which, like those of the past, bear in upon each particular work and shift it out of presence; but now Ingres controls the pressure himself.

The second displacement occurs within the image taken on its own: the disconnection of the odalisque from her surroundings breaks the image into two *separated* zones. They should connect – the theme of synaesthesia, where the fan once more stands for the sense of touch, the fountain and the zither for hearing, the hookah for taste and the censer for smell, ought to describe the unity of the body with its surroundings, across the channels of sense; the synaesthesia should bespeak *interpenetration* of exterior and interior worlds. But, as in the *Grande Odalisque*, the promise of plenitude is contradicted, for the image is less interested in presence and abundance, than absence and desire: the spatial and ontological unevenness of the painting, where an almost unreal beauty is superimposed on to a completely unreal setting, prevents fulfilment to the image and instead guarantees its lack.

III

There can be little doubt that the artificiality of the *Grande Odalisque* and the *Odalisque à l'esclave* was a matter of policy on Ingres' part. That Ingres' conception of the desire and the absence intrinsic to (his) painting was fully conscious, and not simply intuitive, is proved by one of his most complex meditations on the 'sources' of art, the series of paintings collectively known as *Raphael and La Fornarina*. The version shown here (illustration 80) measures the interval between two major representations: *La Fornarina* (an emergent outline on Raphael's canvas), and this *new* portrayal of Raphael's mistress, imagined by Ingres. To these it adds a further set: the gaps that exist between the emergent form on the easel and the final appearance of Raphael's *La Fornarina*; between this newly imagined appearance of Raphael's mistress and the head of the *Grande Odalisque*, from which the jewelled headband has been transported; between the imagined mistress and the *Valpinçon baigneuse*, whom she must much resemble if viewed from behind and to the left, as she is by the figure entering the studio.

    Raphael and La Fornarina is usually seen in the context of those exercises in the hagiography of artists' lives fashionable in France at

80 Ingres, *Raphael and La Fornarina*

least since Ménageot's *Death of Leonardo*. But this is to misunderstand what the work is really exploring, namely the lack set in motion by the displacement of images in a fully self-conscious tradition, and the evacuative consequence for each individual work of its articulation with tradition. *Raphael and La Fornarina* is all about the impossibility of closure or self-completion for the image in tradition; at the same time it is about *physical desire*; and at the extremely sophisticated level to which this work addresses itself, its subject is the connection between these different kinds of lack – the intrinsic openness and permanent postponement of the image-in-tradition, and the perpetual displacements of the image-in-desire.

For the most perspicacious commentary on Ingres' *Raphael and La Fornarina* we must leave art history and return to art, to Picasso, and to the twenty-four variations on *Raphael Painting La Fornarina* included in his *Suite 347* (illustration 81). Picasso has the deepest understanding of the play of absences that is provoked by Ingres' linearism. He is well aware that the Line is the most ontologically ambiguous of forms, since despite its minimal or frugal nature it is able so intensely to stimulate the viewer's senses that the merest of signals and markers are 'fleshed out' at once into presence. He fully understands that this truth about the Line is nowhere more evident (as the graffitists through the ages have always known) than in the representation of sexuality; and also that the presence conjured up by such rudimentary signs is entirely illusory, since the body on which the signs are 'placed' can be endlessly rearranged with no restriction from anatomy and no loss of impact, by the simple connective line. Picasso also understands, completely, the nature of the trope of displacement through which Ingres acts upon tradition: his inclusion of the 'tondo' tacked to the wall illustrates everything that has been said, in the present discussion, about the

81   Picasso, *Number 314*, 5 September 1968, I; from *Suite 347*

self-absenting nature of Ingres' allusions – here, to the *Madonna of the Chair* and *La Fornarina*, so arbitrarily condensed that they then become fissile, separate and equal contenders for possession of an image whose 'presence' is at the same time evacuated by linearism. Picasso knows far more about Ingres than Ingres' commentators. He is intimately familiar with Ingres' rhythm of two dimensions against three, and the irrealising effect of that rhythm on Ingres' art. This he humorously states in the playing-card flatness of Ingres/Raphael, knave of hearts, and in the independently rotated 'spheres' of La Fornarina's breasts. And above all, Picasso understands the fate of artistic latecoming, understands it perhaps even more urgently than Ingres, as a struggle which in the end (for Picasso) can only be resolved by radical violence – art as an act of defiant procreation conducted under the gaze of history and authority, the Church, the Inquisitor, Papa Roma; just as he knows that a prime instrument for overcoming the fate of belatedness is sexual desire, the body (of Ingres, of Picasso). By attributing to Ingres his own sexual energy, as undiminished by age as it had remained undiminished for Ingres, Picasso crosses the temporal interval that separates his time from the time of Ingres, in exactly the same conquest or telescoping of belatedness through which Ingres, imputing to Raphael his own specific sexuality (not phallocratic, as with Picasso, but precisely the sexuality of lack, displacement, interval: not the phallus, but the brush), had made Raphael his own contemporary and youthful rival of the Muse, turning Raphael the father into Raphael the son, Raphael the brother.

I mention the variations on Raphael painting La Fornarina as a preliminary aid to our comprehension of the work many have seen as the climax of Ingres' career, the *Vow of Louis XIII* at Montauban (illustration 82). To its first viewers it was a quintessentially conservative painting, bastion of resistance against the rise of Romanticism, a celebration of all the orthodoxies: monarchy, Catholicism, family, nation. I think they were right: it is about these things, but even more it is about the interflow of desire that unites these institutions in the individual subject. In the first place, the painting is Ingres' most complicated activation of the trope of displacement, or desire. Much of its force is lost on an age that has learned to overlook Raphael, but we must remember that in Ingres' century the work of Raphael was widely regarded as being of a supernatural perfection: even as late as 1882, Crowe and Cavalcaselle could begin their study of his painting with the words 'Raphael! At the mere whisper of this magic name our whole being seems spellbound. Wonder, delight, awe take possession of our souls, and throw us into a whirl of contending emotions.'[11] All of the quotations in the *Vow* would have been immediately recognised by the viewer; the nature of their *articulation* would also have been understood.

For us, things must be spelt out. The idea of a dual scene, with the natural world below and the divine revelation above, is that of the *Transfiguration*. The Virgin is a twin creation, equally summoning the *Sistine Madonna*, who stands, and the *Mackintosh Madonna*, who sits. The putti invoke their counterparts in the *Madonna di Foligno*, where a single putto holds a cartouche, in the *Sistine Madonna*, and in the *Madonna of the Baldacchino*, from which Ingres also takes his angels. For the figure of Louis XIII, Ingres moves to Philippe de Champaigne, but not even the king is

82 Ingres, *Vow of Louis XIII*

allowed to escape the chain of Raphaelesque displacements, for his pose ultimately derives from the kneeling woman who appeals with outstretched arms to the distant Pope on his balcony, in *Fire in the Borgo*. There is hardly a detail in Ingres' painting that does not evoke his great precursor; and evoke not just in a generalised way, but in a chain, a series – more like a tone-row than a chord. The invocation of the *Sistine Madonna* in the upper sector interprets the putti below (a first displacing image), but the putti then lead on a second displacing image, the *Madonna of the Baldacchino*; so that when we look at the *Vow of Louis XIII* our view brings into play several images that are indeed very different: we attend not only to the fusions, but to the discrepancies of the components. Hence the importance of the spatial and ontological break between upper and lower canvas: to a limited degree they are welded, but not at all in the manner of the complex sutures present in the *Transfiguration*; they are joined rather by chiasma, with a portion of the lower and 'real' scene (the architecture) continuing into the upper and 'unreal' spectacle (the vault); and at the same time the two halves of the canvas are *dis*joined precisely by the angels, by woman and desire.

As with the odalisques, Ingres irrealises the Madonna through abstraction. The design of her face (illustration 83) is a provisional solution to a problem of balancing facial features that would remain with Ingres for the rest of his career. The chosen configuration of eyebrows, nose, and mouth, is highly precarious; the slightest shift in any of the elements necessitates so many mutual and compensating adjustments that entirely different overall effects are generated at once (illustrations 84 and 85). Of all the mysteries of female representation to which Ingres dedicated his being, the frontal view of the face is the least susceptible of resolution – it was exactly this that ensured the permanence of Ingres' fascination. The face of the Madonna in the *Vow* implies a suite of *permutations* in which no combination can be final or definitive; it opens on to a vista of alternative dispositions incapable of closure or completion. The face is presented as a very emblem of displacement and desire (which in the ordinary experience of men and women it is: target zone to which each individual directs his or her acutest discrimination, the face is the site, *par excellence*, of the *alternative*). Reduced to primary components, as it is here, and as it is in the erotic gaze, the face is scanned as unique only to the degree that it simultaneously entrains the sum of its possible variants, amongst which eros arbitrates, or rather hesitates; precisely because variation is at work, eros is always in perplexity and can never with assurance award the prize. The Madonna of the *Vow* is painted as though Ingres were following Leonardo's injunction: 'sel pittore vol vedere bellezze, che lo innamorino, egli n'è signore di generarle'[12] – if the painter desires to see beauties which will make him fall in love, then he is a master capable of producing them. But for Ingres the beauty he seeks exists in the terms of his desire, as lack and deferral – if he is in love with the women of his inner pantheon, it is because, in their openness of form and the energy of displacement they arouse, they can never be possessed.

IV

One should never let oneself be beguiled by Ingres' persona of orthodoxy and rectitude. If one had enjoyed the advantage of being alive in the era of the great Ingres–Delacroix debate, there is every chance that one would have supported Delacroix's party.

83 Ingres, *Vow of Louis XIII* (detail)

84 Ingres, *Madonna with the Blue Veil*

85 Ingres, *The Virgin with the Host*

One would have found Ingres' posture of permanent reaction unbearable. One would have despaired at his blindness to the intellectual activity of his age, and would have dismissed his much-publicised reverence for *les bonnes doctrines*. One would have been dismayed by his greed for academic honours and titles, and been embarrassed (bearing in mind the breadth of culture, the sophistication, and the detachment of Delacroix) by his basic lack of urbanity. But the more one examines, from the present century, Ingres' works of even the highest reaction, the more one feels, behind the persona of M. Bertin, subterfuge in the guise of orthodoxy, and discrepancy – amounting almost to a kind of secondary revision – between the public pronouncements and the actual work. In the *Vow*, an apparent reaffirmation of traditional values, Ingres outbids tradition by allowing himself to be flooded by Raphael – each detail of the painting cites the canon, chapter and verse; and through this extremism of his summoning of tradition, Ingres achieves a self-evacuation that is absolutely his, and completely self-defining – in Kojève's phrase, 'the desire of a being is what constitutes that being as *I*'. His self-emptying before tradition has no counterpart in Raphael, or at least in the Raphael posited by Ingres; so that by exaggerating both Raphael's priority and his own belatedness, Ingres forces an asymmetry between them and asserts, unmistakably, his own distinctness.

It is camouflage which forms the essence of the *Apotheosis of Homer* (illustration 86), a work whose high academicism barely succeeds in concealing Ingres' most ambitious use of the trope of totality. It is not an easy work for the late-twentieth-century viewer to appreciate. Our own painting tradition stresses the expanse and the disframing of the canvas, so that the framed stasis of this image looks to us rigid and cluttered: the eye tends to break this enclosed mass and to detach single figures, such as the attractive and almost free-standing Phidias (on the right, extending his arm and mallet). We can perhaps get a better purchase on the *Apotheosis* if we approach it as an expression of the sense of latecoming that haunts Romanticism. It is all over. All the essential problems of art had been solved by the seventeenth century (on this point, both Ingres and Delacroix concur); and they had been already solved by Antiquity, and the solutions then destroyed. Of the work of Apelles, who is seen approaching Homer and leading Raphael by the hand, nothing survives. The *Zeus* and the *Athene Parthenos* of Phidias are dust. Homer's blindness acquires a particular pathos in this context of destruction: like us, he is unable to see the masterworks of the classical age; and Antiquity is presented as a paradise lost, existing in a different dimension to the modern and fallen world. The *Apotheosis* curiously touches here on the themes of Delacroix, and Delacroix's sense of the fatal or terminal quality of the classical world; the imminence of its end, the murder of Archimedes, the coming of Attila. To the extent that the moderns remain in contact with this vanished civilisation, they retain some of its greatness: Poussin points directly towards Homer as though to reprove or chastise his contemporaries; Molière holds, and Racine actually resembles, the mask of antique drama. But the further they enter modernity, defined exactly as the loss of such contact, the more the nobility and generality of countenance evident in such figures as Phidias and Apelles gives way to ironical peering and sardonic expressions, at their nadir in the busy scribbling and sarcastic 'smile of reason' of Voltaire.

It looks orthodox enough. The nineteenth century has now fallen so far below the cultural level of the past that it is unable to send forth a single representative from its own time: or such is the official story. In fact the trope of totality works to overcome the sense of modern humiliation and abasement; and here Homer's blindness reverses its meaning: the paragon of Antiquity cannot see, and though in the narrative of flattery Homer is the alleged source of European culture, his influence extends in the first place to Pindar (on the right and holding out his lyre) and to the tragedians (Aeschylus, Sophocles, Euripides) on the left. This is the enthronement of Homer, not Zeuxis, and the central zone of power and origin has no sway over painting – or over Ingres. Apelles and Phidias were great, but their work is dust: the anxiety

86 Ingres, *Apotheosis of Homer*

through which the latecoming artist may view his precursors changes to pity at their waste.

For Ingres, only two figures bear directly on his own art: Raphael, and Poussin. Together they might well constitute a force of priority dangerous to their successor, but Ingres pursues a policy of divide and rule: Raphael is elevated, Poussin demoted. Poussin's urgent gesturing toward Antiquity establishes that he, too, is a latecomer on whom the burden of the past gravely falls. Following what has emerged as the customary action of the trope (David's *Mars and Minerva*, Ingres' *Imperial Portrait*) the predecessor is seen as weak against his own strong precursors, depotentiated by his own temporal place, and indeed Ingres gives to Poussin a precise position in time, the year of Poussin's self-portrait (which Ingres faithfully transcribes). The burden of latecoming thus focusses singly on the great precursor, Raphael: but with Raphael Ingres feels such kinship, particularly in 1827, with the success of the *Vow* still ringing in his ears, and in a painting so directly modelled on the *School of Athens*, that the elevation of Raphael to the exalted platform of Antiquity amounts almost to a covert self-promotion.

Raphael–Ingres is led on by an Apelles who, compared with Phidias, appears as a spectre or wraith, his lack of visual definition exactly marking the absence of his painting and the loss of his artistic vision. It is a ghost who leads Raphael into the area of darkness and blindness around Homer; an apparition, not a real contender. And this ghost cannot have known Raphael; Raphael 'belongs' here to Ingres, not Apelles. What we are witnessing is the deliberate weakening of Antiquity's claim to strength. At the centre of the image sits the *blind* Homer, where Homer's blindness stands for the greatest consolation the spectacle of Antiquity can afford the latecoming painter: that none of its paintings survived. Such an interpretation of the blindness is supported by the figure of Phidias, far more an inhabitant of the visible world than Apelles, but whose gesture of finger against brow indicates that the source of art can only be revealed by a screening out of external vision: at the level of the narrative a simple homage to Homer, Phidias' insistence on blindness or evacuation of the mind as a precondition for innovative art also refers to the painting's overall trope, of surrounding and cordoning off the totality of influence.

Here it joins the idea of an inner theatre of the imagination where eros and the body form a counter-force to the pressure of tradition. Phidias himself is already cast as an image of ideal virility, as though artistic and physical beauty were somehow cognate; but the articulation of tradition and desire is expressed more obviously and forcefully in the Victory and the Muses. By showing the *Iliad* and the *Odyssey* as governed or protected by the female body, Ingres reaffirms his belief in the capacity of desire to make every precursor his own contemporary – the theme of *Raphael and La Fornarina*. The temporality of eros is always the present, or rather the *imminent*: eros can never possess its object, but only approach it, again and again, on the endless track of desire, and thus history has no weight – in as much as the precursors enjoyed their own day of sensuality, they exited from history into desire's always postponed future, reaching out of their own time toward their successors and joining their successors in the trans-historicity of bodily time.

If sublimation is the name customarily given to the metamorphosis of eros into art, then Ingres' portrayal of the eros or Muse behind Homer's art shows the metamorphosis in reverse: a counter-sublimation, or desublimation (it is the same in the case of *Raphael and La Fornarina*). Ingres goes behind Homer to Homer's inner source, to which he gives a visibility that Homer himself cannot know. The protocol is still that of flattery – Ingres seems to aggrandise the work of the precursor (Homer, Raphael) by discovering behind it a primal and sexual energy; but with the characteristic duplicity of Ingres' genuflections he claims the source for himself and for the sighted world of which he is currently master. The result is that Ingres' own desire is portrayed much as Picasso saw it, as a defiance of authority, a knavish theft of the Muse; and this corresponds to the whole atmosphere of the *Apotheosis*, a bowing before tradition that at the same time steals tradition's mantle. What could be more consoling than the power the latecomer is able to exercise exactly because he comes at the end, of consigning this predecessor to paradise, and that to purgatory? The trickster strategy of the *Apotheosis* is to appear rigidly orthodox, while the serious business of transgression is carried out under authority's nose. In this it is like the *Imperial Portrait*, another study in totality and bathos – but we notice a change of tone. For the youthful Ingres, styles are currents of sheer play; but for Ingres in middle age, Ingres as M. Bertin, the sensation of play, barely distinguishable from hubris, is accompanied by the stiffest expression of orthodoxy. Ingres cannot afford any longer to be *seen* at play. And although a benign eye can still find the hubris and the play behind the *Apotheosis*, no one can say that it *looks* like playful painting. How it must have appeared to the young Turks of 1827 hardly bears thinking about.

The *Apotheosis of Homer* is virtually Ingres' last gasp in the category of history painting: as he grows older (at the time of the *Apotheosis* he was already forty-seven), and as his persona of artistic and social rectitude grows even more rigid, innovation can no longer be sustained. Instead of creating afresh, Ingres *assembles*: the *Martyrdom of St Symphorian* was preceded by magnificent individual figure studies: their final collocation is entirely lacking in coherence. As the sexual impulse declines and as Ingres can no longer arouse in himself the negative pressure of desire, the figure of repetition – formerly a strong device of displacement in desire – undergoes a sorrowful sea-change, for it comes to express regret at the passing of desire, a nostalgia for the old images, to which Ingres clings in persistent, fading loyalty. From one point of view *Le Bain Turc* (illustration 87) is one of Ingres' most vigorous exercises in displacement. The key figures are withdrawn from presence by priority's claimants: most conspicuously, by the *Valpinçon baigneuse*, now given the breast and waist of the *Bayonne baigneuse*, and accompanying herself on the *oud* from the *Odalisque à l'esclave* (left of centre); by the angel from the right of the *Vow*, drowsy, almond-eyed, and – as she had appeared to Ingres in his first studies for the *Vow* – naked. The expanded thigh of the *Grande Odalisque* crops up in the middle distance, behind the beauty who joins together the *Venus Anadyomène* and the garden dancer in the Baltimore *Odalisque à l'esclave*. We may even make out a transmogrified and buddha-like *Mme Moitessier*, complete with starfish hand.

But this is above all a painting about repetition (rather than displacement), and also about the connection between repetition and death (next to the signature we read the crucial words, AETATIS LXXXII). Although Ingres presents us with new women, women we have not seen before except, perhaps, as fleeting distortions in the portraits and portrait sketches, the image guards its principle of *constancy*, in the sense given this term by psychoanalysis. In the words of Laplanche and Pontalis, 'Con-

87   Ingres, *Le Bain Turc*

stancy is achieved on the one hand by the discharge of the energy still present [in the psyche] and on the other hand, by avoidance of whatever might increase the quality of excitation and defence against any such increase as does occur.'[13] The painting does indeed discharge the energy present in Ingres' inner pantheon, but discharges it homeostatically, without excitation and almost without wakefulness, like a nocturnal emission; new images appear, but with none of the trumpet-flourish of arousal that had announced the entrance, for example, of Thetis (or of Zeus). The new apparitions are vaporous and insubstantial, and only the old ones stand out against the mist. These latter figures are copied faithfully from their originals, where that fidelity of repetition marks Ingres' defence against increase of tension and against innovation; not displacement in desire, but the replacement of desire by inertia, the binding of energy to a constant and determinate level.

Le Bain Turc is a painting about male desire, certainly: but to view it only in such terms is to limit its reference to what is obvious. It is a painting of much wider scope, the one painting where Ingres steps outside the specialisations of his erotic imagination and into a truly universal image of the *extinction* of human desire; of the abolition of individuality as the individual yields, in dying, to the inevitable return to the inorganic state. Death, in Ingres, wears the mask of nirvana, of pleasure in the form where it seems, in Freud's phrase, 'actually in the service of the death instincts';[14] a pleasure of repetition that works to prevent the disruption or tearing of being in desire, and to surround the place of disruption with a protective layer or shield: the circular shield of the tondo.

V

Ingres' innovative energy had long since passed to portraiture. In this he resembles his master, David. For David, portraiture had been, with the exception of the martyr-portraits of the Terror, an activity apart, quite distinct from history painting, and a storehouse of vernacular forms to which David could repair when the strain of taking his place in the great tradition of the history painting had become inhibiting and destructive. But for Ingres this distinction between the genres had never existed. From the first, from the *Rivière* series onwards, Ingres had felt portraiture to exist in the same field of precursive influence as history painting, and to the portrait Ingres brings strategies which for David had been required only by the *grande machine*. After the fall of Napoleon Ingres stayed on in Italy and was obliged for ten years, until the Parisian triumph of the *Vow*, to produce innumerable portrait sketches of the visitors, of all nationalities, who passed through

Rome and Florence. Even in these *fa presto*, ephemeral productions, Ingres deploys the tropes of his major paintings. He keys the daughter of the Stamaty family (illustration 88) to the *Madonna of the Chair* and to the *Grande Odalisque* who fuse on the nearby wall, introducing the same displacement-series that had operated in *Raphael and La Fornarina*. To this signature of desire-in-the-image he adds the voiding of form that comes from his control of line.

Two distinct transcriptive registers of 'gears' are brought together in the same frame: facial features and modelling are stated elaborately, in hundreds of minute traces that create a broad spectrum of tonality, ranging from the near-black round Mme Stamaty's face to the white of the keyboard and lustre of her daughter's hair: the fidelity here is high, and passes through a rich array of tonal shadings between the two extremes. But costume is stated laconically: here shade is suppressed and textures are reduced to outline, to long, isolated strokes of the pencil which precisely exclude tonal variety. Just as the paintings hesitate between the dimensions of two and of three, requiring (for example, the head of Mlle Rivière) two distinct scansions, neither of which can lay

88   Ingres, *The Stamaty Family*

successful claim to the image as a unitary presence, so here the disparity of notations elicits a double scansion, first in tonality, attending to modelling and shadow; and then in flatness, attending to the whiteness of the paper as a continuous plane traversed but not broken into by the lines.

Ingres may even distort a sitter under the pressure of his internal pantheon and its strange morphology: *M. Leblanc* (illustration 89), in a sketch where the break between transcriptive registers is already pronounced, is irrealised still further by the deflections wrought by an inner image of the face made pointed, compressed from the sides, with thick eyelids round feline eyes; an image responsible for similar distortions in the cat-like lovers in *Paolo and Francesca* (illustration 90) and in Henry's elfin countenance in *Don Pedro of Toledo Kissing the Sword of Henry IV*. Such disavowal of presence is necessarily more striking in a portrait sketch than in a history painting. By virtue of its rapidity of execution, the sketch is temporally congruent with the time of viewing, and the velocity

89　Ingres, *M. Leblanc*

of the glance; by virtue of its connection with the fashion plate, to which Ingres adds his own acute sensitivity to changing fashion, it possesses a force of contemporaneity which curiously persists even when a particular fashion has passed from favour: even today it is hard not to sense the *chic* of Ingre's sitters. Exactly because of the inherent tendency of the portrait sketch towards an aesthetic of presence, this medium enables Ingres to state his primary innovation as a painter – the concept of desire-in-the-image – with exceptional cogency. But the sketch is nevertheless limited by its usual estrangement of sitter from the background. In Ingres' 'tourist' sketches, the sitter poses in front of the city much as in a photographer's studio the sitter is posed against a conventional backdrop. For deeper exploration of the portrait form we must turn to his portrait painting, and to the peculiar relation Ingres establishes between the sitter and his or her environment.

90   Ingres, *Paolo and Francesca*

The idea that the portrait must imply a surrounding ecology is part of Ingres' legacy from David. David's sitters are adapted to a contextual *Umwelt* that is highly social, indeed political. Although *Mme Chalgrin* is shown without any of the usual domestic appurtenances by which the portraitist customarily establishes the nuances of social place and rank, even that absence of props is laden with implication (illustration 91): her environment is Paris, the Paris of the Robespierre régime, where no citizen can afford to secede from the polis into the seclusion of the home. Her costume is stridently republican: over a dress of black, colour of the Third Estate, the white scarf and blue sash combine against the vibrant red of the background to form the tricolour of the Revolution. Her strained, impassive expression and the resignation of her folded arms indicate acceptance of the changing times; it is almost the attitude of a person under arrest, of a person awaiting sentence. The people's justice is swift and time is precious: David's lightning

91   David, *Portrait of Mme Chalgrin*

execution indicates that the citizen hardly has the time, any more, to sit for or to paint such a thing as a portrait. In all of David's portraits of this period one senses the urgency and distraction of political events: life is happening all on the outside, and the inwardness of the sitter is not at all self-contained or a resource, but rather a reflection, of contingent interest, of the crucial outer events. In the later portrait of *Mme Sériziat* (illustration 92) we can see that the time of danger has passed. Thermidor is over, yet the significance of the countryside is still that, there, one might escape the pressure of events in Paris. Mme Sériziat has been gathering flowers, but her rustic gaiety is assumed; it is that of a city-dweller on holiday, at a *second* residence. The economy is still in ruins – the material of her dress is plain and shows quite primitive stitchwork; opulence can be expressed only through accessories – sash, headband – but the point is that it can and that it will be expressed, openly. Her smile (like that of her husband in the painting's

92 David, *Portrait of Mme Sériziat*

partner, also in the Louvre) shows the relief of those who managed to spend the fatal summer of 1794 on estates away from Paris and who are now able to return in safety. Domesticity, which before had been an outlawed refuge, is once again a pleasure: it is the era of the Directoire. And as we have seen, the *Three Ladies of Ghent* (illustration 55) demonstrates the persistence of David's belief that the nature of the city and the polis is the key to his sitters' inner world: a narrow provincial milieu, jealously guarding appearances; dour, self-repressed individuals, passing from a youth prematurely aged into sour respectability.

Ingres' subjects are not at all like this. Nothing in the outer world troubles or distracts their sleek, feline self-sufficiency: they are sensualist, and they are relaxed. Where David had placed domesticity in a tense relation to the polis, Ingres cuts domestic space off from the political outside. His sitters are not of the nobility and cannot display, like those of Thomas Lawrence in England, the confidence or the authority of an *ancien régime*. Seeking compensation within four walls, in an interior space where we will find no windows or outer doors, the body surrounds itself with objects that fall within the body's immediate orbit: gloves, fans, shawls, rings, necklaces, bracelets, watches and their chains, lorgnettes, the 'personal effects' that give to the new bourgeoisie its limited sense of earthly permanence. All these objects have been consecrated by the body in an intimate contact, and the fabrics which that body prefers are those – velvet, plush – that preserve the impression of every touch, the shawls and silks whose patterns and reflective folds change with and amplify the least movement of the body in its domestic confinement, the satin pillows whose depressions and indentations record and dramatise the weight and contour of the body against which they press (illustration 93). The historical period covered by Ingres' portraiture, and as much in France as in England, is affected by a mania for framing the perquisites of everyday life: for pocket watches and for slippers, for plants and for china, for cutlery and for pianos, covers and cases are sought. In Ingres, the bourgeois body is shown as having developed a kind of casing that embeds it and tends its traces, and the portrait itself becomes a record of this casing for the person, or rather its further extension, since the portrait too records and preserves the body's traces, and hung within the domestic space its status is exactly on a par with the rest of the encasement.

The body is caressed, almost cocooned, by its environment, or better, its enwrapment. Amplified, this enwrapment becomes the seraglio, and the *gemütlich* comfort of *Mme de Senonnes* (illustration 94) will be the voluptuous languor of the odalisques, in their easeful interfusion with their surroundings, across the channels of sense. In the greatest of Ingres' female portraits, the voluptuous harmony between person and personal encasement shows us the origin of his orientalism in the plush interiors of the Parisian town house, but as with the odalisques, this imagery of sensualism and presence is broken apart. The body of Mme de Senonnes is bizarre, incongruous. We have already mentioned the impossibility of her face, a featureless screen on to which facial characteristics are tiltedly projected; but let us also mention her hands (illustration 95). Less famous than those of Thetis or of Mme Moitessier, they are no less strange: thinned out and lengthened at the fingertips, then unboned, then highlighted with bright, strangely mismatched rings, they too echo invertebrate or sub-aquatic life. The distorted hands of Thetis had been balanced by the unreal anatomy of Jupiter, and anyway legitimated by precedents in Pompeian and Herculanean painting, and in the cameo. Here the distortion has no pretext, for Mme de Senonnes is not a visionary goddess, but a hostess whose social generosity has been extended, as we see in the visiting card tucked into the mirror-frame, to her guest, the painter. Ingres' undermining of presence, in the bourgeois por-

93 Ingres, *Portrait of Mme Marcotte de Sainte Marie*

traits, is all the more disconcerting since his own persona is that of a polite caller; the placid ease of the bourgeois interior is invaded by an oneiric quality that nevertheless still observes the etiquette of the visit. Even the most intimate zones of the bourgeois body's encasement are recast in terms of Ingres' playful collisions of two dimensions and three: the shawl, a planar surface which, when crumpled, irretrievably obliterates its two-dimensional design; the rings whose solid curves Ingres collapses into lines stretched across fingers that have lost their grip on the third dimension; the cushions whose high reflectiveness exaggerates the impress on their surface of the sitter's volume and weight – all these familiar items of daily life become puns, like the sitter's countenance, on dimensional interface.

In quattrocento space, the relationship of object to space had been one of finely calibrated location, and two dimensions and three had dovetailed exactly, through the laws of perspective: a

94   Ingres, *Portrait of Mme de Senonnes*

two-dimensional plane could look on to depth, like a looking-glass. For Ingres, the looking-glass is the place where bi- and tri-dimensionality come completely unstuck – where they *cleave*. The head of Mme de Senonnes, in her mirror-reflection, tilts *forwards* and *down*, but the 'real' head looks *out* and slightly *up*. In the virtual image, the ear-ring seems small, with only two links: the 'real' ear-ring is pendant, encrusted, and large. Under the old régime of presence, the mirror-image had served to confirm and to solidify the world it reflected – the mirror-image expanded implications present in its original, in the manner of corollary or inference; but here the viewer cannot easily derive the mirror-image from its alleged 'original': so, far from unifying or stabilising the interior space, the mirror bisects it, and the viewer is faced with two versions of the same sitter which do not correspond. Viewing must attend to (it cannot ignore) a gap between images, must attend to their mutual displacement, and to the lack which their discrepancy

95 Ingres, *Portrait of Mme de Senonnes* (detail)

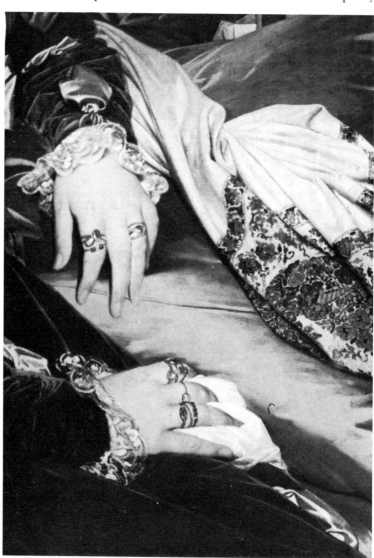

opens up. The mirror fractures the sensory and *gemütlich* encasement of the bourgeois body, just as the painting's surface divides it into disparate allegiances: to design and to volume; to flatness and to depth. Even the framing comes to trouble the spatial coherence. With David's three-quarter length portraits the mind hardly troubles to calculate the possible extension of the sitter's body below the lower edges of the frame: it is taken for granted that the space represented within the painting extends beyond the frame, that it is continuous with what we see, and that it has merely been abridged. Here, the existence of a space beyond the lower edge of *Mme de Senonnes* is insisted on by the lines of the dress, which ask for protraction, as does the vertical bar of the looking-glass: but having posited an excluded lower space, the painting then says nothing about it, and instead of abridgement the lower edge implies a continuation that is at the same time impossible to follow.

Comparable distortions of presence persist in the portrait of the *Comtesse d'Haussonville* (illustration 96).[15] The interior is well stocked with its comfortable encasements: the table-ledge, duly draped and fringed; the chairs, deeply upholstered; the plants, twice enclosed; the body itself, corseted, bedecked, beringed. That the domestic refuge is sequestered from the outer world is eloquently expressed by the visiting cards: not slotted into the mirror as a permanent advertisement of social currency (the style of the 'bourgeoisie'), but discarded and placed to one side (the style of 'nobility'). The social distance between painter and sitter is much greater here than in the portrait of Mme de Senonnes, but the physical and imaginary intimacy is more intense. The end result of Ingres' long quest to achieve a balanced design for this difficult and asymmetrical figure is that the image of the Comtesse d'Haussonville is perfectly coherent in two dimensions, on the flatness of the picture plane, where the authority of the composition (almost) persuades us to overlook such anatomical aberration as the Comtesse's braceleted arm, which moves in from the elbow not to the right shoulder but rather to the right breast; or the concealed side of the Comtesse's neck, which (if we judge from the mirror) spreads out into the shoulder almost at once, a short neck on a high shoulder (whereas in the 'real' Comtesse there is no right shoulder at all). Yet the effect of this two-dimensional coherence is that the figure cannot be rotated in space, and when Ingres does rotate the Comtesse, by means of the mirror, the virtual image seems to reflect a different person, of different height, with a different coiffure, and almost wearing a different dress. Attending closely to the mirror-image, one finds still more evidence of fracture: a yellow tulip with closed petals is answered by a white and open tulip in the glass; the red carnation may have its reflection, but not the pink; a flower-container may be reflected, but not its handles. Certain objects – the central jardinière, the binoculars – seem unable to reflect, while certain flowers seem to exist *only* in their reflection. Mirrors do not behave in this way: but desire does, and it emerges that Ingres responds to the Comtesse d'Haussonville as he responds to an odalisque: a being in promised interfusion with her sensory environment, from whom the promise is then called back. The environment and its creature are sundered, where the disconnection of 'figure' from 'background' signals the entry of desire and lack. The more the viewer tries to restore plenitude to the image by adjusting real and virtual images towards unity, the greater the experience of interval between them.

Thematically, in this particular painting, the interval corresponds to the instability that exists between a social relationship of distance (an afternoon call) and a relationship of imaginary

96 Ingres, *Portrait of the Comtesse d'Haussonville*

intimacy (Ingres' intimacy with this figure and this pose). Some of the contradiction between the two may be resolved in terms of polite compliment – the caller congratulates his hostess on her appearance; but the flattery is a matter of the surface, and Ingres eyes his sitter in ways that contravene the social code. The pose of the Comtesse establishes a middle distance between the formal and the confidential: it combines charm (or coyness) with detachment, but it brings them together, defining the woman as one who has a special right to unite these qualities. Ingres enters into the fusion of the pose and 'disambiguates' it: he moves in too close – the charm or coyness becomes an intimacy in which Ingres annexes his sitter into his inner pantheon; and he moves back too far – the detachment becomes calculation, the cold gaze of the artist–surgeon. In each of these extremes the woman loses her reality, in the sense of the role she establishes for herself, as mistress of the middle distance, controller of the distances. Ingres inflicts on the Comtesse the hallmark distortions of his arousal, or at least of his secret interest. Here the theme of encasement, of drapery, corset, of the screening gown, corresponds to a social mask, where observance of the forms may usefully cover the explicitness of desire. At the same time, Ingres draws back from his inner vision of the Comtesse into an ascesis or gaze of meditation that contemplates in equanimity the inner image *and* the outer world; he observes in action the process by which, in his imagination, the inner and the outer are connected; and he paints not from a warm response, or from the kindling of desire at a spark from the outer world, but from much further back (or 'in'), from a point of *self*-observation that records how, in his own subjective process, a staid and aristocratic hostess can galvanise the inner pantheon.

Ingres' celebrated *froideur* is genuinely chilling because it is not simply the detachment of a male predator eyeing his prey; it is that of an ascesis so extreme that it has gone behind the scenic stage of the imagination to examine the mechanism, the actual structure of desire. It is true that the vantage point of self–observation had been achieved at least as early as the *Jupiter and Thetis*, but there Ingres had concentrated exclusively on the sexual theatre, which he portrayed in a spirit of humour, understanding, and excitement. Here the viewpoint is certainly as inward, but the vista includes both the inner sexual arena *and* the outer arena of bourgeois and everyday life. Ingres sees both: observes how, in his specialised imagination, they interact; and what he paints is the interaction. We underestimate the portrait of the Comtesse d'Haussonville if we think of it only as a place of juncture between propriety and male desire, as a piece of seduction; it is far more inturned than that, deeper, and as an analysis of desire in visual subjectivity it is implacable. What is essential in this work is its relentlessness: Ingres may indeed combine, in Baudelaire's phrase, the gaze of the lover and of the surgeon, but the object of that gaze is less Woman than his own subjectivity, painted in open self-dissection.

VI

It is with some trepidation that I approach the last work by Ingres to take its place in the present discussion (the critic, too, has his portion of anxiety): *Mme Moitessier* (illustration 97). It cannot help provoking a response in superlatives: Ingres' supreme production; the great lyric image of Europe in the era of high capitalism. I suspect that no single painting of Ingres speaks so directly to the twentieth, and particularly to the late twentieth century, when the lessons of abstraction have been fully assimilated. Indeed, one advantage of the immense prestige which at present attends this work is that through the aura of reverence we can sense some of the

97   Ingres, *Mme Moitessier*

emotion which in the period of Ingres surrounded the paintings of
Raphael, whose reputation is currently in such dark eclipse that it
tends to make Ingres' own dependence on Raphael largely
incomprehensible. The relationship between tradition and the
individual talent is, in the case of this painting, highly complex.
Not that its sources are difficult to trace – essentially it is a
Herculanean painting (illustration 2), reformulated in the idiom of
Raphael by means of a little-known and unfinished Raphael
design rather wretchedly worked up by his studio (*Joanna of
Aragon*; illustration 98), and translated into the fashions and bodily
encasements of the Second Empire. What counts in Ingres'
relationship to his precursors is that now the relation actually
works in reverse: so far from its being the case that the sources press
in on the painter as a weight that must somehow be lifted, the only
significance the viewer in fact can find in the Herculanean painting
and in *Joanna of Aragon* comes in back-projection from *Mme
Moitessier*: in themselves the earlier works have no independent
strength. The movement of reversal is crucial. One might argue

98 Workshop of Raphael, *Joanna
of Aragon*

that the transformations have been so radical that to place the 'sources' next to *Mme Moitessier* can only be an exercise in creative psychology, in mysteries of pollenation that need not concern us as we look at the final result: but this would, I think, be wrong. *Mme Moitessier* may recall Herculaneum and *Joanna of Aragon* only in the mind of art historians, but those exact sources are themselves treated by the painting as synecdoches, parts for the whole: the provenances invoked by the portrait are in the first place, and as a deliberately generalised category, Antiquity, and in the second, also generalised from the specific, Raphael. Antiquity, Raphael, *les bonnes doctrines*: *Mme Moitessier* – and despite those vertiginous qualities which engage the twentieth-century eye – is still and primarily an orthodox and indeed a doctrinaire painting of the French Academy. Yet so complete is Ingres' absorption of Antiquity and of Raphael that the tyranny of time and of latecoming is almost undone in a trope one might designate as *reversal*.

This particular trope or turning on tradition is much used by the later Delacroix, and I will be exploring its structure in detail later on. Here one may state its principal aim and effect, of so capturing and retaining the styles of the predecessors, while at the same time subjecting them to massive revisionary movement, that the latecoming artist seems actually to achieve priority over the past: if we look at Ingres' Herculanean and Raphaelesque sources, it becomes possible, for just a moment, to believe that time is flowing backwards, and that Ingres is being *imitated by his ancestors*.[16] It is an effect that can be achieved only when an artist has so completely disciplined himself in his tradition that he understands fully the nature of his own style's departures and returns within tradition's compass, and in Ingres it comes only with age: though the trope need not automatically be associated with resignation. The degree to which *Mme Moitessier* invokes tradition can be gauged by comparison with work that aims only at contemporary effect, such as the social portraiture of Frederico da Madrazo. Both Ingres and Madrazo are acutely responsive to the implications of clothing and of posture as markers of rank and social persona; both are fascinated by the modernity of modernity; and both are interested in exploring the uncertainties of distance, associated with a conception of the feminine perhaps peculiar to this period, that come from a simultaneous insistence on aloofness, and on physical intimacy or invitation. But the freshness and immediacy of execution so vivid in Frederico da Madrazo obtain only in certain limited aspects of Ingres' portraiture: here, in the jewellery, the fan, and especially in the dress of Mme Moitessier, rapidly and effortlessly captured, and firmly situated in the modes of a particular time, the mid 1850s. The upper body of Mme Moitessier is painted in an entirely different register (for which we will find no counterpart in Madrazo). Ingres began to paint his sitter in 1844.

Her dress is the work of a week, or a day; her body took Ingres twelve years to perfect.

The result of such prolonged labour is not only, of course, the fabulous hand (*squid, orchid, hydra*), but a clash of transcriptive registers that resounds throughout the painting (and at this point Ingres is strangely close to Vermeer). The notation for the dress is literalist – each floral spray has been precisely copied, where the complex patterning of the fabric guarantees that there has been a minimum of intervention on Ingres' part: the distortion of the rosettes through each pleat and fold cannot have been calculated and therefore obey no command other than high-fidelity registration. The face and the arms of Madame Moitessier exhibit, by contrast, a maximum of intervention: the image has been purged and repurged, painted, erased, overpainted and re-erased, reduced through unending distillations which conclude in a form whose centrality is achieved by elimination of everything that is contingent, accidental, or immediately alive. The arms and face retain all the colour but none of the radiance or vibrancy of real flesh: this is tinted ivory, not skin over bone, and indeed Mme Moitessier is one of the least vertebrate or skeletally supported of Ingres' women: there is no sensation whatever of the stretch of skin over muscle, or of skin as integument; it is pure contour. The distance between the high-fidelity notation (the dress) and the low-fidelity or laconic notation is then repeated behind Mme Moitessier in her reflection (illustration 99), a purgation of purgation where form is reduced almost to glyph, to the mere possibility of form. This brings the levels of notation or registration up to three, but (as in Vermeer) what is striking is that they are three separate and distinct grids governing local provinces of the image without *interaction*. The discrepancy between real and reflected image is vast – the only clue, for example, that Mme Moitessier wears a scarlet ribbon over her lace headdress is a tiny splash of red at the edge of the 'real' image's hair (a detail alas lost in monochrome reproduction). There is no way that the uncanny hand, with its independent fingers, can match the clenched fist of the reflection; nor is it possible that a reflection in profile can easily be derived from a head that is turned by less than a quarter. The key area, however, is the *juncture* of the real and the reflected images, for now Ingres introduces a fourth register for the gilded framework of the mirror, an elliptical, short-hand notation: in this register there is actual omission of visual information, where the omission cannot be ascribed (as it might still be in the case of the reflection) simply to 'change of focus' (or to the dimming of reflective metal). The zone in and around the mirror brings the divergent registers together in outright discord, and if we scan outward from this zone the entire image deconstructs itself: the spectator cannot even find a viewpoint, and must occupy at least two positions – at eye-level with Madame Moitessier and directly facing her; and (to perceive the reflection at such distance from its 'original') far to the right, and possibly outside the right edge of the frame.

It is a brilliant and an eerie performance. Having made the traditional promise of portraiture, to resurrect the living presence of the world, Ingres produces this fissile and disruptive master-work, the most evacuated of his odalisques. The viewer cannot hold it, fuse it, possess it: to each glance of possession it responds with a shift in temporality, in register, in viewpoint, in a vertigo of displacements that return the viewer to her or his own desire, to the body in dispossession. Every attempt to reproduce a plenary world is an attempt to overcome desire by holding and framing the flux into a form where it can be fixed and possessed (as a 're'-presentation); and nowhere is the urge to banish desire more evident than in the Zeuxian gaze of Western realism. Ingres' work,

99 Ingres, *Mme Moitessier* (detail)

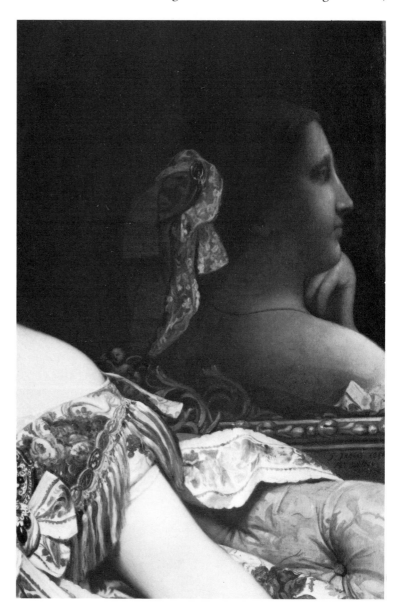

and despite its protestations of orthodoxy, runs deeply counter to that Zeuxian ambition. Presence is always in trouble, in his work; and it is by tending and cultivating desire, by (a)voiding representation, that he works. In the radicalism of his innovation, the artist with whom Ingres at times seems to claim spiritual kinship is Picasso (and particularly if we look at the reflected head of Mme Moitessier). But his real kinship is with Delacroix, though both men disavowed it; and it is to Delacroix that we now turn.

6 *Desire in the Bourbon Library*

Nel mezzo del cammin   Dante

I

AT THIS POINT I have had to face a difficult decision. Within the
confines of the present book it is not possible to discuss the work of
Delacroix in its entirety. Discussion must be selective; and I have
had to choose between concentrating on Delacroix's easel paintings, and Delacroix's *peinture murale*. I regret the choice; but having
to choose, I choose the most important of the decorative cycles, the
ceiling of the Library of the Chamber of Deputies in the Palais
Bourbon: and this on grounds of neglect. The neglect is not
wholesale: we have Maurice Sérullaz's excellent *Les Peintures
murales de Delacroix* (1963), which reproduces the Library cycle in
detail, and supplies careful documentation of its commission and
production.[1] But even the admirable Sérullaz neglects the work of
interpretation. It is not part of his brief; and though such omission
no doubt has its rationale it is still to be regretted, for it is part of a
general critical neglect of the later Delacroix.

Delacroix's major Salon entries of the 1820s and 1830s remain *in
situ* in the Louvre: they are impossible, as it were, to avoid. Slightly
more determination is needed if the viewer is to inspect Delacroix's
murals at Saint-Sulpice, but an altogether more forceful sense of
pilgrimage is required by Delacroix's decorations in the Salon du
Roi and the Bibliothèque de la Chambre des Députés at the Palais
Bourbon, and at the Luxembourg. The Bourbon Library presents
the pilgrim with difficulties all its own. Even when the hazards of
access have been overcome, arduous conditions of viewing are
encountered: poor and at times appalling lighting interferes with
clear perception; the images are so placed that the viewer's body is
in constant torsion, straining to take the Library cycle in as a whole:
the hush of trespass inhibits the free movement of the glance, while
the dead weight of bureaucratic pomp encourages the sensation
that the viewer is an interloper in sanctuaries of power and
privilege. Photography removes some of these difficulties but
introduces others: the cycle in the Bourbon Library is extremely
expensive to reproduce as a total series, with the result that
favoured items – *Attila Destroying Italy and the Arts, Orpheus
Civilising the Greeks*, and *The Education of Achilles* – tend to be
quoted out of context and divested of the complexity they possess
as members of a highly intricate semantic pattern; the removal of
the physical difficulties of viewing, the torsion, the partial and

fragmentary views, deeply disturbs the primacy of the glance over the simultaneous prospect or gaze, and undoes the serial logic of the cycle.

To help redress the balance, the present chapter will attempt a comprehensive reading of the whole series of twenty-two paintings that are bounded at one end by *Orpheus* and at the other by *Attila*. To orient the reader, a diagrammatic map is supplied, yet the reader is asked to regard the map as a guide of limited usefulness, for what it necessarily brackets out are the physical constraints imposed upon the body in its actual viewing practice. The reader must imagine himself transported to the Library itself (illustration 100). He is under surveillance by guards: the Library is an adjunct of the state, and the *képi* gives assurance of order. To counter the sense of trespass he must adopt the attitude of the civil subject and gaze with judicious respect at a series of paintings which, even if he possesses photographic memory, he will not be able to take in as a whole. In line behind security ropes, real or metaphorical, he must now step into the thoroughfare that passes from Orpheus to Attila, and back.

II

Surely it is clear what the polarity of Orpheus and Attila intends: the fragility of civilisation (Kenneth Clark: 'No one realised better than Delacroix that we had got through by the skin of our teeth'[2]). The security of culture must be maintained by force, since force can destroy it; and again the viewer catches sight of the *képi* near Orpheus if the guard is in the south, near Attila if the guard is in the north.

For Orpheus is seen not only as the harbinger of the arts, but of humanity, and at his advent the species remains ab-original: the first men, thus origin; yet deficient, or aberrant. They crouch, they huddle, they squat, and in the case of those nearest to the viewer, the anality of their posture must surely indicate the most primitive physical and psychical organisation (illustration 101). Surrounded by animals, they retain their animal characteristics, and their primarily acoustic existence (marked by the faun-like or satyr-like ear of the figure opposite Orpheus) has not yet been shattered at the eye by the symbolic characters Orpheus points to on his scroll (which is what his lyre has become). This substitution of scroll for lyre is an interesting modification of the traditional iconographic association of Orpheus with music: 'Orpheus came forth so skilled in the Greek language that he composed in it verses of marvellous poetry, with which he tamed the barbarians through their ears; for though already organised in nations they were not restrained by their eyes from setting fire to cities full of marvels.'[3] It was through lyric that Orpheus had tamed the savages, yet inherent in the

North

HEMICYCLE B
Attila Destroying Italy and the Arts

CUPOLA I: SCIENCE
1 *The Death of Pliny the Elder*
2 *Aristotle Describing the Animals Sent by Alexander*
3 *Hippocrates Refusing the Gifts of the King of Persia*
4 *Archimedes Killed by the Soldier*

CUPOLA II: PHILOSOPHY
1 *Herodotus Questioning the Tradition of the Mages*
2 *Astronomy Invented by the Shepherds of Chaldaea*
3 *The Suicide of Seneca*
4 *Socrates and his Daemon*

CUPOLA III: LAW
1 *Numa and Egeria*
2 *Lycurgus Consulting the Pythoness*
3 *Cicero Denouncing Verras*
4 *Demosthenes Addressing the Waves*

CUPOLA IV: THEOLOGY
1 *The Tribute Money*
2 *The Death of John the Baptist*
3 *The Expulsion from Eden*
4 *The Captivity in Babylon*

CUPOLA V: POETRY
1 *Alexander with the Poems of Homer*
2 *Ovid among the Barbarians*
3 *The Education of Achilles*
4 *Hesiod and the Muse*

HEMICYCLE A
Orpheus Civilising the Greeks

Entrance

South

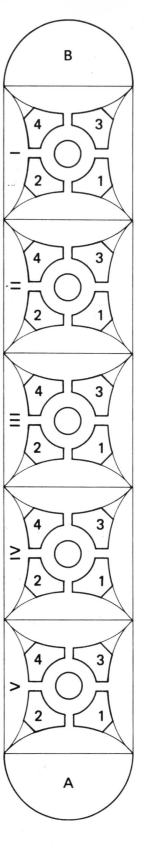

Library of the Chamber of Deputies, Palais Bourbon

concept of the Lyric is an ambiguity as to the sensory positioning of lyric form. The Lyric's fusion of words with music hovers between eye and ear, yet the substitution of the scroll for the lyre effectively proposes the viewer as one who, like Orpheus, is master of prospect and vision: it was through the sounds into which Orpheus translated the words of the Lyric that he penetrated the acoustic world of the barbarians: yet higher than lyric-as-lyre is lyric-as-sign, signs for the eye, and it is from this score or scroll of signs that Orpheus *reads*. The revision of iconographic emphases, brought about by the substitution of scroll for lyre, establishes the viewer as one who is conjoined with Orpheus through the eye, and separated from the barbarians, at the ear; and the revision is an interesting one, since its alteration or tilting of the lyric balance between eye and ear begins to draw attention to the incongruity of *Orpheus* as

100   Library of the Chamber of Deputies, Palais Bourbon

founder of a civilisation that is being described in terms of vision, as image. The lyre/scroll substitution functions as a *lapsus* in which an initially or potentially subversive aspect of Orpheus – the non-representability of his music in the image – is overcome by transforming Orpheus into a manipulator of visible signs, like the painter; yet the *lapsus* also reopens the possibility of Orpheus as eluding the representation, since what he is transmitting to the barbarians – sound – cannot be received by the viewer. Staying with the official level of the image, this underside of the *lapsus* does not yet disturb the theme of Foundation, and I shall postpone its exploration until later; justifying this by moving to the ways in which Orpheus-as-eye is held in place by the polar image at the opposite end of the Library, Attila as destroyer of the arts (illustration 102).

Which arts? The shifting position of Lyric reappears, for the figure closest to Attila holds both lyre and scroll. Again the balance is tilted towards the eye, since the themes of conflagration (at the right) and of broken architecture (at the left) indicate Attila as iconoclast, destroyer of the visible world and its visible signs; an indication confirmed by the figure of the woman who grasps the *caduceus*, attribute of Mercury, god of signs, who through words had also, like Orpheus, tamed the barbarians.[4] For painting, the 'arts of Italy' must mean the visual arts; and since the visual arts of

101   Delacroix, *Orpheus Civilising the Greeks*

Antiquity have indeed been destroyed and no painter can represent them, the meaning of the 'arts of Italy' must pass, by default, to the second Italy and to the arts of the Roman Church. It was in the Vatican that Raphael had painted Attila and his barbaric hordes, and to Raphael the painting makes direct allusion, taking from Raphael's painting of Attila the burning city at the right, the equestrian depiction of Attila, and taking from *Fire in the Borgo*, also in the Vatican, the germ of the figure group at the extreme left, where the older generation is carried on the back of the young.[5] Like those savages who 'were not restrained by their eyes from setting fire to cities full of marvels', Attila is a figure of *blind* fury, of unseeing; and by representing civilisation in terms of the eye – the visible lyre, the written scroll, the burning City which, through the Papacy and through Raphael eventually had restored to it its lost visual splendours – the painting effectively disavows Attila, the blindness at its centre. Yet there is again an underside to the disavowal, for though unseeing Attila is himself the most completely and arrestingly visible of the painting's figures; and while this may confirm his 'capture' – the fully visual representation of the one who destroyed the visual arts has to be in some sense an overcoming of his blind energy – it also unsettles it, since the painting (for its own organisation) *needs* this overpowering outline of Attila, and from the realm of the visible it therefore sanctions the splendour of his violence and his iconoclasm, which indeed, as the painting's own energetic centre, ultimately justifies the image.

102 Delacroix, *Attila Destroying Italy and the Arts*

Opposition is probably the strongest container of meaning, as it is perhaps the strongest generator of meaning;[6] and by opposing an Orpheus who masters vision as well as music to an Attila who destroys the visible, Delacroix locks the two together as polar complements: Foundation, and Holocaust. Yet the same device can be found equally to reinforce the excluded, anomalous, or subversive connotations of each image, by exactly the same process of mutual definition. On their own both *Orpheus* and *Attila* might be images with a strong official meaning that is confusingly yet only slightly *blurred* by connotations which cannot be fitted into the official text: if the works were to be taken singly, those connotations would be marginal, haphazard, and discountable. But the polarity of *Orpheus* and *Attila* raises that margin of surplus meaning into full view through a figure of chiasma: the excluded meanings of one are heightened and confirmed by the excluded meanings of the other. To put this another way: there are certain elements in *Orpheus* that question the legitimacy of Orpheus as representative of civilisation defined in terms of the visible. Music, and sound, disturb the coherence of Orpheus as bearer of culture, and form an excluded counter-sense in which Orpheus-as-music rejoins the savages as creatures of a primarily acoustic world. On its own, the counter-sense of *Orpheus* might be disregarded: but the same pattern is present in *Attila*. His blindness and apartness from the visual world take up the otherwise stray or unsponsored meanings of the Orphic music and articulate them at the patent, official level of *Attila*: the sanctioned theme of blindness activates and emphasises the otherwise inert or negligible theme of Orphic music; and this reflex action, in which the patent level of one polar image energises the covert level of its partner, then redoubles. The problematic status of the Orphic music challenges the coherence of a representation of Attila's blindness which depends, for its power, on the splendour of this violence, which officially the image of course condemns; but which it cannot help also seeming to celebrate.

The cycle at the Bourbon Library is made up of these two paintings, *Attila* and *Orpheus*, placed in individual half-domes; and twenty subordinate images, placed in circular groups of four, inset into each of the five domes that stretch between the northern and the southern end-points. If one assumes that the viewer will begin viewing the cycle by examining and mentally juxtaposing the end-points, one must also say that whatever conclusions the viewer may reach as a result of the juxtaposition, they will still be provisional, for the viewer knows – even if he is not actually inspecting the subsidiary images – that his viewing has not yet taken into account the paintings in the five intervening domes: no matter how astute his interpretation of *Attila* and of *Orpheus* may have been, the moment of closing that interpretation must be postponed. Moreover, when the viewer scans the cycle, whatever position in space he takes up, he must also be aware that the subsidiary images are so placed that he can never see them all at once: if he stands at the north, only the southern surfaces of the overhead domes are visible; if he stands at the south, only the northern surfaces can be seen. What this physical constraint imposes is a state of *perpetual* postponement – the opposition of *Attila* and *Orpheus*, images which must imperatively be 'taken' together, but which absolutely cannot be *seen* together, persists throughout the cycle.[7] The repercussions of this split (between physical vision and conceptual organisation) are vast: they sound in every register of the painting; and indeed as one progresses through the cycle and begins to sense the orchestration of its various registers, a principle of anticipated unison begins to emerge, as the most tantalising of the cycle's many prospects.

III

Let us suppose a meticulous and schematically minded observer who works the series from end to end, in the manner of the ideal Sistine viewer. Nearest to *Attila* he will find the four scenes which make up the dome of Science. In the case of *Archimedes Killed by the Soldier* (illustration 103) it is clear that the figures function as direct transformations of the cycle's protagonists: Archimedes with his scroll, attribute of Orpheus; the soldier with his spear, attribute of Attila. In so far as the *Orpheus : Attila* opposition remains stable, then the import of the image retains that original clarity: the philosopher, surrounded by all the appurtenances of sightedness –

103 Delacroix, *Archimedes Killed by the Soldier*

books, parchment, wax tablets, lectern – belongs to the domain of civilisation and visuality; the soldier, blocking the window, aperture of light, and almost piercing it, is the bringer of Attila's blind violence. Yet the opposition does not of itself possess sufficient stability to stay anchored in its original sense, for Archimedes, despite his unquestionable nobility, displays all the symptoms of a chronic self-negligence. His mantle slips, un-noticed, towards what one would term the ground if the space were not itself so precarious: the whole study, with its lectern and treacherously balanced scroll, its perches of ledge and step, and its irrational perspective, plunges down also. The slackening of otherwise powerful muscle, compared with the vigorous torsion of the aggressor, indicts him as dangerously absorbed in medi-tation, where thought is the body's enemy: this is a body debilitated and ultimately destroyed by the mind, and the eyes of Archimedes, to which all vitality has apparently devolved, cannot guard even their own architectural counterpart, the window, while the eyes of the soldier, lined with black, are lit with the vigilance of an animal predator. Such inclination of the balance against Archimedes certainly alters or reverses the official sense of the image, but the reversal does not end here, for it flows backwards to interpret the images of Orpheus and Attila: the children or disciples of Orpheus and bearers of his scroll lose, through his agency, the feral strength that had been theirs before his advent; the children of Attila are less the destroyers of alien culture than the excluded or preterite bearers of the physical strength which Orpheus had outlawed, and philosophy had ignored.

Reversal is not confined, however, to this backward and 'revisionist' direction, since if we move from *Archimedes* across the dome to its counterpart, *Archimedes* is found to revise also into its future. At first sight *Aristotle Describing the Animals Sent by Alexander* is a simple corrective to the flaw of *Archimedes* – its disjunction of power and knowledge: in the philosopher who is also tutor to Alexander, power and knowledge are brought together and realigned (illustration 104). This complementary revision accords with the notion of balance that is beginning to emerge in the cycle's polar images: Attila returns the feral power Orpheus had banished; Orpheus enforces the symbolic order which Attila destroys. Yet whatever provisional stability is established by the ideas of supplement and equilibrium, that stability is again derailed by the central action of the painting, the gaze of Aristotle on the youth who brings him the mountain-goat. The power Aristotle possesses, though benign with regard to Archimedes, is that of despotism: the elevated position of foot and knee evokes the classical throne-posture of 'the East' (such as we see it, for example, in Delacroix's *Justinian*); the beard and inclination of the head, tilting with the *numen* or nod of power, recall the figure of Delacroix's Sardanapalus; Aristotle is attended

by the emblems of knowledge as death – the animal skull, the
gleaming shells, and the pen which now wields the power of
Alexander's, of the soldier's, and, as distant yet distinct reverberation, of Attila's sword. The youth, whose face expresses the pain
of a wounded incomprehension, is as vulnerable before this power
as the goat and the gazelle whose skulls may shortly hang on
Aristotle's wall: and by rhyming the torsion of his body against
that of the goat, the image presents the youth as an equivalent
animal, captured, interrogated and dissected into script by
Aristotle's knowledge-as-power (Aristotle's humanity is evident
only in the look of pity which tempers his necessary cruelty).
Moving back to interpret the 'polar' images, Aristotle activates the
connotational strand which had suggested that the destruction of
animal innocence was the price to be paid for the Orphic scroll, and
in as much as the pen thus signifies the rending asunder of a prior
harmony, it reinterprets Attila as a *transformation* of Orpheus; not
only as avatar of the vengeance and *sparagmos* which feral strength
will turn on Orpheus as his punishment, but as a later vehicle of the
violence already contained in the Orphic enterprise, from its own
beginnings.

Disturbance of the *Attila : Orpheus* polarity continues in the rest
of the first dome, consecrated to Science. *Hippocrates Refusing the
Gifts of the King of Persia* (illustration 105) may officially celebrate
the noble stoicism of the Greek scientists, yet Hippocrates' head
and features are sufficiently similar to those of Archimedes for the
negative aspect of 'refusal', for which Archimedes must pay such a
heavy penalty, to appear here as well, as wilfulness or arrogance;
and since the presence of three ambassadors from the East, with

104   Delacroix, *Aristotle
Describing the Animals Sent by
Alexander*

golden gifts, coffer, and shepherd's crook, inevitably recalls the iconography of the Magi and the Nativity, what Hippocrates is also refusing is religious gnosis. Later in the series, if we choose to follow the present sequence, the Orient will function as a fount of archaic and sacramental knowledge: in denying the East, Hippocrates anticipates the fall of the classical and agnostic world; the golden staff will later become Attila's punishing sword. And as with *Attila*, it is the beauty of barbarism – here in its Sardanapalus aspect of gold, pearl, and naked flesh – which to a considerable extent justifies the image, so that Hippocrates is further rejecting, so to speak, the representation in which he himself appears.

What might in itself be taken to be the virtuous obstinacy of the classical age is darkened further if we move between *Hippocrates* and *The Death of Pliny the Elder* (illustration 106). Pliny is cognate here with Aristotle, and the degree of shifting reversal present in the dome can be gauged when we consider how incongruous it is that Aristotle, rather than Pliny, should be seen writing a Natural History. Yet if Pliny interfuses with Aristotle, then he must submit to the flow of associations from Archimedes and Hippocrates also, and though Pliny's intellectual endeavour can hardly be accused either of arrogance or self-negligence, the excess of his virtue certainly appears as hubristic – he has challenged Vesuvius. Such moral commentary is presented in a subtle guise: the transfer of roles between Pliny and Aristotle accords to Pliny's curiosity a primitive power which makes that curiosity seem a just or worthy challenge to the eruptive power of the volcano: Vesuvius will win,

105   Delacroix, *Hippocrates Refusing the Gifts of the King of Persia*

yet Pliny will survive, through the scroll he is dictating; he will outlast the eruption, by bringing to the natural violence of the world a power of inquisitiveness as enduring and in its fashion as violent (it is the intellect which destroys Pliny's body, and not only the mountain) as anything in nature. In this sense, the figure of Pliny is a transformation both of Orpheus (scroll, script) and of Attila (violence, conflagration), and as the units of meaning slip and reverse around this first dome, corresponding adjustments take place in the hemicycles of its master-images, whose initial and static opposition progressively yields to a dynamic revisionism: what Orpheus or what Attila means will depend on which point within the intervening domes we are presently considering.

106 Delacroix, *The Death of Pliny the Elder*

The principle of revision produces rather more radical slidings of meaning in the second dome (as we go from north to south), dedicated to Philosophy. Seneca was an antique precursor of 'enlightened despotism', and his political alignment with Burrus had ensured that during the period of their alliance, knowledge and power functioned coextensively within the Empire. As a representative of reason 'backed' by state and military power, the figure of Seneca accordingly joins the figure of Aristotle. The period of harmony between intellectual and state power had ended, however, with the accession of Nero, and Seneca's consequent suicide (illustration 107) also aligns with the figure in whom power and knowledge are dissociated, Archimedes. *The Suicide of Seneca* thus sustains at least two quite contradictory readings: a cautionary tale of the ultimate powerlessness of Philosophy in the face of brute power; and a didactic statement of the necessity of joining political power with reason. Which version shall predominate (and both seem equally possible) is determined by the point at which viewing enters and leaves the painting of Seneca: enters it from the first dome, whose images define in advance the value to be ascribed to Seneca's death; and leaves it to cross over to Seneca's co-victim in the oppression of thought by the state, Socrates (illustration 108). The two philosopher–legislators are linked by the fact of their martyrdom – the remaining quadrants of the second dome are devoted to the Eastern question; this natural doubling, combined with the

107   Delacroix, *The Suicide of Seneca*

physical adjacency of the Greek and Roman martyrs, makes it in fact likelier that these two images will interpret each other, overriding the associative threads which lead in from the flanking domes. Yet Socrates' death, subject of intense interest to the Enlightenment, is precisely what Delacroix chooses not to represent. Socrates is shown instead with his Muse.

How shall we take this hovering attendant? To the extent that the Muse functions as a winged Fame, thought is shown as immortal, or at least as transcending physical destiny – which may confirm in *Seneca* the connotation of sacred martyrdom, evident in the suggestion of halo which darkly flickers (as we look closely) behind Seneca's head. What we then see are two martyrdoms, both of which anticipate Christian martyrdom, but still fall short of that, belonging as they do to the pagan and not to the redeemed world. But the 'Muse' is rather more complex than a *Fama*: as *angel*, a spirit back-projected into the pagan world from its Christian future, the 'attendant' *delimits* Socrates' power, in the fashion of the angel in the *Purgatorio* who confines the philosopher–kings to the Valley of the Preoccupied;[8] as *daemon* – the word actually chosen by Delacroix to describe this attendant figure[9] – it exactly questions the 'angelic' nature of Socrates' inspiration, and ambiguates the inspiration as both celestial *and* infernal (a duplicity eloquently communicated in the daemon's face and hand-gesture).[10] For the viewer who still experiences the influence of the cycle's master-images, *Socrates* must seem frankly indecipherable: although Socrates is Orphic in his status as founding philosopher, he is nevertheless attended by a daemon of un-differentiation, a spirit not containable within any of the

108 Delacroix, *Socrates and his Daemon*

relevant sets of oppositions (*pagan:Christian, from above:from below*, as well as, *male:female*). Such exclusion from the differentiated categories of reason belongs more properly to the realm of Attila – but things are not as clear-cut as that.

What one naturally sees here is a 'progressive clarification' of the meaning of the images: one image interprets the next, as well as the one before; and this process of revision can be compared with irony, in which one discourse positions another discourse contained within itself. Yet a notorious feature of irony is that the contained or quoted discourse tends to efface the points of origin – its own origin, the moment at which the citation or quotation begins, as a sub-set of the master-discourse; and the origin of the master-discourse itself, which irony has a capacity also to erase.[11] In terms of the Bourbon cycle, the subsidiary or lesser images tend, through the ambiguity of their own montage, to erase the master-images of Orpheus and Attila which officially contain them; and at the same time they tend to make interminable the generation of meaning which arises from their own montage. Staying with the present example: Socrates' daemon sufficiently participates in both master-images, *Orpheus* and *Attila*, to destabilise the global set; while locally, within the revisionary effects produced by the juxtaposition of *Socrates* with *Seneca*, the daemon so infiltrates Seneca's suicide that one cannot be certain whether the suicide represents the dark folly of a pagan misalliance of power and reason, or a genuinely proleptic martyrdom, anticipating and claiming in advance the laurel, or the halo, of Christian death.

The movement from stable imbrication – all subsidiary images repeating and confirming the terms of the *Orpheus:Attila* polarity – to indeterminate or fluid irony, is repeated throughout the Philosophy series. If Socrates is asking that the cup pass from him, and if Seneca is pictured in terms of ecclesiastical martyrdom, then *Herodotus Questioning the Tradition of the Mages* (illustration 109) and *Astronomy Invented by the Shepherds of Chaldaea* (illustration 110) are clearly caught (somewhere) in the iconography of the Nativity. But how? The relation of this religious discourse to the master-set is far from clear, since it is Attila who belongs to the Christian era; yet Attila is as likely to have wanted the destruction of the texts of Herodotus, and of astronomy, as the destruction of Italy and the Arts. In what is increasingly the dwindling of the global polarity's power of interpretation over the cycle, the viewer's own interpretive activity arises, and here many hermeneutic possibilities open up, each of which promises to re-close the cycle whose container seems now so porous. In the representation of shepherds who are at once barbaric (pearls, skins, naked flesh) and intellectual (inventors of astronomy) there may seem, for example, to be a conscious rapprochement between the forces (the Physical, the Intellectual) which thus far have tended to be mutually exclusive; and this attitude of compromise may seem to persist in Herodotus' return to the archaic and Eastern source of knowledge. But such interpretation, though backed by many cues and clues, has little with which to validate itself. There are indeed few limits to the ingenuity viewing will bring to bear on images that seem to elude the bounds of sense; but the more interesting question is the means by which interpretation *can* authenticate itself here, in the absence of clear anchorage with the cycle itself, and especially from *Orpheus* and *Attila*, its rapidly depolarising end-points.

This question is raised, and forcefully, by the dome's own relation to the iconography of the Church, since the quotation from a discourse to which absolute authority has at least in the past

109 Delacroix, *Herodotus Questioning the Tradition of the Mages*

been attributed (Sacred Iconography) behaves exactly *like* a quest for authentication or validation; one might compare it (tentatively) with the use of biblical quotation which serves to anchor and authorise, for example, the body of discourse known as the sermon. Yet whereas the sermon deliberately and patently invokes Scripture as a court of higher appeal, positioning Scripture above itself and declaring itself as lowly *midrash* or humble sub-set of the Sacred Word, this is hardly the way that Christian iconography is invoked in the dome Delacroix consecrates to Philosophy. Justification for such 'higher appeal' is lacking: why should it be here? None of the figures – Socrates, Seneca, Herodotus, the Chaldaeans – belongs to the Christian world; Orpheus is altogether outside the Christian orbit, and Attila is only questionably within it. Without sanction from *some* element in the master-images, the 'authentication' provided by Christian allusion functions as the mysterious eruption of *another* controlling agency, seeking interpretive power over the images; an eruption strangely evident when, at an altogether arbitrary point in the series (and the contrast here is with the schematic clarity and intellectual sanction of corresponding images in the Sistine Ceiling), we encounter Adam and Eve in Paradise (illustration 115).

This sounding of the echoes of Sacred Iconography could hardly be more unlike the kind of clarity one associates with Michelangelo. Instead of completing the images by allowing them to reverberate in sacred history, the 'echoes' here tend to make the images conspicuously incomplete. They less repeat than they postpone meaning, since although a set of images is invoked which might, conceivably, control and arrest the proliferation of meanings, perhaps in the manner of Christian type and anti-type (Seneca

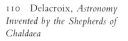

110 Delacroix, *Astronomy Invented by the Shepherds of Chaldaea*

and Socrates the forerunners of Christ, the Chaldaeans and the Mages prototypes of the Nativity), the power of that 'controlling' set emerges only in a secondary guise, as a mysterious alternative to the types and anti-types created in the first place by Orpheus and Attila; it emerges at interstices, at the echoing edge of figures whose primary allegiance must be to other members of the ceiling-cycle; and it emerges therefore *in absentia*, as an *unstated* discourse of control, as opposed to the fully stated, though increasingly unstable, master-discourse of *Attila* and *Orpheus*.

The instability does not, however, spread in all directions at once, or introduce a force of generalised de-coherence: the immediate result is uncertainty within a specific parameter of the paintings, their view of what we may loosely term 'sublimation'. This we can follow most clearly in the image of Socrates, for here the Muse or daemon acts, like the Muse in Ingres, as the copula between the immediate or bodily present, and the temporal span of Tradition. By painting the Muse, incarnation of the primal energy that Socrates sublimated into philosophy, Delacroix effectively reverses the direction of sublimation (normally 'from low to high') and desublimates or plunges downwards to the primal substrate ('from high to low').[12]

Pictorially, the master-figure of this downward plunge is Attila, and although in the official view of the cycle Attila is culture's destroyer or apocalypse, in this downward and desublimating movement represented by the ascription of Socrates' inspiration to an enigmatic daemon, Delacroix himself acts as Attila to Socrates' Orphism: he unweaves the sublimating tissue of culture, and uncovers its deeper origin. Here Delacroix sides *with* Attila and *against* Orpheus: it is as though he were saying, 'What propels culture is really a feral power, something primal and animal-like; and if we follow this realisation through, we can see that Tradition is always secondary to something that stands before it, and in so far as a modern and belated individual can discover in himself that feral energy, Tradition becomes weightless, since the real place of culture is the body, which is always present to us, no matter when in time we come; and I, Delacroix, will show this to you by going behind Tradition to its source, in which I can also participate. By reversing cultural sublimation I shall necessarily appear as an iconoclast, a kind of Attila; but this action is necessary and unless it is performed we will feel intolerably belated and fallen.'

This paraphrase, necessarily reductive, does nevertheless correspond to the repeated pattern or claim of the Philosophy series. Behind Socrates stands the Muse. Herodotus seeks after ancient knowledge, a belated questioner of the Mages, a sharer in Delacroix's own fate of cultural latecoming. The potentially crushing weight of tradition is overcome by bringing forward the archaic source of wisdom; while the source is itself positioned from the future, by these images left over from a Nativity scene; shaped from within the Christian era which only Delacroix, not Herodotus, occupies. The authority of the past is diminished from the past and from the future, and the same is true of the *Chaldaean Shepherds*: though appearing as a fount of atavistic knowledge, the Chaldaeans cannot know the Nativity they seem to herald; just as Seneca cannot know the iconography of martyrdom which belongs only to Delacroix, the Christian (or post-Christian) painter.

Although these acts of placement may seem belittling to the cultural past they also restore to culture's legacies a manageable and personal scale; they *humanise* tradition. Yet at the same time something is distinctly destroyed, which one might call the Absolutism of culture. This must perhaps be destroyed, if tradition is to be scaled down to human and habitable size; but the loss of absolute co-ordinates amounts also to a loss of dignity and certainty, and this too the cycle investigates. The meanings of things come unstuck; meaning becomes fluid and unstable; we cannot be sure how to view the 'founders' of culture, once we lose the absolute co-ordinates (marked by the 'official' but increasingly unstable images of Orpheus and Attila). What one notices here is Delacroix's sense of *responsibility*: he removes the absolute character, the weight of Tradition, but he also takes stock of the kind of relative vision that ensues; and the price he sees to be paid for removing that Absolute is a perception of something like chaos, or the rule of Attila. In Attila, Delacroix is painting a likeness of his own enterprise, where the point is that our inability to decide whether Attila is culture's destroyer or its redeemer, provides an exact measure of what it means, in terms of moral uncertainty, to be a Modern, that is a Romantic, painter.

V

Moving from Philosophy into the next dome, consecrated to Law, we find what is essentially a continuation of the 'desublimating' analysis of culture. The legislators – Demosthenes (illustration 111), Lycurgus (illustration 112), Numa (illustration 113), and Cicero (illustration 114) – are known to history by their cultural work, the laws and political concepts they brought into being; but again Delacroix goes 'behind' cultural production to various archaic or pre-cultural origins.

Perhaps the simplest way to describe the group is to say that it finds the irrational base to reason's actions, a theme explored by each painting in turn. Demosthenes harangues the waves, but not only to practise his oratory (illustration 111). He is made to resemble a sea-god – 'The Athenian orator paces the sea-shore, holding his robe against the wind with one hand, the other hand

raised in a gesture which will subdue his audience as powerfully as
the trident of the sea-god subdued the waves.'[13] His rhetoric is seen
therefore as numinous, grounded in divinity, and his words form
themselves not in the assembly or the chamber of debate, but at the
outer boundary where culture dissolves into primary nature: the
shore. The rhetoric of the waves will later sway the city, but it is
not *of* the city and at this stage hardly belongs to the human or the
civilised world; the word is on a par with the wind and the waves,
the white noise of the unsymbolised. Lycurgus is seen sacrificing at
Delphi, to the guardian of the oracle who will answer in the speech
of the god; it is these words, magical and irrational, which will
ground the Lycurgus legislation (illustration 112). Similarly
Numa, the first king of Rome, is seen conversing with the water-
nymph Egeria, his mythic companion and consort (illustration
113). Numa speaks, and we must suppose his words are natural and
human; yet his hearer is a being both superhuman and subhuman;
her body, garlanded with river-plants, half returns to the element
of water; so that the words of Numa, founder–legislator of Rome,
are again formed away from the territory of civilisation, and
spoken to a spirit who barely emerges from primal nature. The
representation of Cicero differs from the rest in that we see rhetoric
in its phase of action rather than of inspiration, but Cicero's
performance thus stands for all the speeches of the legislators; and
it is dark speech, uttered in a forum whose walls resemble
aqueducts, a forum which indicates the city but which is still open
to wind and sky, an elemental city; and again, though the words
are addressed ultimately to a human audience, and the senators are
in their places, in the first place they are spoken to the statue of

111   Delacroix, *Demosthenes
Addressing the Waves*

Roma, the dark colossus whose silhouette dominates the assembly (illustration 114).

In every case, rhetoric is seen as an activity behind which there stands *something else*, from which rhetoric derives its force, and of which it is a sublimating or an 'upward' transformation. The more primitive energy of the sea, of the wind, of water, and of sacrifice, is sublimated but never altogether severs itself from daemonic origin; and in representing this process of Orphic sublimation, Delacroix necessarily runs counter to the 'upward' or elevating

112   Delacroix, *Lycurgus Consulting the Pythoness*

113   Delacroix, *Numa and Egeria*

direction of culture, so that the cycle in which Orphism is celebrated is portrayed from the down-plunging or regressive viewpoint of Attila.

One misunderstands the cycle, however, if one thinks of this combination of Orpheus and Attila, or of sublimating and vandalising tendencies, as a synthesis or 'balance' in which Delacroix pays his dues to both masters. To be sure, the possibility of such synthesis grows stronger as the series develops and as its initial polarity (based on exclusion) dissolves. Yet this possibility of inclusiveness, or getting the best of both worlds, is never in fact contained *within* the representation. The global terms of such a synthesis, *Orpheus* and *Attila*, stand outside the series in their distant hemicycles, so that the process of forging the synthesis is never accomplished within any one painting, and is always mobile – moving towards, yet never finally reaching or stating the synthesis. In this particular dome, of Law, the actual product of culture – the legislation of Cicero, Numa, Lycurgus, Demosthenes – is shown to be incomplete: their speeches do not themselves represent the source of their power, the waves, the sacrifice, the nymph, the statue. The pictorial figure of the Muse forcibly indicates this absence, for although she stands for the rhetorical power possessed by the speeches and the legislation, she cannot herself stand within the symbolic work she inspires (Egeria, Pythoness, Roma).

This follows closely the classical conception of the art of rhetoric, where language is said to follow the figures of thought – logic – until thought is distorted by the figures of speech, which are

114   Delacroix, *Cicero Denouncing Verras*

held responsible for moving the hearer.[14] Within this conception of rhetoric, the power to move the hearer is therefore never *part* of what is represented, but rather is part of the means or medium of the representation: rhetorical power stands outside what can be represented; it is external to representation, and its place is therefore exactly occupied by the Muse, the force acting upon the poet from outside himself. The Muse marks the place of an insufficiency within representation and of a gap or shift in the world where rhetorical power, conceived as unrepresentable, *comes through*. In so far as the great founders of culture have failed to comprehend within their cultural work the ultimate source of that work's power, each of the legislators has therefore fallen short in the Orphic project of sublimation: there remains something that cannot be raised to a higher power, a residue outside representation.

VI

Postponement, the position of lateness, is transformed into religious terms in the next dome, dedicated to Theology, where the earliest scene, *The Expulsion from Eden*, is already too late, and man has fallen into wandering and exile (illustration 115). To identify the subject of the painting in any confident iconographic fashion introduces a note of distortion, however, for in this dome we are faced with the question of how successfully we can, in fact, translate the images into words. The 'iconography' of *The*

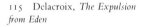
115 Delacroix, *The Expulsion from Eden*

Expulsion from Eden and *The Captivity in Babylon* (illustration 116)
ought to be stable, backed as it is by the combined authority of
sacred texts, and of centuries of Christian art. Yet if we view the
dome *in situ*, in its actual position off-centre in the series of the
domes, the stability promised by such traditionalism goes off
balance, since by this stage it is clear that no individual painting or
group of paintings can stand alone: the paintings are reshapings of
one another, transformations of the 'deep' structures stated in
Orpheus and *Attila*.

It is not difficult to see ways in which the *Expulsion* and the
Captivity are transformations of a single root, of Exile; and the idea
of such transformation is familiar to Christian art, through the
model of 'type' and 'anti-type'. But the certainty which had once
been present in type/anti-type juxtaposition is now precisely
unavailable: the viewer must produce the 'root', of Exile, from his
own interpretive resources. Nothing from within the dome
confirms that the viewer has got the root 'right'. Indeed, the
presence of the harp, hanging on the tree by the waters of
Babylon, can be claimed equally by two interpretive grids: the
grid supplied by Theology (the psalms); and the grid supplied by
the *Orpheus : Attila* polarity (the harp as Orphic lyre). In fact the
harp acts as a place of crossing *between* two routes of interpretation,
each of which can make its bid for appropriation: we can say that
the harp is traversed, but not held, by interpretation. Each has
sufficient inaugural power to claim the harp as offspring, yet
neither can realise the claim, and in that failure of master-discourse
to 'attach' the harp to itself there emerges the possibility that the

116 Delacroix, *The Captivity in Babylon*

two rival claimants – the discourse of Theology, and the polar discourse of *Orpheus* and *Attila* – may themselves be mutual transformations, in a flow of constant metamorphosis where no co-ordinate is truly primal, or stable.

This (heretical) possibility is developed in the two remaining paintings of the Theology dome, whose iconography is suffused with what might be called contradictory signposting, or reversing directions. *The Death of John the Baptist* (illustration 117) is a ferocious dismemberment, recalling on the one side Attila (the sword) and on the other Orpheus (the idea of *sparagmos*). It stays within the orbit of the polar images even in its details, for the attribution of barbaric grace to the executioner, who wears the headband of an athlete, matches the magnificence attributed by Delacroix to Attila; while the fate of being dismembered before Salome, the dancer of destruction, matches the fate of Orpheus at the hands of his followers. Yet however persuasively the polar images may claim the image, the image is claimed also by a scriptural authority which does not feature anywhere *in* the polar set. As a result, Scripture is revised in the light of *Orpheus* and *Attila*, as though the Bible were itself a sub-set of the cycle; while the polar terms of the cycle are, equally, subsumed into and revised by Christianity. Essentially the viewer is on his own to arbitrate between the conflicting centres of authority; more accurately, the viewer is constructed *as* an arbiter whose acts of interpretation, irresistibly called into play by such indeterminate montage, nevertheless remains *in suspense*, for nothing from Delacroix tells the viewer how the dice shall fall.

117 Delacroix, *The Death of John the Baptist*

The Tribute Money is still more remote (illustration 118). The theme of high and spiritual culture emerging out of animal life – the coin of God and of Caesar issuing from the fish – takes us to *Orpheus*: and the theme of 'compromise' – one side of the coin for the lower powers, one side for the higher – has hovered round every image where we have seen attributes or associations of Orpheus and of Attila joined together (the promise of 'equilibrium'). Yet the viewer is now in an outer orbit (I am tempted to say an outer space) of interpretation. How *can* this image be read? It may be that the play of meanings is of extraordinary intricacy. The fish is itself an ancient emblem of Christian faith, and to relate that emblem to *Orpheus*, master of the transformation of animal into spiritual vitality, is to locate the Orphism in Christianity (this seems to me a strong possibility). The double coin, one side for Caesar and the lower powers, the other for God and the spirit, may indeed stand for the energies of the cycle itself (on one side Attila, on the other Orpheus); and this too is not beyond the bounds of sense. But none of these possibilities can be confirmed – *that* is the point; and out of this disinclination or inability to validate a *specific* interpretation the cycle produces one of its deepest and most mysterious effects, the *solitude* of viewing. Each of its images comes from a common stock of tradition, and all (European) viewers are joined, as a public, by this activation of tradition. Yet the codes of recognition are operated by a wild idiosyncrasy: *The Expulsion from Eden* is inserted, out of sequence, between episodes from Antiquity, so that in order to produce meaning at all from these

118 Delacroix, *The Tribute Money*

paintings, the viewer is at the same time taken *out* of public role, exiled from the common inheritance, privatised.

VII

It would be right to call such assault upon the coherence of inheritance iconoclastic, and the part played by destruction in the processes both of painting and of viewing will be examined in a moment, when we come to examine further the cycle's *radical* revisionism, its championing of Attila. Although no determinate reading can, I believe, be finally constructed out of the Theology series, what is clear is that Delacroix uses the series to collapse together two temporal frameworks, from the pagan and the Christian worlds. Lycurgus is next to Numa, Seneca is next to Demosthenes, and in this collage of anachronistic episodes the only persistent temporal co-ordinates are *early* and *late*. Between these two almost all of the figures of the cycle oscillate, in the scansion that runs from Attila to Orpheus, and back. What counts is that 'early' and 'late' are not calibrated from absolute moments or co-ordinates: mutual, or relative, 'early' and 'late' can surface at any point in time and in any episode.

The overall temporality of the series is therefore that of *dislocation* in time, a theme that is explored most extensively in the last of the domes, dedicated to Poetry. What is significant is that the Muse appears to *Hesiod* (illustration 119), for in Hesiod all men are born out of time: the beings of the golden age are followed by those of the silver age, then the age of bronze, the age of heroes,

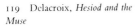

119 Delacroix, *Hesiod and the Muse*

and finally the present age of humanity, and iron. The pattern is not simply one of degeneration.[15] Hesiod's portrayal of time describes humanity as permanently afflicted by a sense of temporal displacement: men come too early and too late: late, since the golden age has passed, and early, since the next age of gold, in Hesiod's cyclical patterning of epochs, belongs to the future.

If we interpret *The Education of Achilles* (illustration 120) through *Hesiod and the Muse*, the figures of the boy and the centaur begin to lose the aspect of union (culture reconciled with animality) that is stated, compositionally, in the 'Géricault' rhyming of human with equine form. The centaur is a creature split across two worlds, and however deftly the forms of the horse are stitched into the forms of the human body, even the most successful representation must include areas of impossibility, where the eye will find the join. Destined to be surpassed by his student, the centaur is like the boy in that both will be rendered obsolete by the Homeric hero, Achilles the man: it is Homer's Achilles, the figure of representation and literature, who justifies this excursion into precocious or dawning time, and in as much as Homer is an avatar of Orpheus, both the centaur and the boy are figures of *nostalgia*, projected out of the later time. Yet the later time is also too late; Alexander, recovering the works of Homer (illustration 121), is already a victim of luxury and the effeminate East, and between Alexander and the slave who holds the coffer there is a gulf of incomprehension comparable to the gulf which had separated Aristotle from the goatherd. Culture will *not* integrate its higher and its lower energies (despite the dream of Achilles and the centaur, which is also perhaps a dream of ideal

120 Delacroix, *The Education of Achilles*

childhood, of ideal relation between fathers and sons). In *Ovid among the Barbarians* (illustration 122) we see two non-communicating species: Ovid, wise, accepting without protest the primitive nourishment, yet defeated, enfeebled, too spent to assume the role of prodigal son; and the barbarians, graceful, vigorous, yet also grudging, mean-spirited, suspicious of this stranger whom they approach less as they would a fellow human than some stray beast.

As we move into *Orpheus* from the last of the domes, and take into it the meaning of temporal displacement generated by the four paintings in the dome of Poetry, we will find an Orpheus who does not so much represent an inaugural moment of culture as one who, like Hesiod, like the centaur, and like Ovid, the Scythians, and Alexander finds himself crossed by two periodic bands: a golden age which to the succeeding generations appears both brutal and idyllic, and a later or silver age which is both a refinement and a debasement. Belonging to both periods, Orpheus is seen as temporally displaced, and if the viewer goes on to read the cycle in reverse, from south to north, enough evidence will be found to confirm a reading in which all of the figures, even Attila, are afflicted by the same condition, of coming too soon or too late. There are many ways such a reading might be elaborated, but rather than develop a 'retrograde' (south–north) reading I want to step back from the making of interpretation to examine some of the conditions or restraints which operate on hermeneutic activity in the cycle as a whole.

121 Delacroix, *Alexander with the Poems of Homer*

My first observation concerns the cycle's own position with regard to the tradition whose creators it represents, and in particular the cycle's sense of tradition's authority. Enough has been said about the Hesiodic theme 'too late and too soon' to make it clear that for Delacroix there exist two moments which taken together define the work of culture: a primitive state from which culture emerges, and a later or higher state where it risks the return of that which has been repressed. The model is a familiar one to the century of Freud, yet what is unfamiliar and indeed difficult for us to understand precisely because of Freud, is that for Delacroix art is not simply the one-way hydraulic movement upwards into sublimation. If that were the case, there would be none of the ambivalent assessment of 'progress' which the cycle everywhere displays. For Freud, sublimation may produce its discontents, but it also produces its pantheon, and if Freud had painted the cycle it would doubtless have looked much more like Ingres' *Apotheosis of Homer* (or the Albert Memorial). Freud has it that as we move on from the primal substrate, the burden of our anxiety and our sense of falling from grace necessarily increase, but the cause of our anxiety is also our consolation, and the man who is born late in culture and the

122 Delacroix, *Ovid among the Barbarians*

man who has sublimated long and deep may both look upon the product, Culture, as renunciation's reward. But while this may be a comforting (if not a comfortable) doctrine for the psychoanalyst or for most men, it is a doctrine that offers no comfort at all to the artist who has to survey two thousand years of cultural enterprise, and an inheritance he must revitalise if he is not to experience his own death as an artist.

The analyst, like the viewer, takes up a position with regard to tradition which in many ways is the *opposite* of the position assumed by the painter. For the viewer, whose aim must always be to see clearly what is before him, the eye must learn to discriminate more and more accurately the images before it, and art, the experiencing of this progressive differentiation, is for the viewer a place of higher and higher observation. The activity of viewing art is intrinsically Orphic. In this it resembles psychoanalysis itself. No art is more Orphic than that of the patient under analysis, or at least this is the myth to which he or she must subscribe. But for the artist, and crucially for the Romantic artist, for Ingres and Delacroix, tradition can present itself as a force of un-differentiation, of repetition, and expropriation of vision by the art of the past: it is as id, not as ego, that tradition manifests. In Delacroix's cycle, the potentially crushing weight of tradition is countered by a trope which, though similar to the trope of totality (the cycle is literally encyclopaedic: it places a circle round the knowledge of tradition), differs from it by reversing the flow of time, and of sublimation: by insisting on the primal substrate from which culture emerges, Delacroix locates a pre-cultural or 'bar-baric' past in relation to which all the founders of culture, even Orpheus, are latecomers. Temporal dislocation is made to seem the fate not only of the nineteenth-century painter, struggling to create an *I* out of an *It*, but of all the alleged primogenitors, of Culture itself.

Once analysed as a psychic process cultural history loses much, if not all, of its temporal weight (which makes psycho-history such bad history; but here we are dealing with art). Or, to reverse the emphases, Delacroix's 'prophetic' discovery of Sublimation emer-ges at a crucial phase when *something* is needed to re-animate, and overtake, a tradition over two millennia in span. This is to humanise the founding fathers, by perceiving them as identical (in their latecoming) to oneself; it democratises culture, since all men, no matter what age they are born into, must confront the pre-Orphic in their own way; and it modernises Delacroix, an artist whose placing of psychic process 'before' historical process makes him our own, or at least Freud's, contemporary. Yet the 'discovery' also runs counter to the direction of humanisation, since the origin of culture now belongs outside normal or civil experience, to the beasts, the oracle, the wind, the waves; and it runs counter also to the direction of psychoanalysis, and of art conceived in the way psychoanalysis promotes, since if a painter is genuinely to innovate within and against tradition, he must subvert the edifice of culture, break the spell of repetition, and assault the temple of Homer; lest he too become, like Homer, blind.

Part of the cycle's assault on tradition is conducted, as we have seen, at the level of narrative. In the Freudian view the cycle should move one way, from the unregenerate feral self, Attila, onwards and upwards to sublimation's ambassador, Orpheus; and clearly this is not what happens. In almost every scene the narrative is troped by reversal, and each step forward is made to seem also a step back. The obstinacy of Hippocrates casts a shadow over his refusal of barbaric gifts; the intellectual curiosity of Pliny is seen as hubris; Archimedes should have had the foresight to protect himself against attack, and Aristotle, who has had the sense to take sides with the military, comes to trouble the peace of the animals, and of the animal in man. The pagan philosophers, wiser than the scientists, seek a compromise with 'archaic' power: they summon the daemon, they enter alliances with the state, visit the priests of Egypt, and read their fate in the stars; but not even these concessions to the archaic can save them from the religion that will rise in the East and undo the pagan world. The legislators, servants of reason and of the Word, owe the power of their words to wave and river, to the Pythoness and the Muse, and to the darkest of all the Muses, Roma: but none of their speeches will stand up to Jehovah, or the Angel of the Fiery Sword, and no culture can be securely founded when mankind wanders in its exile, awaiting the Messiah who, when He comes, will destroy, like Attila, the classical world. There was no Foundation: all were stranded in time, looking back to an earlier state as fleeting as the Muse, as chimerical as the centaur, and as remote as Scythia. History is seen less as a linear progression than as a state of always being later: in the perception of latecoming, history is viewed not from its future but against its past, and the arrows of time reverse.

This movement of reversal (history switched backwards, into emergence rather than accumulation) occurs at many points in the narrative order, but the word 'narrative' can be misleading here because it suggests the literary text, and in fact no text, however ingenious, can actually *embody* such reversal, unless we imagine some kind of extended palindrome that could be read backwards as well as forwards. But the cycle *is* just such a palindrome, and we can 'read' it either way: in the Orphic or sublimating direction from north to south, or in the anti-Orphic or de-sublimating direction, from south to north. What enables this reversibility of the cycle is the freedom of the glance from the one-way movement that captures it in a text, and at this point consideration of the *glance* can help us to understand what is truly radical in the cycle, and what is at stake in its interplay between vision and the body. The most useful contrast throughout is with the Sistine Ceiling, a work which similarly exceeds the panoptic capacity of vision, condemned as vision is to scan all surfaces through an organ so constructed that only a small point exists in clear focus at any one moment, at the bright and crystalline centre of the larger peripheral haze. To this physical limitation of the eye the Sistine Ceiling makes few or no concessions, since the *oppositional* logic of its organisation requires the viewer mentally to juxtapose its component scenes if their overall structure and meaning are to be understood.[16]

The Bourbon Library precisely lacks this panoptic or all-at-once organisation. This is not to deny that in many ways it revises or re-envisions the Sistine Ceiling: as the glance travels from south to north it traces a fall into anarchy and ruin; as it travels from north to south and as Attila gives way to Orpheus, it traces the path of artistic redemption; and these movements match quite closely their counterparts in Michelangelo. Yet the local movements of reversal which occur in each scene – the back-flowing of time *towards* an origin – disrupt the stately linear progress through cultural history; and once we are fully *in* the cycle, and have become aware of the Orpheus in Attila, and of the Attila in Orpheus, the binary logic of the cycle (logic on which the Sistine Ceiling particularly depends) is altogether subverted. The semantic order of the Sistine Ceiling logic is one of *fixed oppositions*. Sinless Adam *is to* the Adam of the Fall as Noah before the Flood is to Noah after the Flood; the Brazen Serpent *is to* the Serpent of Eden as are both to the Crucifixion; Haman is to Ahasuerus as the Crucified Christ is to God the Father; and so forth. Though gathered and generated through the vagaries of the glance, the meanings of Michelangelo's ceiling are held in a stable matrix. The semantic order of the Bourbon Library is one where meanings circulate and reverse in increasing independence from the waning 'official' poles. Once divorced from that matrix, the meanings of each image are generated according to a principle of *relativity*. They are produced mutually, by montage and by juxtaposition: Aristotle conveys one thing if the glance reaches him by way, for example, of Archimedes, and something quite different if the glance travels by way, for example, of Hippocrates. In the Sistine Ceiling, all the images are positioned through simultaneous opposition; here, the images unfold in a dimension of succession or duration (*durée*) that is determined by the glance. The temporality of the cycle is in its deepest sense *somatic*, since the meanings found in the paintings are not disclosed in themselves or all-at-once, in some eternal moment of the Gaze; they reveal themselves in the *mobility* of the glance, which fashions fluid, provisional senses out of the semantic excess. The flow of meanings disseminates without end, since nothing is up to containing it: the official matrix (*plus*:*minus*, *Orpheus*: *Attila*) has collapsed, and the glance is therefore *necessary*, for only it may carve out paths of order through the ruin of the matrix, and the reverberant confusion.

Yet it is important to recognise that the meanings yielded by the cycle are not chaotic or *unlimitedly* plural, and that what might seem an anarchy of viewing (compared, for example, with LeBrun) is in fact subject to significant restraint. The loss of polarity resulting from the rapprochement or interchangeability of Orpheus with Attila does not destroy the order of viewing, or liberate it in the alleged *jouissance* of modernism, but rather relocates order in the *practice* of viewing, which is to say, in the body of the viewer. In this register of what one might call the viewing body, the figure of reversal which we have seen at work in the register of narrative becomes an *activity*, a *physical* enactment of the themes of 'too early' and 'too late' which governed the narrative, since it is now the viewer who experiences the temporal dislocation directly. Each moment of the glance takes its sense from the meaning created in the glance before, and carries over into the glance which follows: meaning *slides across the glance* from 'before' into 'after', but the *present* of viewing is therefore only a slippage between the anticipatory, or proleptic, and the deferred, or postponed. At no single or final moment are the meanings fully *there*, arrayed in a presence that can contain them all, as the meanings of the Sistine Chapel are contained by its theological Gaze, or Gaze of God. The order of viewing is subject not to presence, but to a desire whose actual vehicle *is* the body, in the questing, interminable drive of its physical vision.

The human eye is stilled only at death: the life of vision is one of endless wanderlust, and in its carnal form the eye is nothing but desire. The confidence of Michelangelo in the possibility of a vision transcendent or freed from desire is marked by his ability to represent everything there is, even that which is beyond representation (God); but for Delacroix vision is located in two terms which exceed that universal embrace: for the viewer, *the glance*; and for the painter, *the trace*. Desire in the trace (and here one must think not only of the Bourbon cycle, but of the easel paintings) is the expression of Delacroix's awareness that no matter how many strokes he may apply to the surface, the moment when the image will be fully captured can never be reached. The brush may be of the finest, but whatever its gauge, the fact that paint is *material* condemns the trace to indefinite postponement of presence: each new stroke only shifts the 'closure' of the image one step ahead. Desire in the glance issues from the viewer's similar awareness that no matter how closely focussed or precisely remembered his visual scansion of the image, the moment of the gaze, or of all-at-once apprehension of the image, can never be attained, for the fact that vision must unfold within the physical organism condemns the glance to perpetual movement and restlessness. The Sistine Ceiling can be seen as an expression of the wish to *end* the rule of desire in vision by offering vision a total representation of Creation, from the beginning to the end of time, where the promise that desire may be ended is underwritten by the representability of God. The Bourbon Library belongs to a different cultural dispensation, where vision is prevented from reaching a panoptic view *of* history by the fact of its location *in* history. Representation cannot include everything there is, from the beginning to the end, because the desire in vision ties it to a body that sees only in this time and from this body: the possibility of encyclopaedic or Sistine-like vision is ruled out exactly because the body is *there*, and if representation is to match the lived reality of seeing, the image must embody the creatural limitation of sight. The Sistine dream of the transfigured body precisely matches its simultaneous or *im Augenblick* structure of meaning; in Delacroix's cycle no such dream can be found, and the body is *accepted* in a way it is not in Michelangelo, as a place, the greatest place, of desire.

If we ask where the cycle stands in relation to the cultural achievement it officially celebrates, the answer must be that the temporality of desire *supplants* the temporality of tradition. Instead of a genealogy of culture where the achievement of the founding fathers of civilisation grows through time like a gathering (and oppressive) dynastic fortune, the cycle gives us a *counter*-genealogy where each of the founding fathers is placed in relation to a primitive or earlier state, a background of the barbaric or the archaic. By 'going behind' the fathers to their pre-sublimated inspiration or pre-Orphic energy, Delacroix humanises the fathers and makes them more like sons, or brothers; they, too, are temporally dislocated, as Delacroix feels himself to be, and their work of culture is belated, like Delacroix's own. In the narrative of the cycle, tradition is precisely not seen as progress, but as a process that is the same wherever we look; while in the cycle's register of viewing, the new order of the glance and of deferred or glancing meaning expresses that process as an actual and physical practice. The symmetry between what is happening in the register of narrative and in the register of viewing repositions Delacroix not at the *end* of a tradition, where he may fear himself to be, but in a temporality of desire which Delacroix claims is tradition's only *true* temporality. By mythologising all cultural activity, including his own, as a process under desire, Delacroix becomes the equal of the precursors, and of tradition. But there is a price to pay, and we can form a sense of that price if we compare Delacroix with Ingres.

For Ingres also, desire is the force that counters tradition and makes his images his own, yet the imagery of desire lacks presence – it is by building desire *into* his images that Ingres protects them from expropriation by tradition. The price Ingres pays is *deformation*: the paintings are deliberately prevented from reaching a state of closure, of perfection, that would run the risk of ending the desire so painstakingly built into their construction. To that extent the work of Ingres is iconoclastic, and in two directions: Ingres must assault tradition, harness it to his own purpose, if he is to be a *creator* of images; and to preserve the desire in his images he must make them self-subverting, self-deconstructing – the iconoclasm applies not only to tradition, but to his own work. Delacroix is an iconoclast also, though in him iconoclasm takes a rather different form. Delacroix claims that culture is a sublimating process, as opposed to a sublimated product: he finds that in every heroic enterprise of culture, two sides are visible – the 'before' and the 'after' of its process, which makes every enterprise both early and late; and at no point of culture do the two reach equilibrium. The benign aspect of this myth of culture is that it personalises the tradition and ends the sense of culture as a gathering burden: burden it may be, but no more so for those who come late than for those who, like Orpheus, came first. The negative aspect of this myth of culture is that while the tradition is humanised and the fathers are made to seem more like sons, the stress on the pre-Orphic as pre-sublimated also dehumanises the tradition, since the energy of culture is said to derive from what culture cannot include, namely the feral or daemonic state which it may raise to the value of culture yet cannot fully contain *as* culture. If this daemonic energy were to be wholly sublimated, then the products of culture really would be products, fully finished monuments which seen together might well appear as a crushing weight. It is because Delacroix portrays culture as never quite able to complete the sublimation, as always broken into 'before' and 'after', and as always out of balance, that he can claim culture as a process, and claim further that the process is the same for all men, including himself. This is his assault on culture-as-monolith, but while it makes the fathers seem less august, and more like sons, it makes the son seem a primitive and a destroyer, and more like Attila.

But how can Attila *paint*? The paradox of the cycle is this: in order to describe culture through the myth of sublimation or 'raising up', and in order to prove the description as valid, Delacroix must show a feral or daemonic energy at work in his own necessarily culture-building enterprise. If what he says about the fathers of culture is true, then his own work must be shown to have 'behind' it or running counter to it, a pre-sublimated energy, and this has to be seen *in* the representation. But how can a product of culture represent the energy which Delacroix claims precedes and can never be wholly contained in culture's representations?

Delacroix's solution, in the easel painting, is an intense cultivation of the painterly trace, a trace so visible that it is shown as always deferring the image's closure, never closing up into a 'finish' that would mean the end of the desire *in* the image. In the Bourbon cycle this solution is not available: the paintings are placed too high above us for the trace to be visible or active. Instead, the cycle cultivates an equivalent of 'the trace' in narrative terms. An official narrative order begins by looking encyclopaedic and 'finished', and it seems to promise an abbreviated history of the classical world: but that sanctioned or approved narrative order then collapses; meanings scatter and proliferate in the disseminations of the glance: no Gaze or matrix holds them in position.

It is therefore the viewer who emerges as the hero of this cycle, and as the truer avatar of Attila than the painter is able to be, for the activity of the Glance – its mobility, its freedom, its powers of juxtaposition and montage – embodies in the most literal sense the paradox of culture as simultaneously constructive and destructive, which the narrative personifies in the figures of Attila and Orpheus. The viewer *acts out* the cycle in the Glance, which both creates and destroys the representations, sustains *and* breaks the tradition. To understand the cycle, we must conceive of its forms in dynamic terms, as matter in process, in the sense of the ancient, pre-Socratic word for form: *rhuthmos*, rhythm, in the mobility and vibrancy of vision's somatic rhythms. It is here that Delacroix locates the physical, pre-sublimated base of culture, in the body which, having created the patterns of culture, can also break them. Such a body is radically different from the conception of the body in representation which the Western tradition classically proffers to us, as something fixed, pictorial, framed. Its vision *exceeds* the fixities of representation, turns and overturns the representations; and though the body of desire never can be represented, its existence beyond representation is finally what both Delacroix and Ingres present to us *across* their images; just as David, across his greatest work, presents its death.

Epilogue

The discussion of tradition undertaken in this book returns us to Hazlitt's question: 'Michel Angelo, the cartoons of Leonardo da Vinci, and the antique, your correspondent tells us, produced Raphael. Why have they produced no second Raphael?' How are we to think of the 'anxiety of influence'? or picture to ourselves the power which tradition exerts over the generations of painters? The present discussion has proceeded in the manner of the case history: given that tradition possesses a certain power it has asked how that power is perceived and transformed in the work of David, Ingres and Delacroix. But what of the nature of that power? Can we even say that its power has a *nature*?

Certainly there exist answers to these questions: that it is the nature of power to act by repression, imprint, *force majeure*; that the canon of master-works housed in tradition stamps itself on its successors in the manner of a seal upon wax, or genetic traits upon a dynasty; that the canon is to be understood as an aggregate of primal points, from which a declension of secondary and derivative forms emanate. Hence the classical models of 'influence'; hence also, one observes, the latter-day picture of tradition as combat, as Oedipal, as the battle between the sons and the fathers. These studies of David, Ingres and Delacroix suggest a somewhat different conception of tradition's action. Rather than say of the canon ('Michel Angelo, the cartoons of Leonardo da Vinci, Raphael') that its force is transitive, effortful, and imposing, or that its authority descends below from on high, we should say that the canon emerges retroactively, in the tropes of homage (submissive or subversive) in which it comes to be located. Rather than see the transformation of the precursors in the work of their successors as the product of resistance, reaction, or protest (as though tradition were antiphonal, with a chorus of authority counterpointed by a chorus of revolt), transformation is to be seen in its unity of action, the power of the canon arising from below, in the gamut of citation's tropes. If that power works for change, it is by granting to change the status of transformation, of deviation from background; where background is not to be considered as something split away from foreground, or sited in independent elevation, but where background itself arises out of foreground, in the moment of being cited. These moments of deviation may appear as natural, necessary, improbable; they may be bitter, hesitant, concealed, savage, solitary, prolonged, or sudden; they

213

may be repeated or unique, isolated or concerted: but we need not conclude that they are the revolt of a preterite against an elect, or of youth against age, or of the refused against the admitted. Deviation here is rather the negative term in tradition's power, permanently inscribed in tradition's field of forces; where the permanence of that inscription is perhaps that which in the end distinguishes a tradition from an archaeology, a mere layering of change.

From this we must infer that while tradition may permit or require the existence of a canon of master-works, tradition is not to be identified or equated with its canon. In a tradition such as our own, in which we ourselves are still able to understand as clearly as Hazlitt the force of synecdoche contained in the terms Michel Angelo, Leonardo, Antiquity, Raphael, the power exerted by the canonical image is not to be thought of as singular, or as that of the archetype, since its influence extends not only from itself but from innumerable points, from the plurality of images in whose field of force the canonical image, together with its successors, is caught. The habit of charting tradition according to the model of genealogies, declensions, and transitive influences accords exactly with the picture of the canon as supreme achievement; yet it is to be regretted that for so long the underlying figure of tradition's power has been that of the apex to the pyramid, of the ramifying tree, the legal code, and regretted not least because this figure immediately calls into being its opposite term: those who 'lack' power against those who 'have it', Romantic versus classic art, the Salon of the *réfusés* against the Salon of the Académie. The history of art produced by such a conception of tradition knows no way of accounting for its power over change, other than the addition of new works to the empowered canon, each new work introduced into the pantheon then founding its own dynasty (and inter-dynastic war). Yet in a tradition, where influence is exerted across an endless proliferation of points and not simply from a head-quarters or by directive, influence is distributed less according to principles of centrality and order, than of ubiquity and irregularity: each new painting is a special case, acting in minute response to the innumerable images which compose its immediate neighbourhood. Each work will contain its own particular configuration of points of change, invocations and half-invocations, repetitions and deviations, a plurality of moments in which the tradition is locally called into being and then turned and troped; and if the history of art continues to write itself through the grand categories of Period, Artist and Style, this manœuvre must be understood as itself only the turning of its own specific, and limited, tropes.

Throughout this book the viewer has been presented as the passive term in the circuits of vision, but this passivity is only a matter of degree (the degree to which vision is something that leaves no trace). For the viewer also, painting is a turning of

tradition: what painting discloses to the viewer is never revealed
across the vibrant or lustrous medium of living sight, but across the
gaps between this sign and the next, this image and the next; in the
absence between the spokes. The Victorians had an ingenious
machine, which they called the 'Wheel of Life': as the drum
rotated at a certain speed, the separate images on the scroll within
began to merge and to move. What tradition supplies the painter
and the viewer is not only the images, but the turning background,
the scroll itself; and though Being itself may not be pictured in any
representation, however sublime, it is perhaps in the turning
emptiness of tradition's scroll that David, Ingres and Delacroix
bring Being to appearance, in the void of the verb 'to see'.

Notes

1. Tradition and its discontents

1 A. Waley, *An Introduction to the Study of Chinese Painting* (London: Ernest Benn, 1932), pp. 50–9.

2 See M. Loehr, 'The question of individualism in Chinese Art', *Journal of the History of Ideas*, XXII (1961), 147–58; J. Cahill, *The Compelling Image: Nature and Style in Seventeenth-Century Chinese Painting* (Cambridge, Mass: Harvard University Press, 1982); and S. Bush, *Chinese Literati on Painting: Su Shih 1037–1101 to Tung Ch'i-ch'ang, 1555–1636* (Cambridge, Mass: Harvard University Press, 1971).

3 For an analogous argument in literary poetics, see W.J. Bate, *The Burden of the Past and the English Poet* (New York: Norton, 1972); and the work of Harold Bloom, especially *The Anxiety of Influence: A Theory of Poetry* (New York: Oxford University Press, 1975), and *Poetry and Repression: Revisionism from Blake to Stevens* (New Haven: Yale University Press, 1976). Bloom's work is interestingly discussed in F. Lentricchia, *After the New Criticism* (London: The Athlone Press, 1980); see also Bloom's riposte in 'Agon: revisionism and critical personality', *Raritan*, No.1 (Summer 1981), 18–47, and *The Breaking of the Vessels* (University of Chicago Press, 1982).

4 On the projective errors of 'academic' reasoning, see P. Bourdieu, *Outline of a Theory of Practice*, trans. R. Nice (Cambridge University Press, 1977), p. 19.

5 Reynolds, *Discourses on Art*, ed. Robert R. Wark (New Haven: Yale University Press, 1975), p. 219.

6 Nietzsche, *Twilight of the Idols*, section 44; trans. R.J. Hollingdale (Harmondsworth: Penguin, 1968), p. 44.

7 *The Works of Ruskin*, ed. E.T. Cook and A. Wedderburn (39 vols., London: George Allen, 1903–12), vol. XII, pp. 353–4.

8 Pliny, *Natural History*, vol. IX, trans. H. Rackham (London: Heinemann, 1948), pp. 302–3, 332–5.

9 Ibid., pp. 306–7.

10 Ibid.

11 Ibid.

12 Vasari, *Lives of the Artists*, trans. G. Bull (Harmondsworth: Penguin, 1965), p. 55. On Pliny's influence on the Renaissance historiography of art, see M. Baxandall, *Giotto and the Orators: Humanist Observers of Painting in Italy and the discovery of pictorial composition 1350–1450* (Oxford: Clarendon Press, 1971), pp. 51–120.

13 See Sir Karl Popper, *Conjectures and Refutations: The Growth of Scientific Knowledge* (London: Routledge and Kegan Paul, 1963), pp. 3–30, 97–119; *Objective Knowledge: An Evolutionary Approach* (Oxford: Clarendon Press, 1972), pp. 1–31; *The Logic of Scientific Discovery* (London: Hutchinson, 1968), pp. 27–48; and Bryson, *Vision and Painting: The Logic of the Gaze* (London: Macmillan, 1983), pp. 13–35.

14 'I should be proud if Professor Popper's influence were to be felt everywhere in this book'; Sir Ernest Gombrich, *Art and Illusion: A Study in the Psychology of Pictorial Representation* (London: Phaidon, 1960), p. ix.

15 Popper, *Logic of Scientific Discovery*, pp. 78–92, 251–8; see also Hume, *Treatise of Human Nature*, in *The Philosophical Works of David Hume* (Edinburgh: Black and Tait, 1826), vol. I, pp. 98–235; and Hume, *An Inquiry Concerning the Human Understanding*, in *The Philosophical Works of David Hume*, vol. IV, pp. 24–120.

16 *Complete Works of William Hazlitt*, ed. P.P. Howe (21 vols., London: J.M. Dent, 1930–4), vol. XVIII, p. 49; for an account of Hazlitt's writings on art, see Bryson, 'Hazlitt on Painting', *Journal of Aesthetics and Art Criticism*, LXXXVII, No. 1 (Fall 1978), 37–45.

17 J. Pope-Hennessy, *The Portrait in the Renaissance* (London: Phaidon, 1966), pp. 41–50.

18 F. Nietzsche, *The Birth of Tragedy*, trans. W. Kaufmann (New York: Vintage Books, 1967), pp. 59–60.

19 See V.N. Volosinov, *Marxism and the Philosophy of Language*, trans. L. Matejka and I.R. Titunik (New York: Seminar Press, 1973), p. 21.

20 See R. Barthes, 'The photographic message' and 'Rhetoric of the image', in *Image–Music–Text*, ed. and trans. S. Heath (London: Fontana/Collins, 1977), pp. 15–31, 32–51. On the 'institution' of literature, see Barthes, *Le Degré zéro de l'écriture* (Paris: Seuil, 1972), pp. 7–24.

21 On the canon in literature, see F. Kermode, *The Genesis of Secrecy: On the Interpretation of Narrative* (Cambridge, Mass., and London: Harvard University Press, 1979), esp. pp. 125–45.

22 L. Wittgenstein, *Philosophical Investigations* (1953; trans. G.E.M. Anscombe; rpt. Oxford: Basil Blackwell, 1968), paragraphs 244–341.

23 Volosinov, *Philosophy of Language*, pp. 83–106.

24 J.-P. Sartre, *Being and Nothingness*, trans. H.E. Barnes (London: Methuen, 1969), pp. 252–302.

25 On 'difference' in this sense, see F. de Saussure, *Course in General Linguistics*, ed. Bally and Sechehaye, trans. W. Baskin (New York: McGraw Hill, 1966), part 2, chapters I and II, pp. 101–6. The crucial elaboration of Saussure's 'difference' occurs in J. Derrida, *L'Écriture et la différence* (Paris: Seuil, 1967), trans. A. Bass as *Writing and Difference* (University of Chicago Press, 1978); *La Voix et la phénomène* (Paris: Presses Universitaires de France, 1967), trans. D.B. Allison as *Speech and Phenomena* (Evanston, Ill: Northwestern University Press, 1973); and *De la grammatologie* (Paris: Seuil, 1967), trans. G.C. Spivak as *Of Grammatology* (Baltimore and London: The Johns Hopkins University Press). The best introduction to *différance* is probably J. Culler, 'Jacques Derrida', in *Structuralism and Since*, ed. J. Sturrock (Oxford University Press, 1979), pp. 154–80. Derrida broaches the subject of *différance* as it manifests in the visual sphere in *La Vérité en peinture* (Paris: Flammarion, 1978).

26 See A. Wilden, *The Language of the Self: The Function of Language in Psychoanalysis* (Baltimore and London: The Johns Hopkins University Press, 1973), esp. pp. 9–51; and J. Lacan, *Le Séminaire, Livre XI: Quatre concepts fondamentaux de la psychanalyse*, trans. A. Sheridan as *The Four Fundamental Concepts of Psycho-Analysis* (Harmondsworth: Penguin, 1979).

27 On the integrity of the stroke in Chinese painting, see Waley, *Introduction to the Study of Chinese Painting*, pp. 72–4; D. Siren, *A History of Early Chinese Painting* (London: Medici Society, 1933), pp. 31–6; S.E. Lee, *A History of Far Eastern Art* (London: Thames and Hudson, 1964), pp. 253–5; A.C. Soper, 'The first two laws of Hsieh Ho', *Far Eastern Quarterly*, VIII (1948), 412–23; W.R. Acker, *Some T'ang and Pre-T'ang Texts on Chinese Landscape Painting* (Leiden: Brill, 1954), pp. xxvii, xli–xliii.

28 Edward Young, 'Conjectures on original composition', in *Collected Works* (London: William Tegg, 1834), pp. 553–4.

2. David and the problem of inheritance

1 See T.S. Kuhn, *The Structure of Scientific Revolutions* (University of Chicago Press, 1970); and *The Essential Tension: Selected Studies in Scientific Tradition and Change* (University of Chicago Press, 1979).

2 Bryson, *Vision and Painting: The Logic of the Gaze*, pp. 37–66.

3 See, for example, Sir Ernest Gombrich, 'Image and code: scope and limits of conventionalism in pictorial representation', in *The Image and the Eye: Further Studies in the Psychology of Pictorial Representation* (Oxford: Phaidon, 1982), pp. 278–97. 'Code' and 'message' reached what is perhaps their fullest expression at a certain stage in the history of structuralism, to which the model is, of course, fundamental. See V. Propp, *Morphology of the Folktale* (Bloomington: Indiana Research Center in Anthropology, 1958); Propp,

'Fairy tale transformations', in *Readings in Russian Poetics*, ed. L. Matejka and K. Pomorska (Cambridge, Mass: MIT Press, 1971), pp. 178–96; A.J. Greimas, 'Le Conte populaire russe (analyse fonctionelle)', *International Journal of Slavic Linguistics and Poetics*, IX (1965), 152–75; T. Todorov, *Grammaire du Décameron* (The Hague: Mouton, 1969); C. Bremond, 'Observations sur la *Grammaire du Décameron*', *Poétique*, VI (1971), 200–22; R. Barthes, 'Introduction à l'analyse structurale des récits', *Communications*, VIII (1966), 1–27; Barthes, 'L'Analyse structurale du récit: à propos d'Actes 10–11', *Recherches des sciences religieuses*, LVIII (1970), 17–38.

4 Gombrich, *Art and Illusion*, p. 2.

5 On the work of David see R. Cantinelli, *Jacques-Louis David. 1748–1825* (Paris: G. van Oest, 1930); K. Holma, *David, son évolution, son style* (Paris: Sorlot, 1940); L. Hautecœur, *Louis David* (Paris: La Table ronde, 1954); R. Verbraeken, *Jacques-Louis David jugé par ses contemporains et par la posterité* (Paris: Loget, 1973); A. Schnapper, *David: témoin de son temps* (Paris: Bibliothèque des Arts, 1980); A. Brookner, *Jacques-Louis David* (London: Chatto and Windus, 1980).

6 See A. Brookner, 'J.-L. David – a sentimental classicist', *Stil und Überlieferung in der Kunst des Abendlandes* (Berlin: Verlag Gebr. Mann, 1967), vol. I, pp. 184–90; 'Jacques-Louis David: a personal interpretation', *Proceedings of the British Academy*, LXI (1974), 155–71; and *Jacques-Louis David*, p. 48.

7 For a discussion of this painting, see Bryson, *Word and Image: French Painting of the Ancien Régime* (Cambridge University Press, 1981), pp. 52–5.

8 On the rise of Poussinism, see J. Locquin, *La Peinture d'histoire en France de 1747 à 1785* (Paris: Laurens, 1912).

9 M. Fried, *Absorption and Theatricality: Painting and Beholder in the Age of Diderot* (Berkeley: University of California Press, 1980).

10 See review of Fried's *Absorption and Theatricality*, in *Journal of Modern History*, LIII (1981), 702–5.

11 On the 'optics of desire' in Racine, see J. Starobinski, *L'Œil vivant* (Paris: Gallimard, 1961); and R. Barthes, *Sur Racine* (Paris: Seuil, 1963), pp. 22–34.

12 See A. Brookner, *Jacques-Louis David*, p. 59.

13 See Fried, *Absorption and Theatricality*, pp. 151–60; A. Schnapper, Belisarius entry in *French Painting 1774–1830: the Age of Revolution* (Detroit: Réunion des Musées Nationaux, the Detroit Institute of Arts and the Metropolitan Museum of Art, 1975), No. 30, pp. 364–5; and A. Boime, 'Marmontel's *Belisaire* and the pre-Revolutionary progressivism of David', *Art History*, III, No. 1 (March 1980), 81–101.

14 See J. Seznec, 'Diderot et l'Affaire Greuze', *Gazette des Beaux-Arts* (May 1966), 339–56.

3. *Mortal sight: The Oath of the Horatii*

1 See E. Wind, 'The sources of David's *Horaces*', *Journal of the Warburg and Courtauld Institutes*, IV (1940–1), 124–38; F.H. Hazelhurst, 'The artistic evolution of David's *Oath*', *Art Bulletin*, XLII, No. 1 (March 1960), 58–63; R. Rosenblum, 'Gavin Hamilton's *Brutus* and its aftermath', *Burlington Magazine*, CIII (January 1961), 8–16; L.D. Ettlinger, 'Jacques-Louis David and Roman Virtue', Frederick Cook Memorial Lecture delivered to the Royal Society of Arts, 23 November 1966; R. Rosenblum, 'A source for David's *Horatii*', *Burlington Magazine*, CXII (May 1970), 169–73; and T. Crow's excellent article, 'The Oath of the Horatii in 1785: painting and pre-Revolutionary radicalism in France', *Art History*, I, No. 4 (December 1978), 424–71.

2 See Aquinas, *Summa Theologica: Treatise on the Angels*, questions 54–58; *Treatise on Man*, questions 75–89; trans. the Fathers of the English Dominican Province (Chicago: Encyclopaedia Britannica), pp. 284–305.

3 See J. Snyder, 'Picturing vision', *Critical Inquiry*, VI, No. 3 (Spring 1980), 499–526.

4 M. Merleau-Ponty, *Le Visible et l'Invisible* (Paris: Gallimard, 1964), pp. 172–204; trans. A. Lingis as *The Visible and the Invisible* (Evanston: Northwestern University Press, 1968), pp. 130–55.

5 P. Berger and T. Luckmann, *The Social Construction of Reality* (Harmondsworth: Penguin, 1979). 'Since this knowledge is socially objectivated *as* knowledge, that is, as a body of generally valid truths about reality, any radical deviance from the institutional order appears as departure from reality'; p. 83.

6 'Does the moon move? *Yes.* When you are out for a walk what happens? – *You see it moving forward all the time . . . –* Why does it follow us? – *To see where we are going. –* Can it see us? – *Yes. –* When there are lots of people in the town what does it do? – *It follows someone. –* Which person? – *Several people. –* How does it do that? – *With its rays'*; J. Piaget, *The Child's Conception of the World* (London; Kegan Paul, 1929), p. 218. On the relationship between Piaget's and Lacan's understanding of the child's theory of knowledge, see H.J. Silverman's foreward to the proceedings of the Stony Brook Conference on 'Piaget, Philosophy and the Human Sciences', in *Piaget: Philosophy and the Human Sciences*, ed. H.J. Silverman (New Jersey: Humanities Press, 1980), pp. x–xi; and W.J. Richardson's paper, 'Piaget, Lacan, and language', pp. 144–63.

7 J. Lacan, *The Four Fundamental Concepts*, pp. 93–4.

8 On mastery of laterality, see Sami-Ali, *L'Espace imaginaire* (Paris: Gallimard, 1974), esp. pp. 24–85. On the 'othering' Lacan posits as constitutive of the subject, see 'Le Stade du miroir comme formateur de la fonction du jeu', *Revue française de psychanalyse*, No. 4 (October–December 1949), pp. 449–55, reprinted in *Écrits: A Selection*, trans. A. Sheridan (London: Tavistock, 1977), pp. 1–7; *Le Séminaire: Livre I* (Paris: Seuil, 1975), pp. 87–103, 185–99; *Le Séminaire: Livre II* (Paris: Seuil, 1979), pp. 39–69.

9 The asymmetry here points to what I think must be considered as an essential aspect of the distribution of power and knowledge: when power is concentrated, and as part of that concentration when there is also concentration of the codes of knowledge, the margins where power is lesser will be constructed as the object of knowledge. In the case of the codes by whose agency a society proposes and assumes its own specific and historically produced visuality, 'where power is, there also is sight'; while away from power, where power is lesser, will be found that which *is seen*: woman as the image for man, but (in proportion to the uneven spread of power) not the reverse. The concepts at work here, concerning the image, sexuality and power, are still only emergent. Bibliography is therefore complex, and must appear somewhat arbitrary. It seems the best place for discussion of power to begin would be with A. Gramsci, *Selections from the Prison Notebooks*, ed. Q. Hoare and G. Nowell-Smith (London: Lawrence and Wishart, 1971), and L. Althusser, 'Ideology and ideological state apparatuses (Notes towards an investigation)', in *Lenin and Philosophy and other Essays*, trans. B. Brewster (London, NLB, 1971). If a difficulty of Althusser's essay is the way in which it sees the 'ideological state apparatuses' as the *stake* rather than the *site* of struggle, this certainly cannot be said of the work of Foucault: see in particular *Discipline and Punish: The Birth of the Prison*, trans. A. Sheridan (London: Pantheon, 1978), and 'Governmentality', in *Ideology and Consciousness*, No. 6 (Autumn 1979), pp. 5–21. In so far as analysis of gender in vision presupposes connection between femininity and 'masquerade', discussion must start from psychoanalysis, where this concept has been carefully elaborated, especially in J. Lacan, *Le Séminaire: Livre XX: Encore* (Paris: Seuil, 1975); and in L. Irigaray, *Speculum: de l'autre femme* (Paris: Minuit, 1974) and *Ce sexe qui n'en est pas un* (Paris: Minuit, 1977). Comparable texts in the Anglo-Saxon tradition might be J. Berger, *Ways of Seeing* (Harmondsworth: British Broadcasting Corporation and Penguin Books, 1972), pp. 45–64; and J. Riviere, 'Womanliness as a masquerade', in *Psychoanalysis and Female Sexuality*, ed. H.M. Ruitenbeek (New Haven: College and University Press, 1966). The

connection between the 'masquerade' and the visual arts has been the subject of much feminist work in film analysis. See what is now a *locus classicus*, L. Mulvey, 'Visual pleasure and narrative cinema', *Screen*, XVI, No. 3 (Autumn 1975); C. Johnston, 'The subject of feminist theory/practice', *Screen*, XXI, No. 2 (Summer 1980), 27–34; and A. Kuhn's survey *Women's Pictures: Feminism and Cinema* (London: Routledge and Kegan Paul, 1982).

10 See J. Derrida, *La Vérité en peinture*, pp. 1–168.

11 Recent work on the *Oresteia* has, however, radically called into question its allegedly 'classical' system of representation. See the forthcoming work of S. Goldhill (Cambridge University); I would not want to anticipate Goldhill's arguments here.

12 A. Brookner, *Jacques-Louis David*, p. 74.

13 J.L. Jules David, *Le Peintre David* (Paris: Harard, 1880), p. 220.

14 On the 'centric ray' see Alberti, *De Pictura*, Books I and II; J.-L. Schefer, *Scénographie d'un tableau* (Paris: Seuil, 1969), pp. 9–35; and L. Marin, *Détruire la peinture* (Paris: Galilee, 1977), pp. 58–81.

15 Few statements of the 'reversibility' of viewpoint and vanishing point can be seen as unambiguous, or as vivid, as the following anecdote, from Antonio Manetti's *Life of Filippo di Ser Brunellesco*. 'As for perspective, the first work on which he (Brunelleschi) showed it was a small panel about half a *braccio* square on which he made a picture of the church of S. Giovanni of Florence. . . . The painter of such a picture assumes that it has to be seen from a single point, which is fixed in reference to the height and width of the picture, and that it has to be seen from the right distance. Seen from any other point, the effect of the perspective would be distorted. Thus, to prevent the spectator from falling into error in choosing his viewpoint, Filippo (Brunelleschi) made a hole in the picture at that point in the view of the church of S. Giovanni which is directly opposite to the eye of the spectator, who might be standing in the central porch portal of S. Maria del Fiore in order to paint the scene. This hole was small as a lentil on the painted side, and on the back of the panel it opened out in a conical form to the size of a ducat or a little more, like the crown of a woman's straw hat. Filippo had the beholder put his eye against the reverse side where the hole was large, and while he shaded his eye with his one hand, with the other he was told to hold a flat mirror on the far side in such a way that the painting was reflected in it. The distance from the mirror to the hand near the eye had to be in a given proportion to the distance between the point where Filippo stood in painting his picture and the church of S. Giovanni. When one looked at it thus, the burnished silver already mentioned, the perspective of the piazza, and the fixing of the point of vision made the scene absolutely real. I have had the painting in my hand and have seen it many times in those days, so I can testify to it'; in *Literary Sources of Art History: An Anthology of Texts from Theophilus to Goethe*, ed. E.G. Holt (Princeton University Press, 1947), pp. 98–9.

16 For this reason, to the theorists of nineteenth-century sculpture who demanded of sculptural form the unity of all its aspects, relief recommended itself as the consummate expression of sculpture's aims, 'All the details of form must unite in a more comprehensive form'; 'All separate judgements of depth must enter into a unitary, all-inclusive judgement of depth. So that ultimately the entire richness of a figure's form stands before us as a backward continuation of one simple plane. Whenever this is not the case, the unitary pictorial effect of the figure is lost. A tendency is then felt to clarify what we cannot perceive from our present point of view, by a change of position. Thus we are driven all around the figure without ever being able to grasp it once in its entirety.' Adolf von Hildebrand, *The Problem of Form* (New York: Stechart, 1907), p. 95; cit. R.E. Krauss, *Passages in Modern Sculpture* (London: Thames and Hudson, 1977), p. 14.

17 Cit. J. Lacan, *The Four Fundamental Concepts*, p. 82.

18 See Reynolds, *Discourses on Art*, ed. R.R. Wark, esp. Discourses III and IV.

1 M.E.J. Delécluze, *Louis David: son école et son temps* (Paris: Didier, 1855), pp. 9–10. See also J.L. Jules David, *Le peintre David* (Paris: Harard, 1880), pp. 217–300.

2 Delécluze, *Louis David*, pp. 178–9.

3 J.L. Jules David, *Le peintre David*, p. 213.

4 See A. Mathiez, *Les origines des cultes révolutionnaires 1789–92* (Paris: G. Bellais, 1904); D.L. Dowd, *Pageant-Master of the Republic: Jacques-Louis David and the French Revolution* (Lincoln, Nebraska: University of Nebraska Press, 1948); J.A. Leith, *The Idea of Art as Propaganda in France, 1750–1799* (University of Toronto Press, 1965); M. Ozouf, *La fête révolutionnaire 1789–1799* (Paris: Gallimard, 1976); J.E. Schlanger, 'Théâtre révolutionnaire et représentation du bien', *Poétique*, No. 22 (1975), pp. 268–83.

5 See R.L. Herbert, *Brutus* (London: Allen Lane, 1972).

6 On the Flouest engraving, see A. Schnapper, *David: témoin de son temps*, p. 100.

7 R. Rosenblum, 'The international style of 1800: a study in linear abstraction', Dissertation. New York University, 1956, p. 125.

8 Delécluze, *Louis David*, p. 120.

9 Quai maintained that 'David n'avait fait qu'entrevoir la route à suivre, qu'il fallait changer radicalement les principes sur lesquels on s'appuyait pour exercer les arts; que tout ce qui avait été fait depuis Phidias était *maniéré*, faux, théâtral, affreux, ignoble; que les maîtres italiens, y compris le plus célèbre même, étaient entachés des vices des écoles modernes; qu'il était indispensable de s'abstenir de regarder aucun des tableaux de la grande galerie, et que dans celle des antiques on devait baisser les yeux et passer outre devant les statues romaines et celles même qui avaient été faites en Grèce depuis Alexandre le Grand'; Delécluze, *Louis David*, p. 72.

10 Delécluze, *Louis David*, pp. 163–9. See also D. Guérin, *Bourgeois et bras nus 1793–1795* (Paris: Gallimard, 1973); and F. Furet, *Penser la Révolution Française* (Paris: Éditions de la Maison des Sciences de l'Homme, 1981).

11 See M. Lamy, 'Seroux d'Agincourt et son influence sur les collectionneurs, critiques et artistes français', *La Revue de l'art ancien et moderne*, xxxix (March 1921), 169–81, and xl (September–October 1921), 182–90; T. Borenius, 'The rediscovery of the Primitives', *Quarterly Review*, ccxxxix (April 1923), 258–70. The contents of Girodet's library are described in *Catalogue des tableaux, esquisses, dessins et croquis de M. Girodet-Trioson*, ed. M. Perignon (Paris, 1825), pp. 83ff.

12 J.L. Jules David, *Le peintre David*, pp. 339–40; Delécluze, *Louis David*, pp. 205–9.

13 Cited in Delécluze, *Louis David*, pp. 89–90.

14 See J. Lacan, *Écrits: A Selection*, pp. 1–7.

15 On the work of Ingres, see C. Blanc, *Ingres, sa vie et ses ouvrages* (Paris: Renouard, 1870); H. Delaborde, *Ingres, sa vie, ses travaux, sa doctrine* (Paris: Plon, 1870); E.-E. Amaury-Duval, *L'Atelier d'Ingres* (Paris: Charpentier, 1878); A.-J. Boyer d'Agen, *Ingres d'après une correspondance inédite* (Paris: Daragon, 1909); and H. Lapauze, *Ingres, sa vie et son œuvre* (Paris: Georges Petit, 1911). Of modern surveys, the most distinguished are perhaps J. Cassou, *Ingres* (Brussels: Édit. Formes, 1947); J. Alazard, *Ingres et l'Ingrisme* (Paris: A. Michel, 1950); in English, R. Rosenblum, *Jean-Auguste-Dominique Ingres* (London: Thames and Hudson, 1957); and J. Whitely, *Ingres* (London: Oresko, 1981). I have found extremely useful the articles by E.S. King, 'Ingres as classicist', *Journal of the Walters Art Gallery*, v (1942), 69–113; by N. Schlenoff, 'Ingres and the classical world', *Archaeology*, xii, No. 1 (Spring 1959), 16–25; and by A. Mongan, 'Ingres and the Antique', *Journal of the Warburg and Courtauld Institutes*, x (1947), 1–13. On the evolution of Ingres' style, see J. Momméja, 'La Jeunesse d'Ingres', *Gazette des Beaux-Arts*, xx (1898), 89–106, 188–208; and the exhibition catalogue by D. Ternois, *Ingres et*

ses maîtres, de Roques à David (Toulouse and Montauban: Musée des Augustins and Musée Ingres, 1955). On the holdings of the Musée Ingres, see D. Ternois, *Les Dessins d'Ingres au Musée de Montauban; les portraits* (Inventaire général des dessins des musées de province, III; Paris: Centre de la recherche scientifique, 1959); and *Peintures: Ingres et son temps (Artistes nés entre 1740 et 1830)* (Inventaire des collections publiques françaises, III, Paris, 1956). G. Wildenstein's catalogue, *Ingres* (London: Phaidon, 1964) has been indispensable.

16 On the compositional structure of the tondo form, see R. Arnheim's perceptive analysis in *The Power of the Center: A Study of Composition in the Visual Arts* (Berkeley: University of California Press, 1982), pp. 115–52.

5. Tradition and Desire

1 Sir Kenneth Clark, *The Romantic Rebellion: Romantic versus Classic Art* (London: John Murray and Sotheby Parke Bernet, 1973), p. 106.

2 See, for example, Ingres' drawing of Pauline Gilibert; in D. Ternois, *Les Dessins d'Ingres au Musée de Montauban: les portraits*, plate 62.

3 A. Kojève, *Introduction to the Reading of Hegel: Lectures on the 'Phenomenology of Spirit'*, assembled by R. Queneau (1944); ed. A. Bloom and trans. J.H. Nichols (Ithaca: Cornell University Press, 1980), pp. 3–4.

4 Cit. Clark, *Romantic Rebellion*, p. 97.

5 Clark, *Romantic Rebellion*, p. 117.

6 On sexuality's existence in and through the sign, see J. Baudrillard, *De la séduction* (Paris: Galilée, 1979), pp. 9–73. Baudrillard's analysis is best read in the context of his general critique of 'natural economy', as presented in *Pour une critique de l'économie politique du signe* (Paris: Gallimard, 1972) and *Le Miroir de la production, ou l'illusion critique du matérialisme historique* (Paris: Casterman, 1973).

7 J. Berger, *Ways of Seeing*, p. 55.

8 See T.J. Clark, 'Preliminaries to a possible treatment of *Olympia* in 1865', *Screen*, XXI, No. 1 (Spring 1980), 18–41.

9 R. Barthes, *Le Plaisir du texte* (Paris: Seuil, 1973); trans. R. Miller as *The Pleasure of the Text* (New York: Hill and Wang, 1975).

10 See R. Schwab, *La Renaissance orientale* (Paris: Payot, 1952); E. Said, *Orientalism* (New York: Random House, 1979); and A. Grosrichard, *Structure du sérail* (Paris: Seuil, 1979).

11 J.A. Crowe and G.B. Cavalcaselle, *Raphael: His Life and Works* (2 vols., London: John Murray, 1882), vol. I, p. 1.

12 Leonardo da Vinci, *Trattato* XIII; trans. A.P. McMahon, *Leonardo da Vinci: Treatise on Painting* (Oxford University Press, 1956), p. 24.

13 J. Laplanche and J.-B. Pontalis, *The Language of Psycho-Analysis* (London: The Hogarth Press, 1973), p. 341; and Freud, Standard Edition, vol. XVIII, p. 9, and vol. XIII, pp. 55–6. See also J. Momméja, 'Le Bain Turc d'Ingres', *Gazette des Beaux-Arts*, XXXVI (1906), 177–95; and H. Naef, 'Monsieur Ingres et ses muses', *L'Œil*, No. 25 (January 1957), pp. 48–51.

14 Freud, Standard Edition, vol. XIX, p. 160.

15 See A.C. Ritchie, 'The evolution of Ingres' portrait of the Comtesse d'Haussonville', *Art Bulletin*, XXII (September 1940), 119–26.

16 In our own time a master of the trope of reversal has been the ferocious Francis Bacon. Placed against Bacon's portraits, those of Velázquez take on an entirely different meaning; the predecessor is so extensively interpreted by his successor that it becomes hard to draw the line between their separate intentions: or, rather, the intentions of Velázquez, always difficult to detect behind Velázquez's impassivity, are temporarily redefined in Bacon's terms.

6. Desire in the Bourbon Library

1 M. Sérullaz, *Les Peintures murales de Delacroix* (Paris: Édit. du Temps, 1963).

See also G.L. Hersey, 'A Delacroix preparatory drawing for the Library Cycle in the Palais Bourbon', *Yale Art Gallery Bulletin*, XXIX (1963), 6–7; G.L. Hersey, 'Delacroix's imagery in the Palais Bourbon Library', *Journal of the Warburg and Courtauld Institutes*, XXXI (1968), 383–403; M. Sérullaz, 'Delacroix's drawings for the decoration for the Library ceiling in the Palais Bourbon', *Master Drawings*, I, No. 4 (1963), p. 41; P. Verdier, 'Delacroix's "Grandes Machines"', *Connoisseur*, CLVI (1964), 233–6.

2 Sir Kenneth Clark, *Civilisation* (London: British Broadcasting Company and John Murray, 1969), p. 314.

3 *The New Science of Giambattista Vico*, trans. T.G. Bergin and M.H. Fisch (Ithaca: Cornell University Press, 1968), p. 42.

4 Horace, *Odes*, Book One, X:

> Mercure, facunde nepos Atlanti,
> qui feros cultus hominum recentum
> voce formasti catus et decorae
> more palaestrae

5 See S. Lichenstein, 'Delacroix and Raphael', Dissertation, University of London, 1973, p. 173ff.

6 On the rhetoric of antithesis, see R. Barthes, *S/Z* (Paris: Seuil, 1970), pp. 33–5, 71–4.

7 See Bryson, *Vision and Painting: The Logic of the Gaze*, pp. 87–131.

8 *Purgatorio*, Cantos VII and VIII.

9 'On voit voler derrière lui et se pencher à son oreille son génie ou démon familier. . . .'; Delacroix, in *Le Constitutionnel*, 31 January 1848; cit. Sérullaz, *Les Peintures murales*, p. 296.

10 Cf. Delacroix's studies for the angel in *Jacob Wrestling With the Angel*, Paris, Saint-Sulpice, Chapelle des Saints-Anges; in J.J. Spector, *The Murals of Eugène Delacroix at Saint-Sulpice* (New York: The College Art Association of America, 1967), esp. plate 34 (Grenoble, Musée de Peinture et de Sculpture).

11 See J. Culler, *Flaubert: The Uses of Uncertainty* (Ithaca: Cornell University Press, 1974); and D. Simpson, *Irony and Authority in Romantic Poetry* (London: Macmillan, 1979), pp. 166–200.

12 See Laplanche and Pontalis, *The Language of Psycho-Analysis*, pp. 431–4; and Freud, Standard Edition, vol. VII, p. 206; vol. IX, pp. 187–9; vol. XIX, p. 45; vol. XXI, p. 79.

13 'L'orateur athénien marche sur le rivage de la mer, retenant d'une main sa draperie chassée par le vent, ébauchant de l'autre un geste, qui plus tard courbera les têtes, aussi puissamment que le trident de Neptune domptait les flots agités'; cit. Sérullaz, p. 304.

14 See G. Kennedy, *Quintilian* (New York: Twayne, 1969), pp. 85–6.

15 See J.P. Vernant, *Mythe et pensée chez les Grecs* (Paris: Maspero, 1980), pp. 13–79.

16 Sir Edmund Leach, 'Michelangelo's *Genesis*: structuralist comments on the Sistine Chapel ceiling', *The Times Literary Supplement*, 18 March, 1977, pp. 311–13.

Index

225

DATE DUE

JUN 24 1994	
JUN 25 1994	
JUN 27 1994	
NOV 20 2008	

DEMCO, INC. 38-2931